VIOLENCE AND PUNISHMENT

D1516819

VIOLENCE AND PUNISHMENT

Civilizing the Body through Time

Pieter Spierenburg

polity

Contents

Introduction

Violence and Punishment within Civilizing Processes

Violence and punishment are intimately related. For one thing, the first may result, for the perpetrator, in the second, especially in modern societies. In its turn, punishment may involve violence. This was notably the case with the public torments inflicted on serious offenders in the early modern period. More generally, as I argue in chapter 6, in all societies the criminally condemned have in common that they feel the state's monopoly of force striking at them in one way or another. Ultimately, even the mildest form of punishment depends on a credible threat of violence. Throughout this book I will illustrate my argument with real-life examples. The reader will get to know why fights between Jews and Christians often took place on the Blue Bridge in Amsterdam; how a yellow bulldog betrayed a killer who had hoped to remain undetected; what happened to a thief whom the citizens stopped by splitting his skull with an axe; why the executioner was to activate the guillotine by cutting the rope that holds up the blade with a sword; what the punishment of Adam and Eve reveals about the work and fears of our ancestors.

Let me first delineate the two main subjects covered in this book, beginning with punishment. I am using this concept both in a broader sense and in a narrower sense than is common in everyday language. In everyday parlance we can say, for example, that a parent punishes a disobedient child with a view to raising it properly. Early modern people often viewed a disaster as God's punishment for their sins. In a modern setting, a woman's friends, for example, may view her extramarital affair as the punishment she gives to her husband for his earlier unfaithfulness. Such uses of the word, the examples randomly chosen, are excluded from my discussion. I am focusing on punishment that is in one way or another judicial. At the same time, however, my discussion ranges more broadly than just the act of punishing itself. The discussion extends to the cultural manifestations and the social embeddedness of punishment, as we see in the drama of the scaffold, for example. Therefore, I am additionally using the concept of social control, most notably when I am dealing with informal regulation within village or neighborhood communities.

Whereas most people take the meaning of the word "punishment" for granted, the definition of "violence" often leads to controversy. In our society this word has a decidedly negative connotation, which induces many to extend the term to all kind of situations considered undesirable. Yet, in popular parlance, in English no less than in other languages, it is usually clear what is meant by violence. Here I am purposely employing a restricted definition, which is attuned to the everyday understanding of the word. I include in the category of violence all forms of intentional encroachment upon the physical integrity of the body. That formula excludes forms of encroachment for medical reasons, as well as unintentional harm such as that caused by traffic accidents. Moreover, I reject notions like structural or psychological violence, which appear to me excuses for an ideological argumentation rather than scholarly concepts.[1] Readers who disagree with me on this point may insert the word "physical" each time there is talk of violence. Though restricted, my definition is not narrow. It includes minor encroachments upon bodily integrity which a court considers too trivial to prosecute. And, perhaps more importantly, it includes state violence such as armed police action, corporal punishment and warfare. This formal definition, however, should not be confused with the book's program. In fact, I am largely ignoring the two extremes of warfare, on the one hand, and minor slaps and bruises in conflicts between citizens, on the other.

Having carefully delineated the two main subjects covered in this book, I am eager to open up the field again. To the extent that I am a criminal justice historian, I am far from practicing this sub-discipline in isolation. Key issues relevant for all historians and social scientists, such as gender, the development of the state and popular vs. elite attitudes, all figure in my discussion as explanatory elements. Moreover, I am exploring several corollary developments to the decline of violence and the transformation of punishment, among which are the refinement of manners and the rise of new forms of festivity. All this follows directly from my scholarly approach. I am not studying a phenomenon, like dueling for example, for its own sake, followed by the question whether A, B or C or a combination of them accounts for its rise and demise. As I conclude in chapter 4 with respect to punishment, social phenomena cannot be explained in terms of cause and effect. Historical explanation means clarifying what a particular custom or belief tells us about the entire "figuration" of which it forms part and the changes in that figuration. Thus, the figuration that involved duelists and their opponents and onlookers also featured the decline of feuding and the rise of elitist notions of stylized combat – and much more. It is always a question of interrelationships.

The theme of honor, central to various earlier works of mine as well as to many chapters of this book, lies at the crossroads of these complex interrelationships. For one thing, honor plays a crucial role in both punishment and violence. In punishment we encounter this theme mostly from the negative side, as dishonor. A criminal sentence often brought dishonor to the convict. Most notably, all penalties meted out by an executioner, even if not physical, made the person suffering them infamous. The infamous treatment of the body, whether male or female, extended to the whole person. Thus, the dishonor brought about by punishment was relatively independent from gender distinctions. This was quite different in the case of violence. Whereas the relationship between honor and the body was equally strong, in violence gender distinctions mattered a lot. For centuries, masculinity was linked up with a violent life-style, whereas women were expected to largely refrain from aggression. The interrelationships between gender, honor and the body, then, and the changes they underwent, form a crucial background in particular for the chapters about violence.

Gender, Honor and the Body

Anthropologists as well as historians have studied conceptions of honor, including the intimate relationship between male honor and violence.[2] Honor has at least three aspects: a person's own feeling of self-worth, this person's assessment of his or her worth in the eyes of others and the actual opinion of others about her or him.[3] The criteria of judgment depend on the socio-cultural context. The relationship between physical force and male honor has been observed in many societies, but it is not universal. Among the Suriname maroons, for example, it counts as a stain upon a man's honor if he fights out a conflict or reacts to an insult with aggression. Only in the case of adultery, is the aggrieved husband accorded a limited right to beat up his rival; all other conflicts have to be solved through the institution of the palaver. This attitude has characterized the Suriname maroons for at least 250 years, Thoden van Velzen argues, and it is connected to the uxorilocal organization of their society.[4] According to the anthropologist Frank Henderson Stewart, the concepts of honor prevalent among the Bedouins, and possibly in the Arab world as a whole, are fundamentally different from the European model. In contemporary Bedouin societies no particular connection between male honor and violence exists.[5] Conversely, as chapter 3 shows, in some

Asian societies the link between male honor and violence appears to be very pronounced.

For now, I restrict myself to Europe since the middle ages. For centuries, honor depended on the body or, in Blok's words, the physical person.[6] Appearance was crucial for one's reputation. Honorable men were symbolically associated with strong, awe-inspiring animals and dishonorable men with small or weakened animals. Thus, an old English law mentioned by the legal writer Bracton says that if a nobleman is found guilty of rape, the penalty is castration . . . for his horse or his dog, coupled with cutting off its tail; or his hawk is deprived of the sharp end of its beak and its claws. Through the disabling of his noble animals, the nobleman himself is symbolically disempowered.[7] We find an analogy between the disempowered human body and dishonor in the writings of a Polish convert to Islam at the end of the seventeenth century. His conversion did not prevent him from frowning upon the Ottoman custom of entrusting political functions to eunuchs: "When they are successful, the most important posts of the Empire are given to them. While they are properly speaking only half-men, this does not alter the fact that they are often at the heads of the armies and they have governed the greatest of the provinces. One sees by this that the jobs are not always given to those with the most merit, or those who are the most capable of possessing them."[8] In view of this close connection between the body and honor, it is intriguing that none of the six volumes of a recent book series entitled *The Cultural History of the Human Body* list "honor" in the index.[9]

Despite this omission, the body, honor and gender are all related. Bodies, being male or female with few exceptions, form the basis of gender; gender gives rise to a dual concept of honor; honor shapes the experience of the body. The inherent circularity assures that no element of this triangle is the principal determinant. The relationship is one of interdependence: if there is a change in one element, the others are likely to change too. Nevertheless, in order to get to grips with these complex interdependencies, we may break them down into developments in three areas: the body and gender; gender and honor; honor and the body.

For the body and gender the crucial periods seem to have been the middle ages on the one hand and the late eighteenth century on the other. Important work has been done on the first period.[10] Although the authors concerned criticize each other on points of detail, they agree that the medieval conception of sex differences left room for much ambiguity.[11] In the view of contemporaries, to be female or male largely depended on character and habits. In accordance with this, the process of generation did not just offer two possibilities. Human specimens such as a virago, an effeminate man or a hermaphrodite could be born just as easily.[12] The body's sexual identity had fluid boundaries. Christ's body in particular was often pictured as half female. His side wounds, a source of food, were likened to Mary's breasts.[13] Although Monica Green recently argued that medieval people did view the differences between women and men as absolute, she also cites a source which actually confirms the contemporary notion that the generation of mixed human types was possible. According to medieval physicians, the birth of an effeminate man or a masculine woman depended on the temperature at the spot in the womb where conception took place.[14] Paradoxically, in the medical description of all human bodies, including women and the mixed types, one body, the male, was used as a referent. The notion of sexual ambiguity persisted into much of the early modern period.[15]

Thomas Laqueur offers a thesis to account for these observations.[16] Although this thesis has been heavily debated, criticism concentrated on his idea of a transition from a "one-sex model" to a "two-sex model" and his supposed neglect of popular beliefs.[17] Here I am focusing on another element, the relationship between sex and gender. Moreover, it appears that recent scholarship in majority still favors Laqueur's thesis.[18] According to him, gender came first in the middle ages. In medieval people's minds, the socio-cultural experience of being male or female, or anything in between, had primacy and biological sex was made to fit it. Essentially, this conception of sex differences persisted during the early modern period. From the middle of the eighteenth century onward, however, the relationship was reversed. Sex came first now. Biology was seen as the basis of character, and biology left room for just two sexes. Sexual identity and, as a consequence, gender identity became much more strictly demarcated. This new view was especially pronounced toward the end of the nineteenth century. By then, according to Robert Nye, doctors and biologists had elaborated a standard anatomical and physiological model of masculinity, defining its features as hygienic norms with which all men should comply.[19] Masculinity and femininity had become binary opposites.

At about the same time as this stricter demarcation of the sexes and gender roles was elaborated, the contrast between male and female honor weakened. Since the early modern period, notions of female and male honor have gradually converged. Of course, they remained distinct to some extent. The process of convergence had two main aspects: the active–passive contrast in gender roles became less pronounced, and men, like women before them, had to take moral standards into account. Women's honor had always been based primarily on issues of morality. Foremost, it depended on a reputation of chastity, but in the sixteenth and seventeenth centuries a clean slate with respect to sorcery was important too. A chaste woman was a modest woman, true to the demand of passivity.[20] For men, on the other hand, the domain of sex originally meant activity: the protection of one's own womenfolk from predators, and trying to seduce others' womenfolk. This attitude prevailed not only among elite men, but also among men of lower social status. Popular customs testify to this at least until the sixteenth century. When a cuckolded husband was subjected to the ritual of charivari, for example, he was mocked as a loser by his fellow men, rather than burdened with moral outrage.[21] Attitudes slowly changed during the early modern period. Restrictive demands on men, especially from religious moralists, became stronger. Obviously, the male gender role continued to comprise a more active stance than the female, but the quest for sexual adventure was increasingly proscribed from it. By the nineteenth century, male honor, too, had become associated with sexual self-restraint, at least among the middle classes.[22]

Thus, a shift in the way the body and gender were perceived was accompanied by a transformation in conceptions of gender and honor. That transformation, however, appears to have come about more gradually, extending over a period roughly from the sixteenth century to the nineteenth. Moreover, whereas the shift in the perception of the body and gender implied a strict demarcation between men and women, the transformation in conceptions of gender and honor implied convergence. Indeed, the two changes were loosely related rather than connected in a cause-and-effect relationship. In this complex web of interdependent developments, the third area to be reviewed, that of honor and the body, was involved too. In that case, we are talking primarily, but not exclusively, of male cultures.

Honor can be inwardly or outwardly oriented. Association with the body means being linked to the body's outer appearance in particular. The outside is considered to reflect inner qualities, so appearance takes primacy. Conversely, in its spiritualized form, honor is linked primarily to inner virtues. It depends on an evaluation of a person's moral stature or psychological condition, in which outer appearance plays a much less significant part.[23] Inward and outward are two end-poles of a continuum. The conceptions of honor prevailing in a particular society are never located completely at one end or the other, but always somewhere between these extremes. In Europe over the last 300 years or so, conceptions of honor appear to have moved in the direction of spiritualization. By implication, their association with the body was strongest before this process of change set in. During most of the preindustrial period male honor depended on a reputation for violence and bravery. An honorable man commanded respect; as a patron, he protected his clients and he dealt roughly with an enemy who dared to encroach upon his property. In the streets he kept rivals at a distance, at arm's length at least. When insulted, he was prepared to fight. Well into the seventeenth century, these attitudes were manifest in almost every European country where the subject has been investigated.[24]

The gradual change in the direction of spiritualization did not just mean the reduction or removal of the element of force from the prevalent conception of honor. The change also had a positive side, in the sense that something else took the place of force. Thus, by the seventeenth century, economic solidity was a major supplementary source of honor for men. A reputation of engaging in sloppy affairs would greatly diminish a man's honor; "thief" was a common word of insult. Clearly, this implies the rise of a new ideal of masculine behavior. As Martin Wiener notes for England, the earliest attacks upon traditional manhood can be traced back to the sixteenth century.[25] In the Netherlands, by the eighteenth century, the honor of male citizens was based in large part upon being a decent housefather.[26] According to still other historians, the decisive moment came at the turn of the nineteenth and twentieth centuries, when a more gentle and domesticated type of man emerged; they speak of the break-through of a new masculinity.[27] It can be argued, however, that taking pride in not being considered a thief was the earliest manifestation of a new masculinity, preceding its later counterpart by some three centuries.

This discussion of gender, honor and the body can be viewed as an example of historical explanation in terms of interdependent long-term developments, instead of causes and effects. Up to now, however, I have dealt with only one out of two types of honor: that accorded to a person by his or her peer group. This is the type most easily lost. If a man fails to live up to the expectations of honorable conduct – whatever they are in the period examined – of his peers, he loses (part of) his honor. Conversely, when a man does more than expected, his honor increases. Thus, in a society in which male honor is based on physical bravado, chasing away a particularly fierce enemy may make a man more honorable. The second, more stable type of honor derives from a person's rank. Its primary manifestation is respect by one's social inferiors. Usually, this type of honor can only be lost when a person is deprived of his or her rank. In another important conceptual distinction, Stewart (1994) refers to the two types as horizontal and vertical honor, respectively. This distinction helps us to extend the discussion about honor and violence, albeit a little speculatively, to the very long term of human history.

The Very Long Term

I examine the very long term in particular in the last two chapters, in which two scholars, the historian William H. McNeill and the sociologist Johan Goudsblom, figure prominently. Whereas the second bases himself explicitly on the theoretical work of Norbert Elias, the first offers many points of comparison with this work. McNeill's *Plagues and Peoples* (1977), for example, can be read as a creative contribution to Elias' theory of the triad of fundamental controls. According to Elias, all interdependent long-term processes ultimately form part of one of three overarching long-term developments: changes in the relationship between humans and the nonhuman (physical and biological) world; changes in the relations among people themselves; and changes in the relationship of all people with their individual selves. The term "control" refers to Elias' complementary thesis that in the long run, in these three areas, the trend is in the direction of greater control. He admits, however, that this is most difficult to substantiate for the third area.[28] McNeill shows how specific developments within the first and second areas involved an increase of controls over the very long term, without any of the participants realizing this. Within the second area it concerned the twin developments of societies becoming more populous and increasingly in contact with each other over longer distances. The concomitant development in the first area concerned changes in the relationships between humans and micro-parasites (bacteria and viruses). Ever larger "disease pools" emerged, in which humans acquired antibodies against more and more diseases and micro-parasites became less virulent.

Processes involving pacification and the relative monopolization of force belong to the second area, that of inter-human relations, while changes in people's propensity for aggression belong to the third area comprising the relationship of all people with their individual selves. The interdependence between these two can be demonstrated most clearly for early modern Europe, with the rise of nation-states and the concomitant decline of homicide. It is worthwhile, however, to briefly examine the very long term. Goudsblom (1998) does so, but primarily for one side of the coin, that of the relative monopolization of force, and hardly for the propensity for aggression. This monopolization is relative because every individual act of violence implies a breach of the monopoly. "Force" essentially stands for the organized, "professional" exercise of violence. Goudsblom hypothesizes a sequence of three world-historical phases in the monopolization of force. During a first phase, all adult males monopolized force, excluding women and children from its exercise. This phase is hypothetical rather than empirically demonstrable; its beginnings probably coincided with the differentiation between hunting as a male activity and gathering as a female one. The means involved were most likely of an ideological and psychological nature: men successfully persuaded women and children that force constituted a male domain. Goudsblom mentions rites of initiation and "taboos" in this respect. During a second phase, an elite of warriors monopolized force, excluding peasants, artisans and priests from its exercise. In this case, the means were primarily of a material nature, consisting of a complementary monopoly on bearing arms. Goudsblom calls the social figurations associated with this phase "military–agrarian" societies.

The third phase is the one that many scholars are most familiar with. Relatively autonomous warrior elites increasingly had to yield to larger organizations. Force came to be monopolized within the framework of the institutions that henceforth were called "states." All specialists in violence were either incorporated into the state or eliminated, and practices like feuding, exercising one's own private justice and keeping armed retainers were increasingly banned. There is no need to elaborate on these well-known processes. I am, instead, concerned with the first two phases of the monopolization of force, aiming to take Goudsblom's analysis one step further. He does not venture to speculate about the question of what these two monopolizations meant for the propensity for aggression among the groups excluded from the "official" exercise of force. Indeed, we will never dispose of, say, accurate homicide rates for the millennia concerned. Yet, it is possible to hypothesize a little about the related themes of male honor and the propensity for aggression.

In this exercise, another theoretical contribution from Norbert Elias forms our point of departure. I already introduced the term "figuration." In the course of interdependent long-term processes the figuration that all people constitute together over generations gradually changes, until it finally becomes another figuration. However, Elias adds, elements from an earlier figuration often remain present, in a slightly transformed manner, in the subsequent figuration or even in still later ones. This theoretical contribution may help to shed light on two riddles in the history of violence: its tenacious link with honor and the surprisingly constant fact that violence, in particular homicide, is so disproportionately committed by males. I hypothesize that both may be considered as remnants from earlier figurations. First, serious violence as a male preserve, observed in many societies until today, is a remnant from the figuration that resulted from the first phase in the monopolization of force. When force was monopolized even further, the propensity for "ordinary" aggression largely remained with men. My second hypothesis locates the origins of the link between male honor and violence in the second phase of the monopolization of force. The traditional, body-related concept of honor originated as the vertical honor of the warrior caste: they took pride in what they were doing and got respect for it. Later on, but still within military–agrarian societies, peasants and artisans adopted elements of this honor code and transformed them into a vehicle of primarily horizontal honor.

Civilizing Processes and the Study of Homicide

From the very long term I return to the more familiar theme of civilizing processes in European history since the late middle ages. Civilizing processes are reflected in both the decline of violence and the transformation of punishment. Here we must inquire into the directions for the study of homicide following from Elias' theory of civilization. Once more, this follows from my conviction that historical explanation means elucidating the interdependence between various long-term processes. Theorizing and gathering new evidence should always go together, in a two-way process. As new empirical data necessitate us to revise our theories, these very theories suggest what kind of data to collect, and how to categorize them and group them together. Thus, the theory of civilizing processes entails recommendations on how to study homicide – one of this book's subjects.

One of the advantages of Elias' approach is that he wishes to keep his analysis as free as possible from the intrusion of moral standards or judgments. Several participants in the earliest homicide debates, notably that between Lawrence Stone and James Sharpe in the first half of the 1980s, implicitly assume that a high level of violence in past communities automatically translates into a low quality of life in them. In particular, they tend to equate violence and lack of affection in personal relationships. While Sharpe appears to think that a low level of tensions in early modern English villages would contradict the thesis of their being relatively violent, Stone tries to bolster up his argument with the statement that life was "not very pleasant" in these villages.[29] Such an equation is anachronistic, however. Elias, drawing on the Freudian notion of a link between love and aggression, claims that impulses for both affection and aggression became subject to constraints as a result of the same overall process. Consequently, we should not be led astray by the current assumptions of our time, according to which violent behavior is always destructive, "dysfunctional" and devoid of meaning. Such an unrealistic view of violence can only distort our historical judgment of aggressive behavior in the past. In our analysis of people's propensity for killing, then, we should concentrate on the mode in which aggression was expressed and the extent to which different modes were socially accepted or rejected.

It would be an exercise in purging moral judgments from our scholarly view if we asked ourselves whether it is possible to commit a "civilized" murder. The question follows directly from a primary concern of Elias' theory – that is, what kind of constraints did people impose on themselves and on others? If increasing affect control, the taming of spontaneous drives and impulses, is indeed the dominant socio-psychological trend over the last seven centuries or so of European history, a high incidence of deliberate killings today would not be incompatible with it. Such a killing requires a high amount of rational planning and restraint of momentary impulses. Elias' theory about affect control, then, would not necessarily predict that we find a declining trend in homicide rates. Instead, the proportion of "killings in affect," as a result of sudden rage, may have declined, while that of carefully premeditated murders may have remained stable or even risen.

Two alternative reactions to this proposition are possible. The first, which I will reject, consists of a separate study of murder and manslaughter. This might be necessary if we want to distinguish "killings in affect" from the "civilized" ones. However, there are no less than four reasons why it is better after all to combine the figures for murder and manslaughter into one homicide rate. The first is that precisely the affect-control component of Elias' theory is highly contested, since it is so difficult to substantiate it empirically (as already said, he admits this himself). Did medieval people really have fewer self-restraints, or did they simply control their behavior in a manner qualitatively different from ours?[30] Second, the empirical evidence on related developments, such as the changing attitudes to slavery, punishment and animal sports, definitely indicates that the dominant trend within the civilizing process moved in the direction of non-acceptance of violence, physical subjugation and the deliberate infliction of suffering generally. If we fail to take this evidence into account, we would go too far toward the extreme of relying only on deduction.

The third and fourth objections against separating murder cases from manslaughter cases are of a methodological nature. The definitions of these two categories may vary, historically as well as in individual instances. Finally, we cannot be sure in individual cases: if we calculate separate rates for murder and manslaughter, we are in fact counting the outcomes of judicial trials. To conclude, our calculations have little validity, unless we combine all cases of killing into one homicide rate. My rejection of the idea of calculating separate murder and manslaughter rates leaves us with the second device for distinguishing between different sorts of killings: to supplement the raw data with an analysis of the entire context in which each single homicide or assault was committed. Of course the state of the evidence has to allow for such an analysis. To get to grips with the context, I am introducing two "axes of violence."

Homicides as well as assaults can be characterized according to their position on two related but distinct axes: impulsive violence vs. planned or "rational" violence, on the one hand and ritual or expressive violence vs. instrumental violence, on the other.[31] Note that these four categories are extreme poles of a continuum. The archetype of a highly impulsive killing is the tavern brawl in which a knife is drawn and one of the fighters is stabbed to death. At the other end of the spectrum we find deliberate acts of violence. A carefully planned murder out of jealousy or revenge, for example, may be called rational, even if the perpetrator is caught. The impulsive–rational axis has to do mainly with the psychological state of the person who engages in violence. The social meaning of the act, on the other hand, is the determining factor in the ritual–instrumental axis. Highly ritual violence belongs to a social context in which honor and physical bravery are valued and linked. Whether homicidal or not, highly ritual violence is guided by implicit cultural codes and often its primary aim is to degrade the victim. It is violence for its own sake. On this axis, the opposite pole refers to violence used in order to get something, as with mugging, rape or loan-sharking. It should be added that the violence used in rape often serves both to subdue and to degrade the victim. Such cases, obviously, should be coded somewhere in the middle of the ritual–instrumental axis.

In principle, the two axes are independent from each other. Consequently, the position of a single act of violence on the first axis (near one end, near the other or around the middle) tells us nothing about its position on the second axis. A highly instrumental stabbing, in the course of a robbery for example, can be done either with a high degree of planning or in a moment of sudden greed. Likewise, an act of violence may have a score near the ritual pole on the axis in question and near the impulsive pole on the other. This is something which several historians refuse to accept; they believe that ritual always implies planning and hence self-restraint. The codes of ritual violence, however, constitute a fixed pattern that is ready in people's heads.[32] A knife fighter knows that he degrades his opponent with a long cut to his face and is perfectly capable of inflicting one upon a sudden fit of rage. Nevertheless, my hypothesis is that any long-term trend would be from impulsive to rational and from ritual to instrumental violence.

The identification of two axes of violence suggests still another hypothesis. Both the highly ritual and highly impulsive violence of past centuries often had a distinct community-character. The first derived its meaning from being understood by all participants, and the second was closely associated with daily sociability. Killer and victim often were residents of the same local community. In a populous place they might be strangers to each other, but they usually belonged to the settled population. Homicides were public events, at the center of community life. To a large extent, this is no longer the case today. Serious violence has retreated partly to the margins of society. A large number of contemporary homicides are connected with a property crime or with illegal economic activity such as the drug trade. This applies to instrumental as well as to rational violence; in the latter case, we can think of the liquidation of competitors. Thus, qualitatively speaking, marginalization was one of the major long-term developments in homicide. The trend was from violence at the center of local communities to violence practiced by groups with a professional interest in crime.

The increasing proportion of killings within the biological family, first identified by researchers in the 1980s, forms another conspicuous development, important for a contextual analysis. If family homicide maintains a relatively stable level even today, this would be compatible with the theory of an increase in affect regulation. As affects and emotions were the subject of increasing constraints in the wider society, the nuclear family came to serve as an island where emotions were cultivated. Historians such as Mitterauer (Mitterauer and Sieder 1977) argue that, because of this development, families have become more crisis-prone. James Cockburn is the only historian skeptical about the thesis of an increasing share of killings within the family. In this connection, he makes two claims. First, he thinks that homicides on spouses in the early modern period were seriously underreported and those on lovers often unidentifiable. Second, according to a somewhat elusive argument, Cockburn posits that infanticide should be included in the category of family homicide. That operation would raise the level of family homicide in early modern England to over 30 percent.[33] I disagree with both claims.

The difficulty of identifying lovers as victims of a homicide is probably peculiar to the uninformative English indictments. For the rest, the biological family and legal spouses have received too much attention from historians studying homicide. Understandably, they have looked for a factor that could be easily quantified. From a theoretical point of view, however, the crucial question is not whether killer and victim were related by blood or marriage, but whether they had an intimate relationship. It is only in the latter case that we suspect the killing to have been the outcome of tensions within this relationship. In the categorization of killer–victim relationships, then, intimates should be kept separate from acquaintances and total strangers as well as from non-intimate relatives. It follows that the question whether or not to rank infanticide with the family homicides is largely irrelevant, because, in any case, it should not be included in the category of killing an intimate person. The children in question never were granted the time to become intimates and their premature death was not the outcome of a protracted conflict between the perpetrator and the victim.

Thus, infanticide rates tell us little about people's propensity for aggression and much more about shame and desperation. When a mother kills her infant child, there is neither a fight nor a robbery. Moreover, the perception of the act by the killer and those prosecuting her may be radically divergent: from its being "something many women might be so unfortunate as to have to do one day, because no other option is available" to "an inexcusable assault on Christian morality." The tremendous differences in the social contexts of infanticide and homicide make the former into a distinct category. Again, an objection is possible: this line of reasoning exceeds the bounds of a historian's neutrality, since infanticide obviously involves the killing of a human being. However, so does the death of a soldier at the hands of an enemy. Historians are constantly classifying, including some acts in a specific category and excluding others, according to their evaluation of the social context. This is fine, as long as the process of categorizing is made visible. Hence, we should always construct murder rates with and without the killing of infants.

The Chapters of This Book

The chapters that follow have been chosen for their mutual coherence and their broad scope. They all apply the principle that historical explanation means elucidating the interdependence of at least two long-term processes. The theoretical work of Norbert Elias is a major source of inspiration (and I write "inspiration" on purpose, because I want to creatively expand on it), but I also discuss other theorists. In each case I have thoroughly revised the essay and updated it where necessary. The chapters constitute a mix of a few of my regularly cited articles and others which were unavailable in English up until now. Three were originally published in Dutch, one in French and one in Chinese. All speak to broad questions and several contain international, even inter-continental, comparison. Also, the three chapters focusing on the Netherlands alone do so from the perspective of issues having a much wider relevance.

Chapter 1 presents my work on homicide in Amsterdam, updated for recent years. The chapter insists that, next to constructing homicide rates, it is of crucial importance to gather evidence indicating trends in the character and context of violence. As yet, few scholars of other countries have taken up this program. Chapter 2 equally examines developments in the Netherlands with an eye on European-wide issues. It includes a discussion of homicide in self-defense – a subject that some scholars discuss with reference to legal rules but which few have studied from texts of jurisprudence. It also examines public attitudes concerning the death penalty for manslaughter, thereby extending my analysis of the criminalization of homicide – a process that occurred throughout Europe but which few scholars have tackled head-on. The third chapter subjects the link between historical violence and male honor to inter-continental comparison. It maintains that the relatively high homicide rates of the United States have to do with peculiarities of the American process of state formation and it ventures into comparison with a few Asian countries such as Taiwan.

The section on punishment and social control opens with an assessment of the theories of Norbert Elias and Michel Foucault, viewed in relation to the history of punishment in particular. In fact, chapter 4 implies a re-assessment, compared to the more outright dismissal of Foucault in some of my earlier work. I argue that Elias and Foucault converge to the extent that they find historical study indispensable for an adequate understanding of present-day society and that they both maintain that power is everywhere. They diverge, nevertheless, when it comes to the pace of penal change. Chapter 5 takes the discussion to the history of informal social control. I argue that, while informal regulation within communities and self-help by citizens were common in the early modern period, internal cohesion and communal controls continued to characterize many workers' neighborhoods until the mid twentieth century. When notions of privacy began to change, informal social controls declined. The essay also discusses the changing appreciation of violence by citizens who attempt to stop thieves and other lawbreakers. The sixth chapter essentially represents a renewal of my vision of the long-term history of the penal system, in Europe as well as America. Next to civilizing processes, it introduces Elias' theory of the long-term diminution of power differentials between social groups as an explanatory factor. It ranges from the sacralization of executions around 1500 to the modern resurgence of punitiveness on both continents, engaging along the way with James Q. Whitman's thesis.

The last section discusses several corollary developments to the decline of violence and the transformation of punishment. Chapter 7 focuses on the refinement of manners in the Dutch Republic. Its broader interest lies in the counter-model to the uses of etiquette and the balancing of power in courtly society as analyzed by Elias. It turns out that, despite an aversion to dueling, the Dutch elites of the seventeenth and eighteenth centuries were eager to adopt French aristocratic manners. Chapter 8 discusses long-term changes in festive behavior. Assessing the theoretical contributions of Victor Turner and Emile Durkheim, it goes back several millennia, but it ends with a discussion of the civilizing of festivals during the last two centuries. Chapter 9 covers the longest period of time. It draws the themes of religion and death into the discussion, imagining what it meant for humans when they first began to realize that they were mortal. The book concludes with a brief personal retrospective, commenting on Norbert Elias' influence on my becoming a crime historian.

PART ONE

VIOLENCE

I

Long-Term Trends in Homicide

Amsterdam, Fifteenth–Twentieth Centuries

Homicide is haunting historians. Some welcome its possibilities for a study of the long term, calling it "the one crime for which the evidence is most reliable."[1] Others, more skeptical, are trying to prove that any visible trend is only a chimera. This clash of arguments and approaches particularly concerns the period before the availability of national statistics. Evidence from that period is indispensable, if we want to make meaningful statements about the long term. Throughout this chapter, I will usually speak of *the* homicide rate, meaning the annual average, over a specified period, per 100,000 population, in a specified area.

The study of homicide rates has progressed much since the first ten years (1981–91) when England was the main focus of research and the long-term decline of violence since the middle ages was first established. Yet some of the problems emerging from the debates of that period have not been satisfactorily solved. In the most recent synthesis of the quantitative evidence about murder by Manuel Eisner (2001, 2003), for example, it is not specified which of the data are based on coroners' records and which on prosecutions alone. He also conflates the categories of family homicide and homicide on intimates. On the other hand, recent syntheses pay much more attention to the trend reversal since about 1970, which was still hardly visible when the pioneers wrote their studies.

The Inadequacy of Trial Figures

Examining the Dutch evidence available when I started my research, we can definitely conclude that frequency rates based on prosecuted homicide alone are unreliable. Combining the work of several historians, we might construct a graph of murder and manslaughter cases tried by the city's court from the beginning of the sixteenth century to the beginning of the nineteenth.[2] This enterprise leads to a surprising conclusion: the average annual level of prosecuted homicide in Amsterdam tended to remain constant, at about 1, over the entire period from 1524 to 1811 (although in the short run there were peaks and quiet decades). The city's population, however, rose dramatically from 15,000 in 1500 to 100,000 in the early decades of the seventeenth century, and to well over 200,000 at the end of that century. Thereafter there were minor fluctuations, but the population always remained over 200,000. Thus, a graph of homicide trials per 100,000 inhabitants would simply be the inverse of the population curve. The figure would be less than 0.5 per 100,000 throughout the eighteenth century. It is highly unlikely, although not impossible, that this graph would bear any resemblance to the real incidence of killing in Amsterdam.

The evidence on default procedures, discussed by Sjoerd Faber and Marijke Gijswijt-Hofstra, is one indication that the real incidence of killing in Amsterdam was higher than the prosecution records suggest.[3] Their data from two archival series allow me to calculate that the rate of homicides with identified killers (i.e. default procedures and prosecuted cases combined) lay between 1.5 and 2.1 during the period 1680–1790 and that it was 0.7 during the period 1751–1801. These figures indicate a declining trend, but the total number of homicides committed was higher than the rate of homicides with identified killers.

Outside Amsterdam, too, the available data indicate that homicide rates based on records of criminal prosecution are inadequate. A project on criminal justice in Leiden, 1533–1811, covers the next-longest period. The sentence registers of that town contain cases involving arrested killers as well as default trials. Peaks in the absolute numbers, however, are always due to increased efforts in sentencing fugitive suspects. When the number of homicide cases is low, there are almost no default trials. In another project the court records of seven sample jurisdictions, mostly small towns and rural regions, are analyzed from 1700 to 1811. In those seven jurisdictions there were only 98 homicide trials altogether, including default cases, during that period. The frequency declined after 1750.[4] In Haarlem, 1740–95, the rate of prosecuted homicide amounted to 0.7 per 100,000 per year.[5] Two widely diverging figures for the city of Utrecht also illustrate the problem. Based on the work of Dirk Berents, we can calculate that the homicide rate in this town in the first half of the fifteenth century was 53.3 (perpetrator rate) or about 50 (victimization rate).[6] Examining the town's register of criminal sentences for 1550–70, however, we arrive at a rate of prosecuted homicide of only 1 per

100,000.[7] It cannot be doubted that this immense drop within 100 years is largely due to changes in the registration of killings.

While these data from prosecution and default procedure records are suggestive, the really conclusive evidence is provided by the body inspection records discussed below. Jüngen was the first to recognize their importance and, to anticipate the discussion, let me cite his conclusion: in sixteenth-century Amsterdam, the ratio of detected to prosecuted killings was 9:1. The obvious superiority of lists of body inspections as a source for establishing the incidence of homicide lies in the fact that these records include cases in which the killer remained unidentified. To conclude, there are three types of sources, each successively yielding a higher number of homicides: court cases involving arrested killers; records listing all cases with identified killers; and lists of body inspections. Figures derived from the first two types of sources should be taken into consideration only when they are relatively high, because in that case the actual number of killings must necessarily be at least as high.

Methodological Considerations

Before I present my evidence, some methodological questions need to be cleared up. For one thing, can we infer from the homicide rate that in the early modern period, when a measure of internal pacification had been reached, violence still was socially accepted to some extent? The homicide rate refers to activities which were not tolerated per definition, since they were liable to criminal prosecution. Consequently, the cases we are collecting belong to unaccepted violence. The solution is to consider the homicide cases as representing the extreme pole of a continuum that begins with accepted violence: quarrels that are laughed about; fist fights in which bystanders encourage the participants more or less indiscriminately; a teasing with knives that everyone takes lightly; a beating within the family that the community does not consider serious. In the overwhelming majority of instances, such acts of violence do not result in the death of a participant.

Viewed from this angle, homicide only occurs when things get out of hand. Homicides are "casualties." The frequency of these casualties is an indication of the frequency of relatively minor and common forms of violence. In the sixteenth through eighteenth centuries, lethal fights were not accepted, but moderate forms of violence were considered relatively normal. If we observe a decline in the homicide rate, and thus in the number of casualties, in the course of this period, it means that the level of routine violence has declined. When this process continues, there must be a qualitative shift at some point: acceptance of moderate violence turns into a rejection among most members of society; as routine aggression becomes rarer, the number of casualties becomes insignificant; the residual homicide rate largely consists of extreme or marginal cases, in either the sphere of erupting tensions or a criminal underworld. That is in line with the evidence on the contemporary proportion of homicides on intimates and killings related to other illegal activities.

Also, with respect to the more technical side of reconstructing the long-term trend, problems lessen if we take theory into consideration. It might be argued, for example, that in our time the cowardice of people who are mugged lowers the homicide rate artificially. Unlike 200 or 300 years ago, nowadays most victims choose not to resist, thereby allowing the instrumental violence accompanying the robbery to be limited to a light form or even just the threat of using it.[8] However, it is doubtful whether in earlier centuries many cases of resistance to an assault on one's property resulted in the death of the victim or the robber. More important is that, if most victims today prefer to hand over their wallet, this is, besides their being insured, precisely because they are unaccustomed to violence. So this is in line with the general trend. A similar argument applies to killing in self-defense. When a case is acknowledged as such, it is a lawful act, so we might argue that it should be excluded from the homicide statistics. Such an argument is unconvincing. Had the outcome of the event been the reverse, it would have been a regular homicide; either way there has been a fight. Manslaughter and killing in self-defense are two possible casualties arising out of the same situation.

Still another disturbing factor consists of the cases which remain entirely unknown. Historians generally assume that homicide is the crime most easily detectable, since it is so difficult to hide the body. Nevertheless, there are people who disappear permanently and some of them may have been murdered. Does this happen more frequently today than in earlier centuries? Reliable statistics are lacking. Whatever is the case, hidden bodies point at planned, rational violence rather than killing in affect. A somewhat similar problem applies to a specific type of murder: poisoning. Some historians assume that the chances that this crime remained undetected increase the farther we go back in time. This assumption, however, is highly questionable.[9]

Two of the possibly disturbing factors are peculiar to modern times. In some countries reckless driving with lethal consequences is prosecuted as a homicidal act, but this is not customary in Dutch judicial practice. In medical statistics, death in a car accident is normally listed as a traffic casualty, no matter how guilty the driver was. Although some traffic casualties may be deliberate murders, I cannot imagine these cases to be very frequent. Modern means of transport also affect the contemporary figures in the form of fast ambulances taking seriously injured victims to an operation room. Most scholars agree that increased medical skill and organization only start to play a significant role toward 1900. On the whole, it is probably safe to say that all factors affecting the homicide rate were fairly constant well into the nineteenth century.

Two classification rules, finally, follow from the demand for comparability of figures. The first is that the victims rather than the killers should be the basic unit for constructing the homicide rate. It can make a difference, even if we have the complete evidence on both. There were instances in which one assailant killed several victims simultaneously, as well as those in which one victim was killed by several persons simultaneously. Especially in the latter case, the urge to assign individual responsibility to the actual killer and his accomplices may vary over time. Moreover, in coroners' inquests and medical statistics, we count bodies – that is, victims. The second rule is always to exclude attempted murder or manslaughter from the homicide rate. The definition of what constitutes an attempt at a person's life varied greatly over time.[10] Naturally, mere attempts are absent from medical statistics on the causes of death.

Homicide in Amsterdam, 1431–1816

Amsterdam meets another methodological requirement, that of studying a relatively populous area over time. Jan Boomgaard presents the earliest reliable and relevant data.[11] Information is available for eleven fiscal years during the period 1431–62. The names of 54 killers were known. Exactly a third of them were dealt with judicially, which resulted in 17 financial settlements and only 1 death sentence. Another 34 killers had fled Amsterdam; 1 had died in the brawl and the fate of 1 is unknown. In six instances the victim was killed by 2 men, and in two instances by 3 men, which means that the total number of victims was 44. These figures amount to an average of 5 killers per year and 4 victims per year. Amsterdam's population by the middle of the fifteenth century may be estimated at 8–9,000.[12] Consequently, the homicide victimization rate was approximately 47.

The Amsterdam court records of the sixteenth century include the inspections, carried out at the orders of the judiciary, of the bodies of persons who had died under suspicious circumstances. During the years 1524–65, they numbered 646 altogether, around a third of which involved cases of drowning. There were 344 homicides; as noted above only 11 percent of these led to prosecution.[13] The average absolute number of detected killings was 8.2 per year. With a population of almost 30,000, this amounts to a homicide rate of around 28. In an unpublished thesis Jüngen supplements these figures with data from four sample years: 1560, 1570, 1580 and 1590. In the inspection reports of those years he found an annual average of 10 homicides and 1.5 uncertain cases. Around 1575 the city's population was probably about 47,500, which results in a homicide rate for the period 1560–90 that lies between 21.1 and 24.2.[14] This suggests that the rate was declining during the sixteenth century.

Around 1600 the Amsterdam court stopped the practice of inserting body inspection reports in the registers of criminal sentences. Possibly, the court began right away to list these reports separately, but in that case the earliest records have not been preserved. There is a gap in our information until the 1660s. Five separate registers of body inspections carried out at the orders of the Amsterdam judiciary are extant.[15] Faber has already consulted this source in order to count infanticide cases.[16] Because most of the inspections involved an autopsy, I will refer to them under that name. Together, the registers cover the period 1666–1817, with gaps for the years 1680–92 and 1727–51. When a register or set of consecutive registers did not begin in January or end in December, I discarded these incomplete years. Because of this, evidence is available for three periods: 1667–79, 1693–1726 and 1752–1816. In my tables the second period is split into two sub-periods and the third into four. Because the body inspection reports were copied in a bound register in chronological order, it is unlikely that cases have been lost. The problem is rather that there are too many.

Not every inspected body was actually dead. Around 1700 the registers include visitations of wounded persons, while throughout the period there are a few reports in which a person's state of mind or the condition of a girl's genitals were the issue. These cases are easily identified. It is different with the corpses. Information on the cause of death was based on the registered conclusions of a court committee, who did the inspections. The registers I studied also included cases of non-violent death. The problem is that the judicial conclusion is missing. The autopsies were performed by the city's anatomy professor assisted by two or three surgeons.[17] They never stepped outside the bounds of their profession, always listing the medical cause of death only. Supposedly, the prosecutor and the judges drew their conclusions, based on information about what had happened. It is only in some cases that this information was inserted in the registers. Thus, we know, for example, that a man found drowned was murdered because the surgeons noted that his hands and feet were tied, or that a woman whose skull was smashed had committed suicide because a clerk wrote in the margin that she had jumped out of a window.

The only way to proceed was to collect information on every variable in the records and to use this information in order to reduce the number of uncertain cases to the lowest level possible. For the bodies of persons not identified as infants, this operation had to be performed carefully. There were four possibilities: homicide, suicide, accidental death and natural death. The identification of the fourth was relatively unproblematic. In the cases concerned, the surgeons either listed some infection or disease, or, when they did not know, they noted the absence of any sign of violence. The problem was especially to differentiate homicide from either suicide or accidental death. Information on the condition of the body or the circumstances of the event sometimes allowed me to assign a case with certainty to one of the three categories. I did so in one more type of situation, not with certainty but still with great confidence: I classified as suicides all cases in which the cause of death was listed as strangulation (and in which it was often noted that the body had had a rope around its neck). The Amsterdam sources contain no hints that gangs of sneaky stranglers were active in the city over a century and a half.[18]

For the rest, we have to make deductions from the sort of injury that the surgeons described. Persons whose death was caused by any sort of blunt instrument could either have been killed or become the victim of an accident. They make up the majority of the cases listed as possible homicide. When a weapon had been used, an accident was unlikely, but it could have been a suicide. When a body had more than one wound or one that could not be self-inflicted, I concluded that this meant a violent death at the hands of another person. Then there were the categories of one stab wound, one cut in the throat and one piercing with a sword. It was decided finally to list them as certain homicides too. Although technically it would be possible to commit suicide in this way, it is unlikely that this was done by more than a handful of people. The frequency of strangulation indicates that hanging oneself was the common method for committing suicide. Some persons, on the other hand, definitely shot themselves, which led me to assign the cases of one shot wound, except when it was in the back, to the category of possible homicide. Fortunately, the use of guns does not seem to have been very common in early modern Amsterdam. Dying from poison, finally, also was assigned to the category of possible homicide.

The resulting file of non-infants who certainly or possibly had been killed by another person consists of 1,091 victims, out of a total of 1,451 non-infant corpses inspected. Reliable population estimates for Amsterdam are available. The number of inhabitants in the seven periods, distinguished respectively, can be put at: 200,000; 200,000; 200,000; 205,000; 220,000; 220,000; 205,000.[19] Table 1.1 presents my

Table 1.1 Homicide (on non-infants) in Amsterdam autopsy reports,
1667–1816 (annual averages per period)

Period	Certain homicide		Possible homicide		Median of certain and total
	abs.	per 100,000	abs.	per 100,000	per 100,000
1667–79	5.5	2.8	1.2	0.6	3.1
1693–1709	18.0	9.0	2.4	1.2	9.6
1710–26	17.1	8.6	0.7	0.4	8.8
1752–67	3.3	1.6	1.9	0.9	2.1
1768–83	3.7	1.7	4.4	2.0	2.7
1784–99	3.1	1.4	2.4	1.1	2.0
1800–16	2.3	1.1	0.9	0.4	1.3

calculations (because every average was calculated directly from the total number and rounded off to one decimal, average parts sometimes do not add up to average sums).

We can take the figures of the last column as the best estimates, approximating the real homicide rate. At first sight it looks as if the gaps in the documentation represent the crucial years, with the rate rising sharply during the first gap and declining again during the second. The figure for the period 1667–79 is especially surprising; it is very low when compared with the sixteenth-century data, but also decidedly lower than the level prevailing a few decades later. It is the only figure contradicting the hypothesis of a steady decline. However, there is good reason to assume that precisely in this period cases were underreported. An urban ordinance dated June 3, 1692, explicitly says that "some surgeons and other people dare to open the bodies or inspect the wounds of persons who have been slain or who have died in an accident."[20] The magistrates insisted that only the official physician and surgeons of the court were authorized to do this job. Presumably, the ordinance was strictly enforced, which would explain the subsequent rise in registered autopsies. On the other hand, such unofficial inspections of bodies as were performed in the 1660s and 1670s would have to have been enormously frequent in order to make the total number of inspections approach the figure prevailing from 1693 onward.

To some extent, then, that period must have witnessed a peak in homicide. That is suggested by the data from criminal records (see below). In the first decade of the eighteenth century, homicide trials were nearly twice as frequent as they had been in the second half of the seventeenth century, and in the 1710s even four times as frequent. Although the peak in prosecuted homicide lasted for a briefer moment than the high tide in

Table 1.2 Characteristics of homicide victims (non-infants, certain and possible) in Amsterdam, 1667–1816

Period	% female	% child or adolescent	% stabbed
1667–79	21.8	2.3	49.4
1693–1709	13.0	2.0	74.6
1710–26	13.2	1.3	82.8
1752–67	27.2	9.6	28.9
1768–83	35.2	7.8	20.9
1784–99	38.6	10.2	17.0
1800–16	33.3	20.0	29.1
Total	20.6	4.7	58.1

the number of body inspections, the two cannot be entirely unrelated. Possibly, when the rise in the incidence of killing became manifest, the court reacted to it by intensifying its efforts to catch suspects. If this was so, we must conclude that, even though the homicide rate of the period 1667–79 probably was kept down by underreporting, the figure for the early eighteenth century represented a temporary upsurge from a lower level which had prevailed before the 1690s. But we don't know exactly how low it was, as any attempt to estimate the number of unofficial autopsies in this period would just be a wild guess.

Since the homicide level was so much lower in the register begun in 1752, we might suppose that this was due to underreporting as well. However, it is unlikely that the practice of unofficial autopsies was resumed in this period. During the eighteenth century, bureaucratization definitely progressed in the city, also and especially in the judicial realm. Moreover, a decreased homicide rate after 1750 would be perfectly in line with the observed trend in the frequency of homicides with identified killers. The modest rise, in the last column, during the fifth period was due largely to the unusually high number of uncertain cases. Decline set in again toward the turn of the century. The rates in the certain and median columns are very low in the last period.

The reports also inform us about the victim's sex and approximate age (distinguishing between adults and non-adults). Table 1.2 presents the most striking results. That women and children were less likely to be stabbed than adult men may not be surprising. The figures become especially noteworthy when compared with the frequencies of table 1.1. The correlations, negative and positive, are nearly perfect: when the homicide rate is high, the proportion of stabbings goes up and the proportion of female and young victims goes down (note that many of the young victims were also female, so the percentages of columns 1 and 2

Table 1.3 Infanticide plus homicide (certain and possible) in Amsterdam,
        1667–1816

Period	Infanticide (annual average)		Total number of killings (annual average)	
	abs.	per 100,000 pop.	abs.	per 100,000 pop.
1667–79	0.6	0.3	7.3	3.7
1693–1709	2.3	1.2	22.7	11.4
1710–26	3.8	1.9	21.6	10.8
1752–67	5.6	2.7	10.8	5.3
1768–83	7.4	3.4	15.5	7.0
1784–99	1.1	0.5	6.6	3.0
1800–16	1.3	0.6	4.5	2.2

cannot be added up). Information on the perpetrators is lacking in most cases, but women who killed men, especially who stabbed them, must have been a rarity. Thus, the high level of homicide in the 1690s through 1720s was due mainly to an increase in knife-fighting among men.

With the group of "recently born children," as the reports call them, the uncertainties are negligible. As a rule, their bodies had been found in the water or at another place outside a private home. Babies cannot commit suicide and the circumstances of their death make an accident highly unlikely. Indeed, the inspection of an infant's body was not primarily meant to establish the cause of death. Using the lung proof (checking whether or not the dead baby's lungs float in water), the doctors decided whether or not the child had been alive at birth. When they concluded that it had never breathed, I did not count the case as an infanticide. This is because I discuss infanticide primarily in order that the reader may know the total number of killings, which obliges me to exclude children who were not in fact killed.

Table 1.3 shows the annual averages per period and adds them up with data from table 1.1 (in order to also establish absolute figures, I opted for certain and possible together). Among the infant group, too, violent death may have been underreported in the first period. The lung proof was in an early stage of development, so the magistrates often may have concluded that an inspection was useless. Among the sixteenth-century inspections there were only one or two bodies of infants.[21] Clearly, the infanticide rate did not follow the trend in murders and manslaughters. Infanticide remained constantly frequent during the 100 years from the 1690s into the 1780s. In the fourth period infanticides even outnumbered homicides and they would have done so in the fifth period as well, had not the number of possible homicides been so high. Despite all this, the general trend in the total number of killings, certain and possible, follows a similar pattern to that in table 1.1. The inclusion of infanticide cases merely makes the decline during the second half of the eighteenth century less marked. Admittedly, the bare discovery of a dead baby does not tell much of a story. For information about the mother's state of mind we have to be content with judicial documentation. One crucial datum, however, was usually recorded in the autopsy reports. There were 406 bodies of infants found in the city and the sex of 387 of them was mentioned. Of those 387 babies, 51.4 percent were boys and 48.6 percent girls.[22] Obviously, the child's sex did not matter for the decision to kill it. That is exactly what we would expect, based on the hypothesis that the victim's identity was no major factor in the crime.

Obviously, for the quantitative study of infanticide, judicial trials alone are an even more unreliable source. It is illuminating to compare the Amsterdam data with Hoffer and Hull's figures for England and New England, based on indictments. The infanticide rates they calculated for different periods almost always remained far below one, even though the authors included killings of children up to nine years old.[23] The Amsterdam evidence shows that the actual incidence of the crime was much higher than the prosecution rate indicates.

The Age of Statistics

The last judicial autopsy was copied into the register in August 1817, six years after the French had thoroughly reorganized the Dutch court system. The register in question has dozens of blank pages at the end. It is unclear whether the body inspection committee was dissolved or their reports stored elsewhere, but I have been unable to find judicial autopsies for the period after 1817. Although an article by Herman Franke allows me to pick up the story again in 1850, his figures are hardly comparable with mine. Until 1911 only statistics on convictions are available; they refer to perpetrators, are nationwide and include attempts. In these statistics the rate of prosecuted homicide fluctuated around 0.5 well into the twentieth century.[24] For the opening decade of the series, this may indicate an actual homicide rate close to the one established for Amsterdam at the beginning of the nineteenth century – on the assumption that the level of detected killings still was about three to four times higher than the level of prosecuted killings.

For the period 1911–2006 we are well informed due to the work of Paul Nieuwbeerta and Gerlof Leistra. They constructed a data base of homicide cases for these years based primarily on medical statistics, available since 1911, supplemented by other sources. The resulting figures are also nationwide, hence not fully comparable to the long-term trend constructed for Amsterdam. By the early twentieth century the Dutch homicide rate was much lower still than the one for the capital city 100 years earlier. National rates fluctuated around 0.4 between 1911 and 1965 (except during the war years 1943–5), then climbed steadily to 1.2 in 1990, stabilized subsequently and dropped again below 1 between 2002 and 2006.[25] Obviously, the Netherlands partook of the trend reversal in Europe that started around 1970 and concentrated during the 1970s and 1980s.

What about modern Amsterdam? The Dutch bureau of statistics has a series of causes of death figures for this city during the years 1979–89.[26] In that period the absolute number of homicides fluctuated without a specific pattern; the average annual rate per 100,000 was 2.1. According to Nieuwbeerta and Leistra, the homicide rate in the three largest cities of the Netherlands averaged 3.5 from 1990 to 2001 and 3.4 between 2002 and 2006.[27] These figures, however, are again not comparable with those calculated from the autopsy reports, since modern statistics refer to residents of Amsterdam who have been killed anywhere, and the historical reports to persons, residing anywhere, who had been killed in the city.

Nowadays, information about all persons killed within a city usually comes from the police. Franke was able to extract from them the numbers of homicide victims in Amsterdam during the years 1987–90: 40, 52, 46 and 45 respectively.[28] With 725,000 inhabitants, this amounts to an annual average of 6.3 per 100,000. Since the late 1990s the Amsterdam chief of police annually announces in January the numbers of the previous year, but these figures do not appear to be kept systematically. In another publication Nieuwbeerta and Leistra calculate a police-based homicide rate of 5.4 for Amsterdam in 1997–9.[29] Hence, the rate for late twentieth-century Amsterdam can be put at around 6. It may be concluded that Amsterdam partakes in the modern rise in the homicide rate by a multiple factor, a phenomenon common to almost all capitals and big cities in Europe.

Moreover, no allowance has been made yet for advances in medical technology and organization, the only factor whose influence is so much greater now than it was in previous centuries. As it happens, Amsterdam sources around 1700 allow me to make an approximate estimate of how great this influence is almost 300 years later. As far as I know, no such device is to be found in historical literature so far. Reports of inspections of the wounds of seriously injured persons are included in the second and third registers of autopsies. In the third their number declines toward the end; the wounded appear to have been inspected on a regular basis up to 1706. Some victims were visited twice, first in their capacity as injured person and one or more days later in their capacity as corpse. During the interval they had been taken care of in the city's hospital. They numbered 63 altogether in the period 1693–1706, which is 4.5 per year. With an average of about 19 homicides per year in this period, those dying of their injuries in the hospital make up 23.7 percent. This is the proportion of victims who might have been saved, had our contemporary medical technology been available. Here we have our measure. It is a crude one, but it is based on historical evidence. In the early modern period about one quarter of all homicide victims died "unnecessarily." Hence, the modern rates would have to be increased by one-third to make them comparable with the pre-1900 figures. For modern Amsterdam this would mean a corrected homicide rate of 8. On the other hand, in the early modern period Amsterdam was a city surrounded only by rural areas. It would be fair to take the entire metropolitan area of Amsterdam today as the unit of comparison. No doubt, this would lower the modern homicide rate again.

As we might expect, the modern rise does not involve infanticide. The literature on contemporary murder hardly mentions the subject at all. Newspapers contain no reports about dead babies found in canals. The series of Amsterdam medical statistics for 1979–89 has a category of children under one year of age (hence much broader than that of newborn babies) and throughout this period only one victim fell into that category. Thus, infanticide is no longer an issue. This is perfectly understandable in an age in which birth control and abortion are common and in which there is a near-universal acceptance of having children outside legal marriage.

Contextual Evidence

Evidence on the circumstances of a homicide case and the sort of violence involved should be called contextual rather than qualitative, because it can be quantified in its turn. The only systematic discussion of such evidence in Dutch historical literature is by Gijswijt-Hofstra. Her research concerns fugitive manslaughter suspects who were granted a safe place in one of the five sanctuaries forming enclaves within the Republic's territory from the end of the sixteenth century until 1795.[30] The overwhelming majority of the cases whose circumstances she discusses were quarrels with lethal consequences. The victims were strangers or acquaintances, not intimates or family. There were no premeditated murders. Every killer claimed he had acted in self-defense and bore no guilt. This is understandable, since such excuses were a necessary precondition for obtaining sanctuary. Besides, a suspect needed to be relatively wealthy to pay for his subsistence and his right to stay. Thus, the cases discussed by Gijswijt-Hofstra are in no way representative for all homicides in the Dutch Republic.

The Amsterdam autopsy reports sometimes contain information on the circumstances of the case, but this is never given consistently. The only way to gather contextual evidence on homicide in Amsterdam more systematically is to return to the trial records. My data base of sentences involving a public punishment, 1651–1750, collected in earlier research, and references generously provided by Sjoerd Faber for the years 1751–1810 form the basis, supplemented by several other archival series. I only considered completed homicide, excluding cases of mere attempt and infanticide. The trials for completed homicide include some in which the suspect was granted (a measure of) self-defense; these are analyzed more fully in chapter 2. Although my earlier research was based on the so-called "justice"and "sentence" books, in all cases I went back to the interrogation protocols.[31] The total data set consists of 143 cases, hence just under one per year. These cases involve 144 perpetrators and 154 victims. For a diachronic comparison I am distinguishing three periods: 1651–1700 (37 killers, 39 victims); 1701–1750 (70 killers, 75 victims); 1751–1810 (37 killers, 40 victims). The peak in prosecutions at the beginning of the eighteenth century largely accounts for the greater frequency in the second period.

The problem of representativeness is less distracting than with Gijswijt-Hofstra's data. When we consider the collected cases as a sample of homicide in Amsterdam, the only systematic bias is that the killers were arrested. It is difficult to assess the chances of getting caught in different situations. I would have supposed that this chance was greater for those who killed an intimate, because they were easily suspect and less likely to flee. However, in 1714, the clerk reviewing the autopsy reports noted that no less than four women were said to have been stabbed to death by their husbands, and another by her son-in-law. None of these reputed killers figures in the criminal dossiers; they probably had fled. Some professional criminals, on the other hand, may have remained in town without being detected. Thus, different types of killers each were able to escape prosecution. Even more important for determining the representativeness of the cases is the one quantitative measure we have. The victim's sex is the only variable present in the trial series as well as the autopsy reports. In the trial series the percentage of female victims is 32.5, which is higher than in the autopsy reports. Clearly, people who killed women were more likely to get caught than those who killed men. However, the difference between the two series is largely caused by an exceptionally high number of female victims in the third period of the

Table 1.4 Killer–victim relationships in Amsterdam homicide trials in three periods

Type of victim	1651–1700		1701–50		1751–1810	
	abs.	%	abs.	%	abs.	%
Intimate	4	10.3	11	14.7	17	42.5
Acquaintance	16	41.0	27	36.0	13	32.5
Stranger	14	35.9	33	44.0	7	17.5
Unclear	5	12.8	4	5.3	3	7.5
Total	39	100	75	100	40	100

trial records. They made up 20.5 percent and 22.7 percent in the first and second period, respectively; a proportion comparable to that found in the autopsy reports. The first and second periods, then, can be considered fairly representative. The period 1751–1810, in which no less than 62.5 percent of the victims were women, has to be handled with greater caution.

The number of female killers in the trial series, ten altogether, was too small to allow a meaningful comparison over time. Together they made 12 victims, 11 of whom were either the woman's own (non-infant) child or another adult female. The twelfth victim was the woman's husband. It means that of all killers of spouses and lovers tried, only one was female.

During an initial stage I distinguished nine possible relationships of the victim to his or her aggressor: spouse; lover; child, parent or sibling; other family relationship or in-law; occupational relationship; fellow in underworld; other type of acquaintance; stranger; relationship unclear. In this categorization, strangers are by far the largest group. Of course, some interaction precedes almost any homicide; the victim was listed as a stranger when the killer did not know him or her before the incident leading to the killing. In most of the unclear cases, the records do not reveal whether the two already knew each other or not; as a rule, these victims were either acquaintances or strangers, not intimates. The category of distant kin and in-laws had only one representative in each period. That makes it reasonable to combine it with the three subsequent categories. The first three together make up the intimates. By grouping the victims in this way, we have reduced the types of relationship to four.

Table 1.4 shows the frequencies over time. The proportion of acquaintances declines slightly but not dramatically. That the proportion of strangers is somewhat lower in the first period when compared to the second may well be due partly to the relatively high percentage of unclear cases in the first period. Obviously, the most conspicuous shift concerns the reversal of the intimate–stranger ratio around 1750.

It is exactly 1:3 in the second period and about 2.5:1 in the third. It may be objected that I just cast doubt on the representativeness of the trials in the third period. However, I am not prepared to consider the observed trend entirely an artefact. For one thing, the percentage of all three subcategories of intimates increased. A trend can be observed also with respect to the killer's age (mentioned often but not always): 27, 30 and 33 years, in the three periods respectively. This trend is compatible with a shift from fights among strangers to conflicts among intimates. Finally, since the number of homicide victims in the autopsy reports was much lower after the middle of the eighteenth century, the trials of the third period represent the most intensive sample. By the early nineteenth century the number of victims appearing in the autopsy reports was only three to four times as high as that found in the trials. The homicide rate had dropped considerably in comparison with a century earlier. It was hypothesized that such a drop would be accompanied by a rising pro-portion of homicides on intimates. That is precisely what seems to have happened, although the dimensions of the change may have been more modest than the figure for the period 1751–1810 indicates.

A few other variables are informative. That of the killer's birthplace, for example, shows a fluctuating pattern. Those born in Amsterdam made up 29 percent, 58 percent and 38 percent, in the three periods respectively. While for the first this is about 15 percent lower than in the general population, for the second it is about 10 percent higher. A number of homicide convicts either had a previous arrest or one or more additional offenses listed in their sentence. Those killers can be consid-ered as the group with a criminal background. They made up about one-half, one-third and one-quarter in the three periods, respectively. If the data on birthplace and criminal background are combined, the con-trast between the second half of the seventeenth century and the first half of the eighteenth is especially marked: among the perpetrators of homi-cide a shift took place from immigrants with a criminal background to residents without such a background.

It is illuminating to consider separately the 1710s, when the frequency of trials was so high. That decade stood out from the total file of trials in several respects. Out of 27 victims only 1 was female. The killers, all male, were relatively young, about 25 on average, and no less than 70 percent of them were born in Amsterdam. None of the trials was for killing an intimate. Indeed, no act of violence in this decade might be called a culmination of tensions. With that observation we have moved to a more interpretive evaluation of the evidence. In the decade 1711–20, 16 cases concerned a tavern brawl or a similar kind of quarrel; 4 were robbery-related; 3 concerned the perpetrator's resistance to apprehen-sion; 1 man had suddenly attacked 3 others for no apparent reason; in

1 case the circumstances were unclear.[32] An upsurge of trials apparently meant an increase in the number of highly impulsive killers caught. Moreover, these killers were relatively young and rooted in the community. Since the homicide rate peaked in this very period, the upsurge of trials also must have meant an increase in the actual frequency of lethal quarrels. That suggests that high homicide rates are the result of a high frequency of tavern brawls, and comparable kinds of impulsive violence, within the community.

A characterization of the court cases with the help of the two axes I distinguished in the introduction is not an easy enterprise. It must be repeated that the word "axis" has been chosen because it is never a question of either–or but always of more or less. No homicidal incident simply can be labeled according to one archetype or the other. Let me briefly review the cases, restricting myself to what is relevant for the discussion of trends.

Throughout the period 1651–1750 violence with a highly impulsive character was dominant. About three-fifths of the killings in that period resulted from conflicts arising in a tavern or street without any discernible previous history. There was no planning involved; just a little took place in some cases, when a quarrel was interrupted and one of the protagonists used this opportunity to go home and get a knife. When two persons fought, a third sometimes intervened, which might make him either the killer or the victim. In other cases the killer had been provoked, because the victim was teasing him. The non-settled population was involved in this kind of violence too. One pickpocket stabbed another to death as they fought over the division of the spoils. Apart from these brawls, about half of the robbery-related homicides of this period had impulsive features. A man had been drinking with another, for example, and suddenly decided to try to take his companion's possessions. Or a woman killed another out of desperation, because she owed her victim money which she could not pay. During the period 1751–1810, on the other hand, only between a third and one-half of the homicides can be called highly impulsive. That does not mean that the remaining cases were close to the rational pole. Careful planning remained rare; it was only a feature of some robberies.

Less can be said about the ritual–instrumental axis. From the available documentation it is difficult to determine to what extent the tavern brawls and comparable quarrels also had expressive features. Most cases of highly instrumental violence were homicides related to property crime. They occurred throughout the period 1651–1810.

The question of the extent to which the killing of an intimate person was an eruption of pent-up tensions must be dealt with separately. It is difficult to relate this question to the two axes of violence. A homicide resulting from a long-standing conflict can hardly be called impulsive, but neither, as a rule, is it planned in advance. Although, supposedly, this crime is more common in modern times, its nature is closer to ritual than to instrumental violence. I am calling this type of homicide on an intimate person "tension-related." The opposite type, described in several Amsterdam trial records, may be termed "anger-related." We encounter it notably among men who killed their wives or concubines. Characteristically, the perpetrator was said to be drunk and annoyed over a specific thing. Sometimes the incident was a beating that got out of hand. Every story of a partner killing is like that up to the 1720s. From then on, tension-related cases surface in the court records, and they become more frequent in the period 1751–1810. All but a few of the cases in that period belong to one of four groups, which are about equally frequent: tension-related homicides on intimates, anger-related homicides on intimates, highly impulsive violence toward acquaintances or strangers, killings related to robbery.

Finally, I am considering poisoning. The first recorded trial took place in 1728, when a man had poisoned his sister with arsenic in order to inherit from her.[33] Another man was tried three years later; he had killed an acquaintance in an attempt to test whether his special poison was as undetectable as he hoped.[34] Earlier, between 1693 and 1709, the surgeons performing the autopsies had found poison in the bodies of four persons and their reports contained another 20 such cases in subsequent years. This suggests that historians' concerns about an elevated dark number for poisoning, by wives or others, may be exaggerated.

It can be concluded that the contextual evidence assembled so far indicates a trend. Straightforwardly impulsive violence predominated until the middle of the eighteenth century, becoming less prominent since then. Notably, the incidence of tavern brawls decreased. Around the same time there occurred a shift from the killing of strangers to the killing of intimates. From the 1720s onward, a number of homicides on intimates were tension-related. The observed trend probably continued after 1810. In his study of royal pardons in the Netherlands, Sibo van Ruller discusses 122 homicide cases from the period 1814–70. Most cases, he says, either were robbery-related or involved marital/love problems. He identified 48 female and 43 male victims.[35]

Conclusion

The claim of a long-term shift in the character of homicidal violence still has to be corroborated by further research and requires evidence for the twentieth century. With my conclusion on the overall trend, from the fifteenth century onward, I am on firmer ground. Homicidal violence definitely declined in Amsterdam at least until the first decades of the nineteenth century. The trend is so marked that the uncertainties become meaningless in comparison with it. The homicide rate, defined as the annual average of violent deaths, excluding infants, in the city per 100,000 inhabitants, was 47 (or even more) in the second third of the fifteenth century. A hundred years later it stood at 28, and it had declined to about 23 toward the end of the sixteenth century. It was very low, just over 3, in the period 1667–79, but this is probably due partly to under-reporting. In the 1690s and the first quarter of the eighteenth century the homicide rate stood between 9 and 9.5. It had greatly declined by the middle of that century: to between 2 and 3. In the 1800s and 1810s it stood between 1 and 1.5.

As for other parts of the Netherlands, only Berents' data can be taken into consideration. His figure, though representing a minimum level, is still quite high. The homicide rate of about 50 for the city of Utrecht in the first half of the fifteenth century converges with the Amsterdam evidence for the same period. Thus, the Netherlands also witnessed the general trend of long-term decline, first observed for England. In the Netherlands the decline was even steeper. The Dutch trend began at a much higher level than the English and the level stayed relatively high well into the eighteenth century. The temporary peak in Amsterdam around the turn of the seventeenth and eighteenth centuries cannot simply be explained by pointing at the metropolis' many taverns and the tavern brawls they facilitated. After 1750 the town still was bustling and, in spite of this, the homicide rate had declined.

In our time the Amsterdam homicide rate is back at 6 (corrected rate: 8). Much has been said about the contemporary rise. For the moment, two crucial qualifications should be made. First, the national homicide rate today is much lower than the capital's. Homicidal violence tends to concentrate in Amsterdam (and a few other big cities) and this was probably less so in earlier centuries. Second, within the capital a considerable share of homicides takes place in the context of a criminal underworld, notably in connection with the drug trade. This trade is rooted less in urban communities than in international networks. Violent crime generally in Dutch society is committed disproportionately by groups who are marginal from an ethnic or cultural point of view. It would seem that the idea of a marginalization of homicide holds for the Netherlands. This means that the contemporary rates are not incongruent with Elias' theory. There is still another way to put it: serious violence today is concentrated in "unpacified islands." Nineteenth-century national societies in Europe were particularly homogeneous. By contrast, the greater differentiation prevailing in the late twentieth century and the twenty-first has led to the appearance of small islands within these societies where the pacification once guaranteed by the state has crumbled to some extent. In order to confirm this hypothesis, independent evidence, apart from the homicide rate, is needed. The argument presented here links recent trends to long-term developments, claiming that historical research may contribute to an understanding of contemporary problems.

2

Homicide and the Law in the Dutch Republic

A Peaceful Country?

Since the 1990s the so-called "polder model" has played a prominent role in Dutch public discourse. Its merits were debated in the media as well as in Parliament. "Polder model" refers to a tradition of conflict-solving and decision-making by way of discussion, negotiation and compromise at every level, from the local to the national and from small clubs to large corporations. This tradition allegedly went back to the middle ages, when the struggle against the rising water required the cooperation of all inhabitants, or else annihilation by flooding would have been their collective fate. In fact, the polder concept constitutes a variant of an older belief, according to which Dutch society, past and present, has always been relatively peaceful, devoid of warriors, fanatics and rabble rousers. Even today, a number of social scientists and some historians maintain that the Dutch are a particularly non-violent nation.

Admittedly, this self-congratulating view pertains first of all to collective and political violence. Social transformations in the Netherlands, so the argument runs, tend to occur quietly, almost without bloodshed. The major examples adduced include the "velvet" transition to the Batavian Republic in 1795 and the easy adoption of the 1848 Constitution under the mere threat of revolutions elsewhere. Even within the sphere of political and social upheaval, however, there is much evidence to the contrary, as historians such as Rudolf Dekker point out: religious conflict in the 1610s amounting to near civil war and culminating in the execution of the defeated party's leader, Johan van Oldenbarnevelt; recurrent tax riots throughout the seventeenth and eighteenth centuries; violence between Orangists and their opponents, with the murder of the brothers De Witt in 1672 as a marker; the Belgian Revolution of 1830 and the ferocious attempt to suppress it; bloody military campaigns in Indonesia at the end of the nineteenth century and again in the late 1940s.[1]

In this chapter I am concerned with interpersonal or everyday violence. The belief in Dutch exceptionalism extends to this field and it has even been claimed that my own work supports the contention of a constantly low level of aggression in the Netherlands. That assertion requires a highly selective presentation of data. A closer examination of the available quantitative evidence, on the other hand, inevitably leads to the conclusion that the Netherlands witnessed some periods when the level of interpersonal violence indeed was lower than that common in Europe, as well as a few periods when it was higher, while it was in the median range most of the time.

For one thing, this can be concluded from the homicide rates presented in the previous chapter. Those for fifteenth-century Amsterdam and Utrecht, close to 50, can be called median, because the data we have from reliable counts for medieval towns throughout Europe vary widely between 20 and 100.[2] Amsterdam's homicide rates of about 28 by the mid sixteenth century, and about 23 between 1560 and 1590, again are in the middle between, for example, Rome with rates twice as high at the time, Stockholm that slightly exceeded Amsterdam, and, at the other extreme, the city of Cologne as well as Elizabethan Kent and Essex with rates of 10 or lower. On the other hand, the peak in the Amsterdam homicide rate between 1693 and 1726 was well above the contemporary European average. During the second half of the eighteenth century the city took part in the pan-European decline of homicide. Around 1800 this decline had led to even lower rates in Scandinavia and England, whereas in Germany the rate remained at a higher level than the Amsterdam one, and in Italy was still higher.

The Dutch medical statistics kept since 1911 yield very low homicide levels indeed, compared to European standards, fluctuating between 0.23 and 0.44 until 1970 (except during World War II). After 1970, however, Dutch homicide rates quickly rose, once more partaking of a general European trend. By 2000 they were again in the median range among European nations West of the former Iron Curtain.[3]

The Seventeenth and Eighteenth Centuries: Qualitative Evidence

Despite the reliability of these quantitative figures, some scholars remain unconvinced by statistics. These should be supplemented with qualitative evidence, although its interpretation is always open to differences of view and scholarly approach. Is it significant, for instance, when citizens are eagerly buying broadsheets about bloody murders, or, on the other hand, when they comment unfavorably on the aggressive habits of other nations? Court records referring to violence that actually took place constitute a somewhat harder body of evidence, although the researcher's selection of cases involves a measure of arbitrariness. It can be argued, nevertheless, that three phenomena were especially character-istic of interpersonal violence in early modern Europe: the formal duel, the popular duel and established–outsider confrontations. This section presents Dutch examples of these three types in reversed order, begin-ning with Jewish–Christian fights. Compared to the rest of Europe, the examples imply intensified, average and lower violence, respectively.

Jews lived in the Dutch Republic from 1598, when a group from Portugal arrived. This Sephardic community, consisting in large part of wealthy traders, remained relatively small. In the course of the sev-enteenth century, they were followed by Yiddish-speaking Ashkenazics from Germany and later from Poland. These were overwhelmingly poor people and many of them had fled either adverse economic conditions or overt discrimination. In the Dutch Republic they met with fewer restric-tions from the authorities, if not from the Reformed Church and the guilds. The degree of discrimination and the level of everyday aggression, however, are two different things. Jews met with increasing hostility and violence from ordinary members of the Christian population.

In the second half of the seventeenth century, the Jewish community in Amsterdam became a visible group, though still of modest size. In 1682 eight adolescents approached the synagogue and attacked Jewish men and women in the streets with knives, injuring a young man.[4] The influx of Yiddish-speaking immigrants from Germany and Poland continued unabated, so that after 1700 Jews had become numerous enough to be more than just victims. From then onwards, fights between Jews and Christians occurred on a more or less regular basis. In October 1716, the Amsterdam court considered the matter serious enough to publish a special ordinance, which mentioned that *smousen* and Christian boys often assembled to fight each other with sticks, stones, knives and daggers. This regularly caused serious injuries to participants, the ordinance continued, while passers-by got hurt and horses ran wild. Henceforth a person's mere presence in such a fighting group would be sufficient for a sentence of whipping. Bystanders refusing an order to leave the scene would be fined.[5]

The court's emphasis on boys appears justified, because many of the offenders tried for Jewish–Christian fights were teenagers. For example, 14-year-old Abram Isaacqs was arrested in June 1718 after his group had withdrawn and jumped on a boat when constables arrived. Citizens who had watched the fight were happy to tell the constables that Abram had been the principal combatant, carrying a dagger.[6] A Christian, appropriately named Christiaan Christiaansz, tried in 1729, was 22. Arrested along the Amstel river on a Sunday, he claimed that he just happened to be going that way when he noticed a fight between Christians and Jews. Seeing that two Jews carrying knives were beating two little boys, he just had to draw his knife against the attackers. Christiaan, however, was also charged with having fought Jews with a dagger on the preceding Saturday and he had already been banished for participation in Jewish–Christian fights the previous year.[7]

The ritual element in all these confrontations is plain, since many of them took place on either a Sabbath or a Sunday. Obviously, the religious and ethnic differences were an important background, but the antagonism had a territorial aspect as well. The large majority of the Jewish community in Amsterdam lived in the North-Eastern part of the city and the Blue Bridge over the Amstel river formed the border between "Christian" and "Jewish" territory. Fights often took place on this bridge. Participants who had drawn a knife or dagger, when caught, usually received a whipping sentence, but the majority probably used blunt weapons or just their fists. Two casualties, both Christian, were reported: an orphan boy in 1720 and an Englishman in 1724. After the first murder the court published the 1716 ordinance anew, but in both cases no perpetrator was caught.[8]

Although judicial activity concentrated in the 1710s and 1720s, Jewish–Christian fighting continued after these decades. The chronicler Abraham Chaim Braatbard observed the phenomenon by mid-century, adding that no serious incidents had occurred. By serious incidents, he probably meant killings or near-lethal stabbings. Increasingly, the relationship between the Jewish community and the Christian world took on a political character. During the 1748 Tax Farmers' Rebellion, Jews prevented the plundering crowd from being active in their territory.[9] In the second half of the eighteenth century, as the Stadholder was friends with a few wealthy Sephardics, many Jews identified with the house of Orange.

In 1795, after the French invasion, three members of a Batavian militia went on trial for murdering an Orangist. They had gone out in their uniforms to provoke their enemies, starting in a coffee house where, according to their own statement, a band of Jews had attacked them.[10] A murder case in 1804 had no political overtones. A mixed group of Jews and Christians, using Yiddish slang words, had a fight with an exclusively Christian group. One of the latter died, but the court was unable to determine who had killed him.[11] Further research is needed to determine whether the existence of a mixed Jewish–Christian gang points at increasing integration. Within the underworld of the later Republican years, mixed bands consisted, in majority, of Jews and gypsies.[12]

Thus, the conspicuous presence of Jewish minorities in the Netherlands led to exacerbated tensions between them and the Christian, Dutch-speaking majority. While the secular authorities espoused a policy of relative tolerance and protection, ordinary people reacted differently. They fought for their own turf. Such frequent and structured battles have rarely been recorded in other parts of early modern Europe. This is different in the case of knife-fighting, which was customary in many countries.

The most detailed evidence for Dutch knife-fighting comes from the Amsterdam archive again, but the custom extended over the entire Republic. A knife fight can be termed a popular duel, because it usually involved two combatants only, who as a rule belonged to the lower classes. The Amsterdam evidence points at a relatively uniform type of popular duel. A previous history of conflict sometimes lay behind it, but often the disagreement arose on the spot. One party, at least, had to perceive an encroachment upon his honor. A disagreement accompanied by strong language or just a sudden insult often started off the incident. For a combat to ensue, one party had to challenge the other. In line with an implicit code of avoiding fighting indoors, the challenge often consisted of an invitation to leave for the street together. Outside, the duel began by mutual agreement, the yell "sta vast" (stand your ground) being the point of no return. If third parties were present, they served as witnesses. Their role was comparable to that of the seconds in the official duel, but their presence had not been arranged in advance.

A high degree of impulsiveness characterized many popular duels. The fact that duelists followed a ritual script by itself tells us nothing about the degree of impulsiveness. The script, with several variants, was in people's heads and they did not have to pause and reflect about it. In many cases, it appears, there was no prior conflict or enmity. Sometimes the duelists had quarreled earlier that day and resumed hostilities. In just a few cases, the court did record the existence of a longer-lasting enmity. For the modern researcher, there is no point in trying to establish whether early modern male fighting was any less impulsive than medieval violence. The long-term trend rather consisted of some groups gradually learning to handle conflict and dissatisfaction without fighting. Indeed, in Amsterdam around 1700, popular duelists belonged to the disreputable segment of the urban working classes. If one of them happened to attack a respectable citizen, the latter tried to ward him off with a stick.[13]

The knife-fighting culture flourished equally outside Amsterdam. If the city magistrates arrested a man guilty of homicide elsewhere in the Republic, they would put him to trial themselves. The court for Brabant also tried knife fighters. Popular duels in this territory occurred near taverns or in the street, but sometimes outside a village. In that case, the words of challenge were "come with me into the hayfield."[14] More important, for my comparison of the level of Dutch violence with that in the rest of Europe, are the scattered data from other countries. Although the available literature is poor with respect to details and circumstances, it does disclose that the popular duel was widespread in early modern Europe. Whereas Englishmen, especially Londoners, tended to settle matters by boxing, Frenchmen, especially in the South, would rather use swords. In Scandinavia, Germany, Italy and Spain, lower-class men fought over matters of honor mainly with knives.[15] With respect to the popular duel then, the Dutch Republic was part of the European mainstream.

Exceptionalism: The Formal Duel

The formal duel, fought throughout Europe by aristocrats and military officers in particular, constituted the principal exception. When it comes to this custom, the Dutch were decidedly more peaceful than the inhabitants of other countries. Italians had invented the formal duel in the early sixteenth century and it spread to Spain, France and England by the latter half of that century. After 1600 still other countries, in particular Germany, followed suit. In the Dutch Republic, on the other hand, the official duel hardly took root at all. Although, from the late seventeenth century, the Dutch elites eagerly adopted aristocratic habits (see chapter 7), these did not include dueling. The Republican political structure forms no sufficient explanation for the duel's unpopularity, since it was common in Venice.

Among the few recorded practitioners, several were foreigners. Significantly, the first Dutch law about dueling, in 1609, applied to French soldiers in the service of the Estates General. It reminded them of Henry IV's laws and obliged them to present all honor conflicts to their superiors for arbitration.[16] Some actual cases in The Hague involved foreign diplomats and officers residing there. In March 1621 the Count of Laval, a French officer in Dutch service, intended to fight a duel with another foreign nobleman, but Prince Maurice stopped them when he saw them leave his palace together. Laval was eventually killed in a duel in Venice in 1642.[17] A scandal broke out in the Dutch Republic in 1628. Volkert Teding van Berkhout, scion of a leading patrician family, had followed his patron, the French Duke De Guise, to Rome. There Volkert fought a duel with another Dutchman, who died a week later. The family in Holland expressed their dismay in several letters, even though physicians in Rome determined that the victim had died of diarrhoea caused by heavy drinking.[18] This incident exemplifies the negative attitude toward dueling prevailing among the large majority of Dutch patricians. Although most universities explicitly forbade students from engaging in dueling, it was uncommon among them too. Students were more prone to challenge each other to ordinary fights or to show their bravery by scraping the street with their rapiers. The academic tribunal of Franeker judged ten cases of official dueling before, and five cases after, 1700.[19]

The Amsterdam court records, which contain so much evidence for lower-class knife fights, are practically silent about the official duel. This is no surprise, since soldiers, the principal practitioners in the Republic, were normally tried by a court-martial. A formal duel in 1682 involved two French ex-soldiers who fought for reasons that noble theorists would find very unlofty. The two disagreed over the division of the spoils after snatching a farmer's purse, decided to settle the matter with swords and borrowed the weapons of two colleagues still in the army, who served as seconds.[20] In line with their indifference to dueling, the Dutch civilian elites seldom carried a rapier as a mark of status. An Amsterdam ordinance of 1668 even prohibited the carrying of any type of sword during the daytime, unless the person in question was in active military service. To be sure, the ordinance was twice renewed, and the second time, in 1677, it was said that many people carried rapiers in spite of it.[21] References to this weapon in the Amsterdam court records often involve foreigners, including some whose status would not have allowed them to carry it in their home country. In 1713 the court questioned a 30-year-old wig maker, born in Copenhagen, who had drawn his rapier when a bouncer had kicked him out of a night club and hit him with a stick. The judges explicitly asked the defendant why he was carrying this weapon even though it did not suit his profession of wig maker.[22]

All this was different in most of the rest of Europe. In Rome, for example, every man who thought himself important carried a *spada*. In the German countries, simple craftsmen attempted to look more impressive with a rapier on their side, often against official laws. These laws were meant to maintain clear class boundaries rather than to eradicate the duel. The legal systems of most countries treated dueling as a special offense, combining the prescription of harsh penalties with the possibility of easy pardons. Dutch legislators, on the other hand, refused to consider the custom as a distinct offense. Provincial placards referring to the duel usually did so in connection with common fighting and assault generally. Reformed moralists and synods associated the custom with the military, urging the Stadholder, as commander-in-chief, to issue a general prohibition. William III complied with their wishes in 1682.[23] The negative attitude of the Dutch was carried over into the modern period. During the nineteenth century, few formal duels were recorded, while published tracts were anti, almost without exception.

Homicide, the Law and the Public

The information about the formal duel is indicative. If any social group in the Dutch Republic was relatively peaceful compared with its foreign counterparts, it was the patrician elite. Since this elite included judges and prosecuting officers, their non-violent attitude affected their treatment of homicide in the lower classes. Throughout Europe, by the mid seventeenth century, homicide had effectively been criminalized. Ancient practices, such as private reconciliation to prevent revenge and the easy granting of princely pardons after an offender's claim of reacting involuntarily upon a provocation, had become marginal. Almost everywhere the death penalty awaited persons convicted for manslaughter, although execution need not follow automatically. In England, for example, many felons still received a pardon, which did not save them from punishment though, because their sentence was commuted to transportation. Execution after a death sentence was the rule in the Dutch Republic, on the other hand. In this country, it appears, the criminalization of homicide had gone further than in other parts of early modern Europe.

This process had considerably narrowed the broad margins within which legislators and courts conceded the claim of self-defense. When caught and tried, a killer had to prove much more than sheer provocation if he hoped to exculpate himself. Thus, the Amsterdam magistrates insisted that a defender should always retreat from a threatening scene if possible. They refused to acknowledge the honor code of the popular duel. For the duelists themselves, as long as the fight remained equal, it was shameful to retreat from it without mutual agreement. A time-out to pick up a fallen knife or to accept a knife from a comrade because one's own broke preserved the equality of the fight, but to the court it merely presented an opportunity to flee. If the man who granted the time-out had not started the fight, he lost his claim to self-defense through it. The court told another defendant, who had fought with one man while two of his opponent's friends watched with drawn knives, that the attack initiated by them did not endanger his life, because it happened at the Nieuwmarkt and he could easily have retreated into one of the many houses there.[24]

We can examine the rules of self-defense in actual practice because of the survival of the records for a few Amsterdam trials in which the issue was discussed. Even an acquittal did not always mean no punishment at all. In 1674 the Amsterdam-born sailor Samuel Samuelsen even got the sword waved over his head – a symbolic decapitation – for a manslaughter committed in Vlissingen eight years earlier. His sentence – as always, read aloud from the scaffold – acknowledged that he had been reluctant to fight. The victim had given him a knife, they had fought a while without injuries, he had left the scene, but the victim had come after him, attacked him again and cut him. All this, still according to the sentence, fitted the label of self-defense but he had to receive a punishment nevertheless as an example to others.[25] In 1716 the court even imposed a banishment of 25 years upon a killer whose claim of self-defense the magistrates explicitly acknowledged.[26]

The case of 31-year-old Jan Baeters in 1730 was more ambivalent. He assisted and lived in with his father, the repairman of one of the city's sluices. Jan was working downstairs when he heard noise upstairs, where he discovered that three men were threatening his father with knives. The father said: "Son, they want to kill me; please help me." One of the assailants assured Jan that he would be a dead man too if he helped, but then the three went back to the lower floor. They told Jan that they would injure him if he came after them. Despite this, Jan climbed down. One of the intruders cut the courageous son, who fell down but managed to draw his knife and to fatally stab the other in the belly. The prosecutor insisted that Jan was guilty of manslaughter: the victim had challenged the defendant while the former stood downstairs and the latter upstairs. When the defendant climbed down, the victim had correctly interpreted this as "a consent to the challenge." Moreover, the defendant's sister, not mentioned in the protocol earlier, had tried to stop him in vain. Jan claimed that he went down merely to resume his work and his attorney added that no witness had actually seen him injuring the victim.[27] The dossier contains no judgment, but if the judges had accepted the prosecutor's argument they would have sentenced Jan to death. His absence from the relevant records means that the court's majority had a different view. Incidentally, the prosecutor's argument betrays an awareness of the popular duel's code, but it ranks this code squarely with criminal intentions.

Nine years later, an innkeeper who had retreated into his *kolf*-playing area and killed his assailant there, was punished with symbolic decapitation. In his inn he had tried to separate and reconcile two knife fighters and he had taken the knife from one of them, whereupon the other attacked him and drove him out. His sentence said that, although it was self-defense, he should have called for help from customers inside. Moreover, he should have taken more precautions – which ones was not specified – against people carrying knives into his place.[28]

In some other cases, the issue, rather than self-defense, was whether the victim had died from the wounds inflicted by the defendant or because of bad medical treatment or poor health. The increased medical chances of surviving a potentially lethal attack in modern times constitute a methodological problem for the quantitative study of homicide trends.

In the past, the inherent uncertainty sometimes complicated the task of judicial fact-finding. In Amsterdam, a substantial minority of wounded victims died days or even weeks after the attack. In some of these cases, the doctors and surgeons were unable to determine whether the victim had died of his wounds or something else, which usually resulted in a sentence of symbolic decapitation. In a 1756 case, when the victim had died after eight days, the committee performing the autopsy wrote a lengthy report, subsequently reviewed by the medical professors of Leiden and Utrecht. They noted that, if large arteries have been cut, the injured person must die within 42 hours. Since the victim had lived for eight days and had smoked a pipe, only small arteries could have been cut and by dripping they had slowly filled up the victim's chest. An incision had been made after six days, which was too late: the victim had suffocated in his own blood. In conformity with this conclusion, the defendant was symbolically decapitated and banished from Holland forever.[29]

While drunkenness counted as a mitigating circumstance in cases of homicide or assault in some parts of Europe, the Amsterdam court was resolute. The magistrates debated the extent of the defendant's intoxication primarily in relation to the process of fact-finding. They wanted clear answers instead of the claim of forgetfulness. To a charge or question the accused routinely replied that he had been too drunk to remember what had happened. Defendants knew that their confession was required for a scaffold sentence. In such cases, the magistrates tried to make the suspect admit that he had not been so drunk after all. In a trial in 1739, for example, they cleverly asked the accused how he could see that the other had a knife if he really was intoxicated. This case was settled when four guards of the watch house, where the defendant had spent the night, declared that he had sat quietly by the fire, not looking drunk at all.[30]

The court was especially shocked when law enforcement agents became homicide victims, noting this as an aggravating circumstance in the perpetrator's sentence. All kind of criminals, thieves and burglars, no less than duelists, might offer resistance when threatened with arrest. In a few cases this resulted in murder, so that the attempt to evade apprehension became their principal offense. In 1719, for example, two constables were spying near a basement where they suspected the sale of stolen goods. When three men entered, the constables followed them and interrupted the transaction. In the ensuing wrestle one of the men managed to stab a constable to death, whereupon all three fled leaving behind the goods they had indeed stolen. The thieves had the audacity to return, demanding that the female proprietor either bought the goods from them or gave them back. No law enforcement agent was present at this scene, but later that night a few other constables managed to arrest the killer, despite renewed resistance with a knife.[31] More often, the perpetrator's resistance to apprehension was non-lethal. Amsterdam nightwatchmen, armed with just a stick and a rattle with which to call upon colleagues and citizens, were particularly vulnerable. Those of the Batavian period still lacked a saber, but they additionally carried nooses. They put one around the neck of a violent recidivist in 1804, but he took a knife from his pocket with which he cut the noose and attacked his captors.[32]

Not every resident applauded the court's reluctance to grant self-defense, and its resolute stand against the popular duel. The criminalization of homicide had taken root among the authorities and a large part of the upper and middle classes, but many others continued to view manslaughter, certainly when it occurred during a fair fight, as a kind of accident. This probably was the case in several parts of early modern Europe, but the Amsterdam evidence is most telling. Historians of post-Restoration England observe a reluctance to prosecute, for all crimes, if the victim found the prospective sanction too severe. On the Continent, where inquisitorial systems held sway, dissatisfaction at the sanction was expressed primarily by helping the offender to evade arrest. From the 1630s to the 1690s, Dutch moralists warned against the sinful view that one may hand over a thief to the agents of justice, but not a manslaughterer.[33] It suggests that, by this time, at least some church members shared the opinion in question. Perhaps they abandoned it by 1700, but in the early eighteenth century there still were Amsterdamers who thought the death penalty unfair for accidental homicide.

When it was family or friends who helped a killer escape, this does not necessarily point at a wider dissatisfaction with the prosecution of homicide. Comrades of Claas Lambertsz, who had killed a Frenchman in March 1703, accompanied him through the city gate, saying "now walk with God."[34] Also in 1703, during Pentecost, a porter of the weigh house had stabbed one of two men who had rebuked him for harassing his female companion. The next day, when he learned that the victim had died, the porter, accompanied by his crying wife and two brothers-in-law, went for help to the home of a colleague, who managed to get the killer onto a coach bound for Utrecht. The fugitive, however, was arrested along the way. During his trial, a letter, urging him to be steadfast because declarations in his favor had been drawn up, was smuggled into his cell hidden in a fish-head.[35]

But even strangers were involved in helping killers. A soldier who had deserted his regiment and his wife in Schiedam for fear of having to run the gauntlet for maltreating a woman, was on trial for a homicide in Amsterdam. It was rumored that he had killed a man in Schiedam as well, but he assured the court that he had made up this story for the lady of his lodging house upon arrival in the city. It would motivate her, he thought, to act quickly in getting him recruited on an East Indian ship.[36] A homicide in August 1713 resulted from a disagreement over a card game among four friends in a bar in the Servetsteeg (Napkin Alley). Afterwards, all the alley's landladies collected money for the perpetrator to facilitate his flight from the city.[37] Two separate homicides took place in front of "Eva's whores' and thieves' bar," in November 1713 and in January 1714. After the second incident, the court took in Eva and a number of customers for questioning. These interrogations allowed the judges to establish who was guilty, but not in the case of the November incident. On the day after it, four of the suspects had returned to the bar to inquire into the victim's condition, conferred with Eva on their further course of action and then disappeared from the city.[38] Such cases were recorded in rural Brabant too. After a lethal stabbing in 1729 an innkeeper had facilitated the perpetrator's flight and refused to provide information to the authorities.[39]

A few cases explicitly reveal that the public tended to excuse knife fighters, but not men who had attacked decent or unarmed citizens. A fracas in July 1674, for example, began when two gentlemen had reproached two other men for beating the women with them. The two not-so-decent men injured both gentlemen with their knives, even though one of the victims carried a rapier. With bloody hands, the attackers retired into a bar, where a woman washed away the blood with gin water. To make the other customers believe it was all right, she told them that the two had fought each other.[40]

Cases in which third persons inquired into the victim's condition for the perpetrator provide another indication of the tolerant attitude to homicide. If a bleeding victim was not dead yet, the stabber thought it wise nevertheless to flee the scene right away. He would usually wait to leave town until he was sure that the victim had died. The persons inquiring for the attacker in hiding usually were intimates or friends of his. Most of the time we do not hear how covertly they put their questions. Occasionally, however, the persons providing information destined for the perpetrator belonged to the victim's inner circle of family and acquaintances, which suggests that even they could agree that the stabbing was an accident. In one case, it was the victim's sister-in-law, for whom he had fought. Instead of informing the court, she visited the perpetrator in his hiding-place, obliged his request to inquire anew into the victim's condition and came back to report that her brother-in-law had died.[41]

In some other cases, however, the victim's family assisted the court in finding the perpetrator and prosecuting him. At the beginning of the trial of Wijnand Arentsz on February 25, 1711, the judges wanted to be sure that they had the right person in front of them. Was he the one who had stabbed a young man on the night of December 8 of the previous year? The victim, who had reproached his attacker for beating the woman accompanying him, had died from his wounds a few days later. Cleverly, the prosecutor first asked whether Wijnand usually took a dog with him when he went out. He replied, "Yes, a yellow bulldog." The next question was : "Do you have a wife to whom you have given a cut to the face, does this wife have a mother and do you have a godfather with a limp?" The answer was positive on all counts. Then the victim's parents came in to testify that a woman with a scar on her face, an old woman, and a man with a limp and a yellow bulldog had come to their house to inquire into their son's condition. The company had been very upset when told that he had died. These indications sufficed for torture, and the shinscrews made Wijnand confess. The conflict had arisen, he admitted, when he was beating his mistress. He had left her after the stabbing, gone home and told his wife that he had injured someone.[42]

Another killer, whose principal profession was theft, counted in vain on the mercy of strangers. In October 1699 he had stabbed to death a journeyman who had organized a *maling* (a crowd taking back stolen goods and harassing the thief) against him several times. On December 23 of the next year, several men pursued him again after he had taken a slaughtered sheep from the hook. When they caught him, he pleaded: "Let me go; I have committed a manslaughter." He wisely refrained from revealing the circumstances, but his pursuers refused to oblige anyway, probably thinking that a thief deserved execution no matter what. That happened indeed, but for the earlier homicide.[43] When discovering a property offense, the public was almost always prepared to act, if not to hand over the perpetrator to justice immediately, certainly to beat him and throw him into a canal.[44] In this way, the activities of law-abiding citizens contributed to street violence. Citizens could be just as ruthless in this as knife fighters and robbers, as the case of Monkey Butt (see chapter 5) demonstrates.

In the Amsterdam court cases of the seventeenth and eighteenth centuries, the citizens who pursued thieves, robbers or violent trouble-makers, on average, appear as the stronger and more determined party. Conversely, we do not hear of an organized intimidation of witnesses or other citizens who had provided a "service to justice," but there are cases in which an individual offender, usually after serving his term, took revenge. A notorious thief and fighter nicknamed "Jantje Kruidenier" (grocer), born in Cologne, almost killed his victim in January 1714. Earlier, he had broken out of the rasphouse twice, once with the help of his wife. During his second stay there, when the witnesses who had testified in his trial came to see him, he threatened them from behind the bars: "I will take revenge on you, even if I have to wait twenty years."

After his escape he indeed stayed in town and on that January afternoon he saw one of the witnesses, a paint seller, passing by. To a woman who sold chestnuts on that spot and apparently knew about the case, he said, "Damn, there he is." She tried to stop him but he pushed her aside and stabbed the paint seller in the back. According to the surgeon who treated the victim, it was sheer luck that the knife had struck against one of the ribs and not gone through into the chest. After the stabbing Jantje roamed around in Cologne, Frankfurt and other places, but he returned to Amsterdam a year later, perhaps to see his wife. She, however, had been imprisoned in Leiden in the meantime. He was hanged in January 1715.[45] Such cases were exceptional. It happened more often that offenders threatened witnesses, smashed their windows and called them traitors, their wives whores and their children bastards. Some female witnesses became victims of revenge too.

Violence then, played a role in law enforcement in various ways, but a non-violent activity, that of helping killers escape, was most diametrically opposed to the authorities' notions of justice. A major, unanswered question refers to the subconscious motives of the helpers. We know just one thing for sure: they assisted killers in getting through the city gate or on a ship. But did they wish the offender to avoid just the death penalty, or judicial prosecution altogether? A simple answer is that they wanted both. The criminalization of homicide had led to an increased frequency of prosecution, as well as the sanction of capital punishment for all guilty offenders. The persons who assisted a killer disagreed with both elements. They were traditionalists, out of tune with the mainstream of their age, or at least with the norm-setting majority of upper, middle and the respectable lower classes. If any of us were the E. P. Thompson of the history of violence, he/she might turn the implicit valuation on its head and call them unarticulated protesters defending a moral economy of unrestrained passion, but the argument would be the same. This answer, however, attributes to contemporaries an awareness of long-term processes that only the modern investigator can grasp with hindsight. In fact, these processes are blind.

This applies to the men and women who lived at a time when private reconciliation was common after a homicide, but it equally applies to the generations living at the end of the seventeenth century and the beginning of the eighteenth. Those who assisted an escape were not somehow aware of being a rear guard in an otherwise inevitable marching on of the criminalization of homicide. Surely these people had ideas inherited from their ancestors, but their primary experience derived from their own time. In Amsterdam, the idea that it was wrong if a killer fell into the hands of justice was associated in particular with offenders who had slain their opponent in a popular duel. The duel, popular and official, was the new cultural element, unknown in medieval times. In the middle ages, the notion that an unpremeditated homicide was an accident referred to a wide range of killings in which men acted to avenge or save their honor. Fairness of numbers in violence was hardly a virtue at all in medieval days. All murders ran the risk of being avenged and could lead to a vendetta. Hence, the idea that a killer did not deserve death was totally foreign to medieval people, because death might follow justifiably through revenge.

Was the notion that a killer did not deserve death an idea that developed in the late seventeenth century then, together with the new emphasis on fairness of fighting? Or did those who assisted an escape share a reminiscence of the recently disappeared private handling of homicides after all, wishing to preserve this venerable custom? The mutual help between the parties related to killer and victim, in providing information, would point in that direction. As yet, the issue is undecided. The best we can say is that an ancient value, that a killer should have some freedom of action after his deed, became tied to a new value, that of the fair fight with equal numbers and weapons, voluntarily entered upon. It was not until society became more pacified and a larger part of the population grew unaccustomed to standing ready to defend themselves with weapons or to accept a challenge to fight, that this symbiosis faded away. From then on, every act of serious violence was treated as a shame on the perpetrator, and a readiness to fight and defend oneself was in itself a sign of being an outcast.

Declining Acceptance of Violence

Since the mid eighteenth century, Amsterdam was a relatively peaceful place, in which rates of homicide and assault had declined and the public appeared no longer prepared to excuse killers. The popular duel flourished especially between 1690 and 1720, which coincided more or less with a temporary rise in the city's homicide rate, the peak period of sailors' involvement in violence and the heyday of the music hall – an age of prosperity, leisure, erotic entertainment and aggression. From then onwards, one-on-one knife fights quickly became infrequent in the city's records, presumably because they largely disappeared from street and tavern life. After a decade or two, moreover, references to citizens wielding a stick against a man attacking them with a knife became rare. This chronology was probably peculiar to the larger Dutch cities. In Brabant, knife fighting remained prevalent until the mid nineteenth century.

The Amsterdam evidence discloses that, in the second half of the eighteenth century, only the relatively marginal Ashkenazic Jews engaged in popular duels. Two of them fought with lethal consequences over the spoils of a theft in 1768. The killer fled as far away as Paris, but after six months he was arrested in Bruges, in the Austrian Netherlands, and extradited, which suggests increasing international cooperation in the capture of serious criminals. When interrogated, the defendant claimed that he had explicitly asked his opponent whether they would go for a cut only, and that the eventual victim had replied that they must fight as skillfully as they knew how.[46] There were probably more popular duels among Jews at that time. Jewish witnesses seemed reluctant to testify about non-lethal knife fights within their community. One such case in 1782 came to light only because a Christian passer-by was injured.[47]

The silence of Jewish witnesses was probably due to a desire to settle conflicts informally within their community. Among the rest of the city's population, references to assistance in the escape of killers practically ceased after the 1720s. This is understandable since popular duelists, whose exploits also disappeared from the records, had been the main beneficiaries of such assistance. It seems, though, that attitudes toward the punishment of homicide were genuinely changing.

A case in 1795 suggests that tavern clients had become indifferent to the fate of "accidental" killers. Two men, Cornelis Meerkamp and Jan Musman, had a long-standing financial conflict. Jan insisted that Cornelis had cheated him of 1,000 guilders, whereas the latter claimed that he owed the other no money at all and had always assisted him. They started to quarrel again when they met in a wine bar. It never became exactly clear what happened when both went outside, but all customers saw Cornelis re-enter the wine bar with a blood-stained knife in his hand. He had used it earlier in the bar to peel a lemon. There was no talk of Jan – who was lethally wounded – having had a knife. Cornelis exclaimed, "Where shall I go to?" Neither the landlord nor any customer reacted or appears to have suggested that he should leave town.[48] The reference to the lemon is illustrative too. Cornelis had apparently obtained the knife for practical purposes in the tavern. It was no longer self-evident that many men carried such a weapon for protection at all times. Violence had become unacceptable to the great majority of the population.

Conclusion

The belief that a tradition of non-violence characterizes Dutch society has no basis in the available historical evidence. Throughout their history, the Netherlands stayed in the median range among European nations with respect to the level of homicide. In some periods the Dutch homicide rates sank to the lower end of the scale, but occasionally they peaked above the European average of the time. Looking at the qualitative evidence for the Republican period, we observe a similar situation. The Amsterdam archive's documentation on the popular duel is abundant, but it was far from being a local custom. Not only Amsterdamers practiced it but lower-class men from all over the Republic and foreigners too. Indeed, knife fighting was common in many parts of early modern Europe and certainly no Dutch exception. Peculiar to Dutch urban society of the seventeenth and eighteenth centuries, on the other hand, was the cohabitation of Christians with large Jewish communities. Whereas the ruling elite was less anti-Semitic than the authorities of some other countries, the populace showed greater hostility. This situation produced violent conflicts, whose frequency and intensity exceeded the level observed in most other parts of Europe.

The Dutch of the Republican period were exceptional – in this case remaining at the lower end of the scale of violence – when it came to the formal duel. Few men proudly carried rapiers in the street and even fewer issued written challenges to fight. While this attitude may well have fostered the later belief in a general tradition of peacefulness, at the time it affected a small group only. In early modern Europe, mainly aristocrats and military officers practiced the formal duel. Most officers in the Dutch army were foreigners, and the nobility played a more marginal role than in the surrounding countries. The really remarkable fact concerns the urban elite's refusal to embrace the formal duel, despite its adoption of French aristocratic manners from the mid seventeenth century. If, occasionally, a member of one of the leading families fought a duel, his relatives considered it a dishonor. Thus, only the patrician elite was relatively peaceful. Its bourgeois origins and its ambivalent position during the Republic's formative period go a long way toward explaining this peculiar trait.

It should be emphasized that the elite's peaceful habitus extended to the domestic, European context only. Members of the leading stratum participated in the violent trade conflicts of the East India Company, the transatlantic slave trade and plantation slavery in the Caribbean colonies and Suriname. At home, its peaceful habitus led the patriciate, after a period of having to be encouraged by Reformed synods and moralists, to become intolerant of lower-class violence and promote the full criminalization of homicide. Paradoxically, this attitude fostered state violence, as courts rarely granted self-defense, so that killers who got caught faced almost certain execution. This offensive of criminalization met with active resistance from popular groups until the early eighteenth century. Yet repression by the state influenced popular attitudes after a time, causing a significant decline in the level of interpersonal violence by the late eighteenth century. But this decline, once again, occurred in most parts of Europe.

3

Violence and Culture

Bloodshed in Two or Three Worlds

The title of this chapter is inspired by that of an article by the cultural historian Peter Burke (1997). He wrote about "carnival in two or three worlds," referring to the city of Rio de Janeiro, which he knows from personal experience. Burke discusses the recent history of this popular festival in Latin America, as well as its European and African roots. The caveat implied in the "two *or* three" stems from an awareness of his limited knowledge of African societies. I will discuss festivals in chapter 8, but now my subject is interpersonal violence. In this chapter, the "three worlds" are Europe, North America and East Asia and I am using the "or" even more hesitatingly than Burke does. My reading of Asian history is limited, but I hope that my remarks will be of interest to more specialized scholars.

Unlike with carnival, in the case of violence there can be no talk of roots. The experience of wounding and killing is a human universal, common to all known societies. The circumstances in which wounding and killing are embedded, on the other hand, vary across cultures and over time (see the introduction). This chapter touches on the European history of violence only briefly, assuming its basic outline to be well known;[1] it proceeds by comparing European developments with those in North America and concludes with a few tentative ideas about East Asia. I will largely restrict myself to serious violence, for which homicide often is a good indicator. There are three key themes to be discussed here: the incidence and character of violence; its cultural context (honor, ritual, the attitudes of various social groups); social structure, in particular the level of state formation.

For European history it was crucial that much of this continent witnessed more or less continuous, though not linear, processes of state formation from the late middle ages onward, with the development of monopolies of force and taxation, bureaucracies and finally nation-states in which power differences between various social groups had greatly diminished. In many other parts of the world, monopolization of force hardly took place at all until recent times; alternatively, processes of state formation were interrupted or complicated by conquest or colonialism. Notably, the area that became the United States witnessed a peculiar development. As the native population was nearly extinguished and their societies were wiped out, the development of political and economic institutions had to start almost from scratch each time Europeans occupied a new part of the continent. In all parts, a relatively sudden "modernization" followed. As I will argue, this is crucial for understanding differences regarding the place of violence in American and European societies until today.

The history of violence in Europe can be traced back at least to the medieval period with its frequent feuding. In a medieval vendetta, unequal struggles, treacherous attacks and ritual maiming were common. As long as such acts served to uphold the family honor through revenge, the assailants were unashamed and third parties showed no indignation. The fact that a national state authority was merely embryonic in the later middle ages explains the widespread tolerance of feuding, upheld by urban statutes and royal decrees. Conversely, the suppression of the vendetta in much of Europe after 1500 was due in large part to the emergence of state organizations. In addition, this suppression owed much to ideological pressure from the church, in Protestant and probably also in Catholic countries.

This becomes clear when we consider ecclesiastical attitudes to private reconciliation. From the earliest times, the ritual of the vendetta had been complemented by rituals of reconciliation, which signified the end of a feud or just the conclusion of peace between the families of killer and victim after a single homicide. The reconciliation ritual involved religious elements such as prostration and prayers as well as a financial compensation which the killer and his relatives paid to the victim's family. From the 1580s onward, Protestant church synods and moralist writers in the Dutch Republic constantly argued that formal reconciliations were un-Christian rituals and that the authorities should always punish those guilty of manslaughter, preferably by death. The secular authorities did not comply with their wishes immediately, but, toward the mid seventeenth century, prosecution and the death penalty were the rule, which sealed the criminalization of homicide. Eventually, the criminalization of homicide took place throughout Europe, but research has yet to demonstrate to what extent church pressure was a factor in various countries. It should be added that ecclesiastical attitudes did not constitute an "independent factor." As early as the eleventh century, church people had tried to regulate the feuding and warring of knights, with only limited and temporary successes. Indeed, how could church people around 1600 have insisted on criminal prosecution, if a system of regular justice – and hence stable state institutions – had not been available?

Religious moralists, in Protestant as well as Catholic countries, also attacked the duel. The link between traditional male honor and the body, as well as the gradual process involving the spiritualization of honor in Europe, have been discussed in the introduction. Here it suffices to emphasize that the spiritualization of honor formed part of civilizing processes and can therefore be explained with the help of Elias' theory of civilization. This means that changes in the concept of honor were related also to processes of state formation. The traditional concept of male honor, so much linked to the body, is prevalent at times and places where there is no strong state. In that situation, you have to rely on your own strength to defend yourself, and men able to accomplish this receive respect for it. In European history, the growing strength of states brought with it ideological changes that altered the concept of honor. Honor remained important for many, but it became spiritualized. The term "spiritualization" emphasizes gradual change rather than a total shift from one attitude to another. Honor is still important for us nowadays, in Asia perhaps even more so than in Europe. In the latter continent, the spiritualization of honor was accompanied by a massive drop in homicide rates from 30 to 50 per 100,000 population per year in the middle ages to between 0.5 and 1.5 in the twentieth and twenty-first centuries.[2]

Violence and Honor in North America

When speaking of (North) America, I am referring to the territory of the present United States and not to Canada or Mexico. In the contemporary world, a conspicuous difference between the United States and Western Europe concerns the incidence of interpersonal violence. Although American national homicide rates have declined from peaks of 9–10 in the 1970s through the early 1990s, to 5–6 from the mid-1990s until today, the latter figure still is about three to four times that prevalent in almost every EU country nowadays. The situation in which American homicide rates far exceeded those of Western Europe has prevailed since the early nineteenth century. Likewise, the United States has been viewed as the more rowdy society of the two during most of this period. That view was associated with the image of the frontier, which has been a major theme in American historiography ever since the work of Frederick Jackson Turner.[3] Although Turner preferred to dwell on the individualism rather than the violence of the frontier, remarks about "savages" as "obstacles" to the colonists' Westward movement recur in his work. But we should move from Turner to modern historiography.

Not all of America has always been a violent place. Notably, Colonial New England appears to be the exception, at least since the last quarter of the seventeenth century. According to Randolph Roth, the homicide rate among unrelated adult whites in New England was over 100 in the first few years of colonization; it quickly dropped to 9 from c.1625 to c.1680 and stood at about 2 during most of the eighteenth century. The rates in Virginia and Maryland, again for unrelated adult whites only, were somewhat higher, but they show a similar trend: over 200 until c.1640, just over 30 between c.1650 and c.1675, and around 10 between c.1675 and c.1760.[4] The meaning of these data is open to debate.[5] Roth considered European-American victims only, because they formed a good indicator for the amount of aggression among the colonists themselves, but of course the killing of Indians contributed to the region's overall violence. In the case of native victims, throughout the United States, we face both a technical and a methodological problem. First, the data on the number of Indians killed are unreliable until the end of the nineteenth century.[6] Second, there is the problem of categorizing the incidents on which we have information. In the unsettled frontier conditions, it is often unclear where to draw the line between interpersonal violence and killing in war (which also pitted English colonists against those of competing European nations). Thus, it would be hazardous simply to proclaim any region of Colonial America to have been a non-violent society.

From the early nineteenth century on, most parts of the United States certainly were more violent than North-West and Central Europe. For one thing, this emerges from Eric Monkkonen's study of homicide in New York City. When compared to data series from London and Liverpool, the New York rates were consistently higher; between 1800 and 1900 the latter fluctuated around 5.[7] Philadelphia homicide rates, reported by Roger Lane, fluctuated between 2.2 and 4.0 during the period 1839–1901, but these figures are based on judicial indictments only.[8] And those were Northern cities. In Antebellum America, the region most known for violence was the South. It is also the region best studied in this respect, based especially on qualitative evidence. The crucial factor here is once more personal honor.

Honor in the Old South has been scrutinized at length by Bertram Wyatt-Brown (1982), Edward Ayers (1984) and Kenneth Greenberg (1996). They show that all social classes within the white population endorsed an honor code which encouraged men to be violent. This code was very similar to the traditional European one and Wyatt-Brown indeed argues that it originated from Europe. Whereas the planter elite in the US South behaved in a manner reminiscent of the old European nobility, their white social inferiors may be compared to fighting craftsmen in medieval towns. In fact, male Southerners cherished an ideal according to which an honorable man must show virility and courage and avenge insults with physical attack. In Europe, by the first half of the nineteenth century, this traditional honor code was confined to marginal regions like the Mediterranean or the Balkans. This was different in the United States. Although the studies just referred to focus on qualitative evidence, the available quantitative data, before and after the Civil War, tend to confirm the picture of a high level of violence throughout the South. The homicide rate in Edgefield County, SC, for example, stood at 18 between 1844 and 1858.[9] In the state of Louisiana, between 1866 and 1884, the rate averaged no less than 32.[10] As always, these elevated rates were due in overwhelming part to the prevalence of male-on-male violence.[11]

The case of the Old South, whose reputation for violence dates back at least to the middle of the eighteenth century, counters the claim that the United States did not become a violent country until Samuel Colt had invented and mass-produced his revolver.[12] Guns were involved in another notorious episode in US history, that of the Wild West. Although some historians have tried to belittle the amount of violence in the West, the work of Clare McKanna proves them wrong. In a useful historiographical introduction, McKanna shows that claims for a relatively peaceful West were either made without reference to homicide rates at all or based on mistaken calculations.[13] His own data refer to three counties: Douglas (Nebraska), Las Animas (Colorado), Gila (Arizona), 1880–1920. Based on coroner's inquests, he calculated homicide rates ranging between 2.6 and 9.7 in Douglas, between 10 and 42 in Las Animas (excluding a massacre in 1913), and in Gila between 34 and 152 among whites and between 11 and 178 among Apaches. However, McKanna does not specify the population figures involved in these calculations. Moreover, his figures have to be corrected, because he includes the category "killed by police," which should be classified as state violence. When this category is excluded, the average homicide rates during the 40 years studied are 5.5 for Douglas in by then no longer so wild Nebraska; 31 for Las Animas; and no less than 65 for both racial groups together in Gila. McKanna additionally provides homicide rates for seven California counties, 1850–1900: between 20 and 92, hence an average of 55.5.[14]

The evidence on the type of violence in the three counties studied is indicative, too: "Homicide in the American West tended to be a crime committed by a male under the influence of alcohol in a saloon or outside on the street, typically late at night. The homicide usually resulted from some *minor disputes* with an acquaintance, and more often than not was committed with a handgun."[15] As triggers of quarrels, McKanna mentions: "too much foam on the beer, unpaid fifty-cent bets, pool games, bar tabs, and a myriad of other minor issues."[16] Note that the word "minor" recurs in both quotations. When the reason for a fight seems minor or trivial to a modern investigator, this usually indicates that honor played its part. An unblemished outward appearance matters in an honor culture. McKanna only recognizes this explicitly when referring to the black population of Omaha: "They [blacks from the South] brought with them an exaggerated sense of honor that would not tolerate a careless comment, a jostle on the street or a derogatory gesture. Such behavior could bring a quick violent response."[17] Indeed, as Ayers and others argue, African-American men of the South had adopted the whites' sense of honor by the end of the nineteenth century and some carried it on to the West. Probably, however, this cultural code also was an independent tradition there.

We can conclude preliminarily that the honor–violence complex was as characteristic of the American Old West as it was of the Old South. It has also been observed in urban settings around the turn of the nineteenth and twentieth centuries. In late-nineteenth-century Chicago, for example, young working-class men of various ethnic backgrounds cherished traditional male honor; in the early twentieth century, honor was reinforced by the arrival of Italian mafiosi in the windy city.[18] Meanwhile, Southern whites continued to invoke the traditional code of honor until the 1930s, employing violence, in particular, when they perceived female virtue to be in danger.[19]

America vs. Europe: State-Formation Processes

In an argument which needs further refinement, I claim that the structurally high American homicide rates are related to the prevalence of a culture of self-help in American society. The persistence and strength of this culture of self-help in their turn can be explained by taking Elias' theory of civilization into account. In fact, my argument extends this theory a little. The case of the United States shows that, even when a monopoly of force – in its outward manifestation, the federal government reacts when the country is attacked – has been established for a considerable time, strong counter-tendencies may operate against the internal effectuation of this monopoly. These counter-tendencies lead to a stagnation in the spread of more "civilized" standards of conduct in *some* areas of social life – in the case of the United States, the area of conflict and aggression.

In order to explain the origins of the culture of self-help in America, we have to take account of a specific element in Elias' original exposition of his theory: the sociogenesis of military and taxation monopolies. In Europe their formation was a gradual process; the dual monopoly did not appear overnight. Its eventual emergence, which Elias analyzed for France in particular, meant that, in the long run, centripetal forces (favoring a central rule by the king) prevailed over centrifugal forces (favoring a country torn apart). The centrifugal forces varied in nature. In an early phase they included the absence of durable chains of communication, which, for example, made it impossible for a king who had beaten a rival duke in an outlying region to rule the duchy effectively. Centrifugal forces also included rebellious groups, notably high-ranking nobles and independent-minded cities. When the king's monopoly was still weak and unstable, such rebellious groups were bent on encroaching upon or even destroying this monopoly. Dukes and counts wished to be autonomous rulers, with the king as no more than their peer. In French history, Elias identified the Fronde (a revolt against the regent Mazarin, led by the nobility and the Paris *parlement*, 1648–52) as the last episode in which an attempted destruction of the king's monopoly was the dominant factor.

Whether the Fronde was indeed the last revolt of that type in French history is a question of lesser relevance. It is more important to identify the other goal. After the Fronde – and at a certain point in processes involving the monopolization of force anywhere – the nature of opposition and rebellion shifted. Political struggles increasingly assumed the character of aiming at co-possessing the monopoly, rather than destroying it. Co-possessing means that it was no longer the king's sole property. The very existence of a military and taxation monopoly was taken for granted, but the Third Estate – or similar groups in other countries – wished to co-determine, together with the king and his advisors, the ends to which it was used. Finally, representatives of the former subjects entirely deprived the king of his monopoly, which itself continued to exist. That was of course what the French Revolution was primarily about, even though a king temporarily returned afterwards. As Tocqueville observed, the state came out stronger from the Revolutionary period. In the nineteenth and twentieth centuries, in France and other European nations, democratization meant that citizens, already accustomed to being disarmed (at least in normal, non-revolutionary circumstances), struggled to co-decide the ends to which the monopoly of force would be employed.

Although the American Revolution replaced a king by a president, the territory which became the United States did not witness the gradual development characteristic of France and other European nations.

In particular, there was no phase of centralization before democratic movements appeared on the scene. Consequently, the political elite as well as common people hesitated, as it were, between the wish to co-possess and the wish to destroy the monopoly of force. One might say that democracy came to America too early.[20] That is, of course, a rhetorical statement, not a value judgment. In the period before, during and after the War of Independence, the majority of the population was accustomed to relying on themselves, their families and local assistance for protection. Local elites and, increasingly, common people equated democracy with the right of armed protection of one's own property and interests. This claim to a right of self-defense was irrespective of the incidence of gun ownership; indeed, it could be made with various kinds of weapons in hand. The "too early" advent of democracy resulted in a kind of political-cultural stalemate: even though monopolization of force within the territory of the United States progressed to some extent, compared to the European situation this was only a slow and partial monopolization.

That many Americans at the time of the Revolution and in subsequent decades were distrustful of a monopoly of force and valued self-defense is primarily a sociological-historical observation, not a legal issue. Hence the notorious Second Amendment to the United States' Constitution is only of partial relevance for my argument. Just semantically, it is so obvious that the Second Amendment tied the right to bear arms to a well-regulated militia that one wonders why it was necessary to substantiate this connection by further historical research. Perhaps the matter requires a European's reading. The fact that the Second Amendment is silent about bearing arms for private use does not run counter to my argument. If we hear voices committed somewhat less to personal self-defense in late-eighteenth-century America, we would expect them to come from men with legal and political authority. In spite of these voices, the cultural belief that individual citizens had a right to protect themselves with arms was widespread. Many owners of handguns and bowie knives claimed this right with renewed vigor in the Jacksonian era. On some occasions, the popular belief is reflected even in legal documents at the state level. Thus, both the Declaration of Rights and the Constitution of Pennsylvania assert that the people have a right to bear arms in defense of themselves and the state. Admittedly, this clause originated in the dissatisfaction of frontiersmen at a perceived lack of support from the state in their struggles with native Americans, but that observation in no way diminishes the significance of the inclusion of the word "themselves."[21] As an irony of history, the "well-regulated militia" eventually disappeared, whereas private militias have existed in the United States since 1799.[22] Today, the idea that individuals cannot and should not rely on state institutions to protect their homes is alive and well. Members of the Michigan Militia say so explicitly in Michael Moore's documentary film *Bowling for Columbine* (2003).

Setbacks to the full monopolization of force in the United States continued to operate throughout the nineteenth century. In large parts of America, foremost in the Old South, one can hardly speak of a monopoly at all in this period. Before the Civil War, the plantation system meant that elite family heads ruled like petty monarchs; on the plantation they had sovereignty over their family and slaves. Southern state governments were reluctant to interfere with the power of masters.[23] Although the masters did not actually wage war on each other, this situation is reminiscent of the European middle ages. Compare an illustration from the novel *Dred* by Harriet Beecher Stowe, showing a black man with a gun. The caption says: "the slave-owners' greatest fear: an armed slave."[24] The fact that this represented anxiety rather than reality reinforces my point that the plantation was a little principality. The prince kept armed retainers, but he would never have allowed the peasants in his domains to bear arms. In other words, the plantation resembled a medieval count's domain, with the state government resembling the suzerain king. After emancipation, planters continued to rule their lands as semi-autonomous domains for a long time. Before and after the Civil War, the jury system further blocked an effective monopolization of force in the South. Whites were almost never convicted for homicide, whether on blacks or on other whites. They routinely got away with self-defense or similar excuses. In an unpacified society, such excuses had a measure of reality. As Ayers explains, you just had to shoot your enemy first, because, otherwise, he would shoot you.[25]

For the Old West, the lack of an effective central authority is plain. It was exemplified by, among other things, the frequent resurgence of vigilante committees. Vigilantism has been defined as "extralegal coercion by a group of private individuals seeking to maintain the existing distribution of power."[26] Coercion may consist of threats only, but often it amounts to actual violence. Although the vigilantes themselves are not necessarily members of an elite group, they do defend the established order. In terms of my theory, they should be seen as a group of citizens exercising collective self-defense and private justice in defiance of the state's claim to a monopoly of force: "People were convinced of a right to shortcut government and overrule officials."[27] This phenomenon was especially characteristic for the Old West, but the range of its history and geography was wider. The Carolina Regulators of 1767–71 are usually considered the first vigilantes. Within an urban context, the phenomenon continued well into the twentieth century. In Tampa, for example, vigilantism began in the 1850s, became an organized form of community justice in the 1880s (when Tampa grew into a town) and continued to claim victims until the 1940s.[28]

A thin line differentiated vigilante committees from lynch mobs. The principal difference, perhaps, is that the first term sounds more benign than the second. The word "lynching" was probably first used to denote extralegal violence against Tories in Revolutionary Virginia. The practice subsequently spread Westward until it reached California by the mid nineteenth century. It was not until the 1880s and 1890s that lynching became associated primarily with white-on-black violence in the South. By then, lynch mobs acted, more often than did vigilantes, against alleged offenders, whose principal wrong had been to challenge white supremacy, rather than "real" offenders. From the early twentieth century on, photographs of the "strange fruit" hanging from Southern trees made lynching into a national issue.[29] Like vigilantism, the "rough justice" of lynching was exercised not so much in the absence of state institutions as in defiance of them.[30]

Armed "detective agencies," conspicuous throughout the United States around 1900, constituted still another example of competition with the state's monopoly of force. Whereas modern private security companies are subordinate to the police, these earlier agencies operated more autonomously. Especially notorious were the episodes in which industrial employers called upon them in cases of labor conflict. This happened in both frontier and more settled conditions. In 1892, for example, when the steel workers of Homestead near Pittsburgh were on strike, Carnegie's Lieutenant Frick hired 600 Pinkertons to bring in scabs (strike breakers). As they approached in covered barges on the Monongahela River, they were met by gunfire from the shore, which resulted in the death of 7 Pinkertons and 9 strikers.[31] In Las Animas County, the Colorado Fuel and Iron Company hired gunmen of the Baldwin-Felts Agency to police their property. Private policing was extremely common there and private detectives were often pronounced police officers on the spot. During the coal miners' strike of 1913–14, the Las Animas sheriff made all 348 guards into his deputies at once.[32] Formally making them state agents should not be confused with state control here. To be sure, labor unrest was also quelled by vigilantes sometimes, or US troops, but the use of private armed corps in this period seems a uniquely American phenomenon. In Europe, employers usually called upon the police or other state agencies to suppress labor unrest.[33]

Thus, in America as a whole and throughout most of its history, the tendency toward monopolization of force has been a weak one in comparison with European nations. That situation continues into the present. Even today, the states and the federal government generally allow more self-protection than European governments. The fact that American politicians are unable or unwilling (this largely amounts to the same) to ban guns testifies to this. It is an intriguing historical paradox that the country which, throughout the twentieth century, boasted the most formidable military might externally was unable to do away with competing claims to authority internally.

Finally, the persistence, until today, of the traditional male honor code, stressing virility, bravery and physical attack, may be taken as a symptom of weakened state-formation processes. As argued before, in a social situation in which people have to rely to a great extent on themselves for protection, aggressiveness and bravery tend to be valued positively, by all or some social groups. Consequently, the traditional concept of male honor is prevalent at times and places where there is no strong state. The link between "macho" honor and weak state formation also makes it understandable that black men adopted the honor code after the Civil War. As argued above, white Americans of the Revolutionary period and after equated democracy with the right of self-protection. Slaves had no such right. Blacks after Emancipation adopted the code of toughness and self-defense because it signified to them that they were independent citizens. Obviously, they could demand respect from their peers only; they were unable to ward off lynching crowds, for example. In Stewart's terms, explained in the introduction, no vertical honor was accorded to them but they could obtain horizontal honor.

From the 1920s onward, this code migrated with the people cherishing it from the rural South to Northern cities. In the 1990s it was still very much alive in inner-city neighborhoods, to be rediscovered and analyzed by the urban anthropologist Elijah Anderson. He observes two competing orientations in poor urban neighborhoods, which he calls "decent" and "street." A street-oriented person constantly has to win and maintain respect and to avoid being "dissed" (disrespected). In many ways, this "code of the street" is similar to the old macho honor code which characterized the cultures of many societies, among them those of North-West Europe during the middle ages and beyond. Anderson further observes that inhabitants of poor neighborhoods with a decent orientation are influenced, nevertheless, by the opposite code: you may want to be decent, but you have to survive among those who are not. Indeed, the code of the street is related to a relative lack of pacification: "the street code emerges where the influence of the police ends and personal responsibility for one's safety is felt to begin."[34] The French sociologist Loïc Wacquant (1997) argues in a similar vein. He speaks of a de-pacification in American ghettos, caused by a retreat of the state and public and semi-public institutions from these areas. This is in line with Elias' theory, maintaining that localized decreases in the public security which state organizations are able to offer may lead to the recurrence of an aggressive mentality. It is also in line with my slight modification of the theory: strong counter-tendencies against the internal effectuation of a monopoly of force lead to a stagnation in the spread of more "civilized" standards of behavior in some areas of social life.

Further research has to refine the analysis offered in this section. I have discussed race relations, for example, primarily with reference to the trajectory of state-formation processes in the South. Slavery undoubtedly fostered the culture of violence in the US South, but beyond slavery, racial prejudices prevented the full social and economic incorporation of black people in American society until today.[35] It should be noted, however, that race relations, violence, notions of honor and self-protection and political dynamics were all interdependent as part of the particular "figuration" that came out of the American Revolution. A final point is that most Western and Central European countries have witnessed increased levels of interpersonal violence since the 1970s, along with greater ethnic diversity coupled with processes of marginalization and exclusion. This has led to a partial revival of the traditional macho notion of honor and respect also in Europe. The United States and Europe seem to approach each other somewhat, even though that does not diminish, in my view, the plausibility of the analysis outlined above.

As a preliminary conclusion about North America, we note three major deviations from the overall development of European societies: setbacks in state-formation processes, persistence of a body-related honor code, and a homicide rate that continues to be relatively high.

A Venture into Asia

When shifting our attention to Asia, the Dutch East India Company (VOC), which kept a fort on Formosa (the Portuguese name which the Company took over), forms an obvious starting-point. The Dutch colonized parts of Taiwan between 1624 and 1662 and then imprisoned the last governor for the offense of losing the island. There is an abundant historiography about the VOC, but a bibliographic search into the subject of violence leads almost exclusively to studies of hostilities in relation to trade rivalries and colonialism, rather than of interpersonal violence. The overwhelming majority of studies, moreover, deals with the VOC's main area of interest in the Indonesian archipelago. Thus, Schulte Nordholt identifies two main phases of "unprecedented Dutch violence" in Indonesia, the first in the late seventeenth century, when the VOC sought to establish trade monopolies, and the second during the years 1870–1910, the period of imperialist expansion and the establishment of a colonial state. When referring to the second phase, he speaks of a regime of fear.[36] Obviously, colonial regimes present a special case, which cannot simply be fitted into the traditional model of state-formation processes, such as the French example studied by Elias. In one of the few attempts at an assessment of the relevance for Asia of Elias' theory of civilization, Stephen Mennell therefore concentrates on the three "classic" areas of autonomous development: Japan, China and pre-colonial India. He concludes that China, Japan and, to a lesser extent, India all witnessed parallel processes involving the rise of a dynastic state, pacification of the elites and a refinement of manners.[37]

The case of China is treated, in greater detail with respect to violence, in an overview article by Barend ter Haar (2000). He explains that already before the founding of the Han dynasty there was a turning point away from "martial violence" (*wu*) toward "refinement" (*wen*).[38] Independent cultural dynamics, he emphasizes, were at work, rather than Confucian ideas. Confucius sanctioned personal revenge, especially by sons of murdered parents, and throughout the Han period blood revenge for close relatives, although often performed by professional avengers, remained prevalent. The Tang were more successful in achieving a measure of monopolization of force. Even then, however, the elites continued to practice private violence for political purposes, which became less common under the Song dynasty. The pacification of the Chinese elites was related to parallel changes in attitudes to the body, involving a distancing from the body. For example, the elites discontinued the practice of sealing covenants by the ritual drinking of human or animal blood. After the Tang there was also a gradual rejection of wearing a military outfit and playing violent games. Finally, state violence in the form of maiming and corporal punishments was mitigated from an early date, with forced labor as the principal substitute. Violent punishment continued to be liberally used, however, toward servants, farmers, children and wives.

Other English-language studies published since 2000 deal with persistent violent traditions during the second millennium. Robinson (2001) shows that even Ming China (1368–1644) was far from a peaceful society. He refers to publications in Chinese, Korean and Japanese dealing with the violence of beggars, robbers and members of fighter guilds who beat up persons for money, plus violence in brothels and gambling dens and through blackmail. His own research focuses on banditry. Even in the capital region, bandits often had links with elite groups. Yet Robinson estimates that the incidence of daily violence in sixteenth-century Europe was higher, which might explain why a visitor like Matteo Ricci considered China a peaceful country. Even in the Qing period (1644–1911), however, the central state lacked control over some regions like the South-East coast, where brotherhoods and elite families were enmeshed in feuds. To this region we can add Macheng county, a mountainous area in mid-China at the border of three provinces. From the expulsion of the Mongols until 1938 this region had an extraordinary reputation for violence. Today it is a center of the Falun Gong movement and its repression.[39] On the other hand, family avengers who were apprehended under the Ming and Qing usually suffered the punishment of *ling chi*, (badly) translated as "death by a thousand cuts."[40]

Thus, the pacification of Chinese society certainly progressed during the five centuries or so preceding the 1911 revolution. According to ter Haar, the entire move away from violence in China was related to state-formation processes and to general cultural change. Neither Mennell nor ter Haar mention the theme of personal honor, which was so crucial for the analysis of interpersonal violence in Europe and America. The theme of honor is prominent in Eiko Ikegami's (1995) study of Japanese history, centered around the Samurai and the changes in their life-style and culture. That the Samurai turned from a warrior class into a class of courtiers, beginning with the establishment of the Tokugawa shogunate, is relatively well known. Ikegami additionally demonstrates that this development was accompanied by a process of spiritualization of honor, not unlike the one which took place in Europe. However, to a greater extent than among the early modern European aristocracy, the social identity of the Tokugawa Samurai continued to depend on their origins as a warrior caste.

Indonesia, on the other hand, is one Asian country where the macho type of male honor still holds sway very much today. For this we can turn once more to Schulte Nordholt. He traces the native honor culture back to the period 1870–1910 when the colonial state was established. In the process, the Dutch made use of a pre-existing system of indigenous violence, involving robbery, extortion and theft and operated by violent entrepreneurs similar to the Sicilian mafia. Such an entrepreneur was called a *jago* and these rowdies continued to be active at least into the 1930s. They reappeared, under the name of *preman*, in modern Indonesia, especially after the fall of the Suharto regime. Today, the various political parties have gangs of *preman* associated with them. In connection with these violent entrepreneurs, Schulte Nordholt mentions the concept of "failed state." Although he does not want to designate modern Indonesia as such, he emphasizes the lack of political control over the army.

These observations should be underpinned with quantitative evidence in the form of murder rates. I have been unable to find historical time series for homicide in Asian countries or cities. For relatively recent figures, we may turn to a report of the World Health Organization. Its

Table 3.1 Homicide rates per 100,000 inhabitants in some East Asian countries

China (selected urban and rural areas)	1.8
China (Hong Kong)	1.0
Japan	0.6
Philippines	14.2
Republic of Korea	2.0
Singapore	1.3
Thailand	7.5

Source: WHO

Table 3.2 Taiwan homicide rates, 1975–1998, per 100,000 inhabitants

1975–78	1.17
1979–82	1.68
1983–86	1.86
1987–90	2.38
1991–94	1.78
1995–98	1.64

Source: Tsung-Hsueh Lu 2002

reliability can be questioned, since it ignores national differences in data collection, but it is often used, nevertheless, for comparative purposes. The rates in table 3.1 are for the latest year available, in most cases between 1995 and 2000.[41]

These are the individual East Asian countries which the report lists (most of the discussion is per world region). Whatever the deficiencies in the figures, it is clear that economically well-developed areas such as Hongkong, Japan, Korea and Singapore have homicide rates much closer to those of Western Europe than to those of the United States. The WHO report does not mention Taiwan, but elsewhere I found a medium-term time series for this country. Tsung-Hsueh Lu provides Taiwanese homicide rates, 1975–98, calculated from nationwide mortality data collected by the national Department of Health (table 3.2).

This is a fluctuating pattern, but apart from the years 1987–90, the rates are in the range below 2.0 which was characteristic for developed Asian countries in the WHO report. Interestingly, Taiwan is comparable in several respects with the contemporary Netherlands.[42] The size and population of the two countries are in the same range (Taiwan: 36,000 square km and 23 million inhabitants; the Netherlands: 41,000 square km. and 16 million inhabitants). Both nations, moreover, boast a modern economy and a parliamentary system. Dutch homicide rates, like those in many European countries, have shown an upward movement since the late 1960s: from about 0.5 in 1970 to about 1.3 in the 1990s.[43] These rates have been calculated from Bureau of Statistics (CBS) mortality figures. Since they exclude non-residents killed on Dutch soil, rates calculated from police data and various other sources are between 0.2 and 0.3 higher.[44] The latter discrepancy may apply to the Taiwanese homicide rates as well. Therefore, it can be concluded provisionally that modern Taiwan has slightly higher homicide rates than the modern Netherlands. The difference is perhaps explained by a greater prevalence of organized crime in Taiwan.[45] Obviously, however, more research is needed if this comparison is to be pursued.

Conclusion

Four general points about comparative world history serve as a conclusion. First, the relationship between state-formation processes, male honor and the incidence of serious interpersonal violence – involving roughly simultaneous change in these three factors – appears to hold for the three world regions reviewed. Second, we must conclude that the case of the United States appears unique: it is a thoroughly modern country with a developed economy, which nevertheless witnesses relatively high homicide rates (generally above 5.0, and in the early 1990s around 10). This can be explained with reference to the peculiarly American trajectory of state-formation processes. The third conclusion refers to honor. Cultures of violence are often related to an honor culture stressing male bravery and toughness. Concepts of honor may change in the direction of greater spiritualization, as has happened in Europe (with a partial revival of the older concept in the contemporary period) and in Japan. Traditional male honor is very much alive today in such disparate areas as American inner cities and Indonesia. The final point refers to the most general level. Processes of long-term change and the trajectories taken by this change in various world regions are meaningful units of analysis and comparison, not – largely imaginary and static – competing "civilizations."

PART TWO

PUNISHMENT AND SOCIAL CONTROL

4

Punishment, Power and History

Foucault and Elias

Imagine this scene, reported by an eyewitness. The authorities have ordered that a scaffold be set up for a public execution. One man, scion of a respectable Frankfurt family, is about to mount it. He has been condemned for robbing and murdering four men and two women. The acquittal of the murderer's mistress increases public interest in the case. Already in the early morning, an immense multitude assembles at the square where the fateful event is to take place. Some of the spectators endeavor to create a picture of the convict, which they intend to sell to others for a profit. The scene reaches its climax: the executioner presents the criminal to the assembled audience and severs his head from his body.

Now listen to a quite different text, the house rules for a prison. Each Sunday morning the warden collects the inmates together and recites from the Bible or another religious book. A preacher is there to instruct them, finishing with a few "histories admonishing to piety." In the afternoon, those inmates who are able to read and write get advanced training, while the warden or a work master teaches this art to the others. During the rest of the week, the inmates have to work. Whenever they are together, the master of discipline constantly watches them. He even has to listen to them in their sleeping places to find out what they are talking about. If the inmates go astray nevertheless, the following punishments apply: for frivolously cursing or swearing, three days on bread and water; for the inability to cite one's prayers, the same; for disrespect of the staff, such as pulling an ugly face or using bad words, one month on bread and water. The list of infractions and corresponding punishments is longer still, but these suffice for now.

A sequence like this is surely familiar to any reader of Michel Foucault's *Surveiller et punir* (1975).[1] That book opens with the contrasting cases of the public execution of Robert-François Damiens in 1757, followed by the house rules of the Parisian Maison des Jeunes Détenus, drawn up by Léon Faucher in 1838. Foucault cites articles 17–28, on the order of the day, and concludes with a remark in the sense of "look how much has changed in only eighty years."

By contrast, the examples with which this chapter opened are no less than 344 years apart and, more remarkably, I began with the more recent example! The reporter, the French writer Albert Camus, witnessed the last public execution in France. The German leader of a Paris-based gang, Eugen Weidmann, was decapitated before a large crowd in Versailles on June 16, 1939. I purposely omitted that the executioner severed the convict's head from his body by operating the guillotine and that the pictures made of the event were photographs. The photographers sold the pictures to the newspaper *Paris-Soir* and their publication caused an outrage, presumably with the "delicate" public who had refrained from watching the event in person. This was the final trigger that led to the abolition of public punishment in France.[2] My second text was a sample of the internal rules for the Amsterdam rasphouse, drawn up by Sebastiaan Egberts on November 21, 1595.[3] The first inmates arrived a few months later. Soon the rasphouse had acquired an international reputation as a model prison, to which visitors flocked from Germany, England, France and elsewhere.

This chronology, I suppose, gives pause for thought. My intention is in no way to suggest that the transformation of punishment took place in quite the reverse order from the one claimed by Foucault. That would be absurd. After all, we should also take into account the long and agonizing treatment Damiens had to endure (and that for scratching Louis XV in his side with a knife[4]), whereas the murderer Weidmann was guillotined without additional atrocities. Moreover, the shift to indoor executions took place in most European countries between 1850 and 1870; the French "delay" constitutes an anomaly that historians have not yet satisfactorily explained. Conversely, the Amsterdam ordinance of 1595 had a less meticulous character than the Paris one of 1838. The former, with its long list of penalties for infractions, focused on submission and obedience and less so on the order of the day. The rasphouse's order of the day consisted of the rhythm of forced labor rather than a precise timetable.

Despite these caveats, my two opening examples suggest that the grand narrative of the evolution of punishment in early modern and modern Europe may be somewhat more complex than the story presented in *Surveiller et punir*. To avoid an empty empiricism, I am considering Norbert Elias' theoretical framework next to Foucault's. As Elias' work is cited and discussed throughout this book, it needs no separate introduction here, so let me proceed with discussing Foucault's work.

Foucault on Penal Change

On earlier occasions, I have proclaimed the absolute incompatibility of Foucault's and Elias' sociological-historical approaches.[5] On second thoughts, perhaps this was an exaggeration. In any case, the two theorists themselves were eager to learn from each other, though it never came to a personal meeting. Any discussion of Foucault's views of punishment should begin with an unprejudiced (re)reading of his *Surveiller et punir*. More than 35 years of debate and interpretation have placed layer upon layer on top of this book. It has been commented and re-commented upon in relation to Foucault's other works as well as the commentators' personal ideas. This has made it difficult to separate the author's original intention from the views of his interpreters.

In fact, when one reads *Surveiller et punir* with a fresh eye, it appears basically as a perceptive, well-written analysis of scaffold punishments, penitentiaries and the techniques of discipline.[6] Consider the chapter entitled "The heyday of physical punishment."[7] Foucault provides us with an inside look into the Ancien Régime's criminal procedure and execution ritual: secrecy is the paramount principle during the preliminary investigation and the subsequent trial; the entire procedure in court is aimed at obtaining the suspect's confession; judicial torture plays a crucial role; the convict is obliged to act as the "herald of his own condemnation" (a clever formula, which summarizes a complex staging enterprise); punishment is saturated with symbolism referring to the crime; religious beliefs impregnate the proceedings at every level; an important function of the execution is to underline authority (although too much emphasis is placed on the person of the king); in particular, the execution serves to restore the sovereignty, shaken for a moment by the crime; finally, Foucault rightly stresses the constitutive role of the spectators watching an execution (providing little evidence on this aspect from the sixteenth and seventeenth centuries, though).

Having discussed the Ancien Régime's system of physical punishment, Foucault proceeds to analyze the forces of change and subsequent developments. He discusses the Enlightenment project for penal reform, the introduction of new criminal codes in France and early experiments with new penal methods outside France, such as Philadelphia's Walnut Street prison. The third part, entitled "Discipline," appears as the book's cornerstone. In it Foucault temporarily leaves the field of punishment, looking for disciplinary enterprises in other sectors of society, notably in schools, factories and the army. The last institution, in particular, enables him to trace the origins of the disciplinary principle back to the seventeenth century. In all cases, the arrangement of bodies in space, the ordering of activities in time and the classification of people into distinct categories constituted the pillars of the regulatory program. This part of the book culminates in an analysis of the panoptic principle, the most efficient system of surveillance, as advocated by Jeremy Bentham and others. The inmates of panoptic institutions knew (or thought) they were constantly watched, so they had no option but to internalize the docility and bodily control expected from them. The new prisons of the first half of the nineteenth century, the subject of the book's last part, essentially constituted the realization of the panoptic project. Next to surveillance, solitary confinement was the most distinct characteristic of these institutions. Foucault rightly stresses that punishment had not simply changed from being directed at the body to being directed at the mind; rather, both mind and body were now the objects of surveillance and disciplinary intervention.

Why has *Surveiller et punir* obtained such a contested status and how is it possible that, upon rereading, one can describe this work as a set of solidly historical analyses? The clue, I think, lies in its very final sentence, a footnote to the last word in the body of the text: "Here I interrupt this book which is meant as a historical background for several studies on the power of normalization and the formation of knowledge in modern society." The formulation is slightly ambiguous, yet its meaning is clear enough. Foucault wrote *Surveiller et punir* as a historical work that would form the basis of a study of modern society. He purposely intended it to be largely empirical; most of the theorizing was reserved for later. Since Foucault subsequently shifted the focus of his attention to sexuality, he never completed that other task.

Foucault and Historians of Crime and Justice

It seems inevitable that widely admired theorists get their interpreters – a feature that Foucault and Elias share. As with other important works, some of those who reflected on the implications and significance of *Surveiller et punir* made statements or discovered theses not fully backed up by the book. In fact, some of my own earlier criticism was aimed or should have been aimed at the Foucaultians rather than the French philosopher himself. The Foucaultians are numerous. For a considerable part, the meta-analysis of *Surveiller et punir* has been construed by scholars from various disciplines who reflected about Foucault's entire work. It would by far extend the bounds of this chapter to consider all those publications, so I will restrict myself to those pertaining directly to the history of punishment.

Most historians of crime and criminal justice reveal themselves neither as ardent supporters nor as uncompromising opponents. Often, they are content with just citing Foucault. They mention *Surveiller et punir* as the only theoretical work – or one of the few – in their field of study and proceed with their own evidence, hardly discussing to what extent this confirms or disproves Foucault's views. Alternatively, they summarize *Surveiller et punir* in a few paragraphs, with little indication of what they think of it. V. A. C. Gatrell, for example, first calls Foucault's analysis of penal change a "materialist" one and then discusses some elements of this analysis in a seemingly approving fashion.[8] A slightly different way of introducing Foucault while avoiding too much debate is to consider his work as a parallel to other traditions of historical discourse. In German historiography, for example, the notion of "social discipline" (*Sozialdisziplinierung*) has been paramount for several decades. The theoretical positions associated with this concept vary somewhat, but in most cases it is assumed that the rise of absolutism was part of an all-encompassing drive toward a disciplined society in which the churches, too, played an important role. In an overview article, Ulrich Behrens refers to *Surveiller et punir* as a reinforcement of that thesis.[9]

Among German historians, Martin Dinges has occupied himself intensively with Foucault's work. In his study of violence and conflicts of honor in eighteenth-century Paris, Dinges uses the French philosopher's views on discourse as the basis for an assessment of the meanings to be attributed to the narratives contained in the Parisian archives.[10] In an article on Foucault's reception in Germany, Dinges concludes that most of his compatriots have failed to grasp the full significance of Foucault's views on punishment and discipline or have misinterpreted his work. Problematic, in my view, is Dinges' consistent labeling of Foucault's critics as people led by a belief in progress. Because the French philosopher, with his emphasis on the rise of a disciplinarian society, "criticized the Enlightenment," his opponents must necessarily be prophets of rationalization and modernity.[11] This argument inappropriately reduces a scholarly debate to a political and ideological clash of views, confusing the analysis of social change with its moral appreciation.

Despite Foucault's insistence that the disciplinary principle continues to affect modern society, few historians have applied his work to twentieth-century developments – that is, as far as prisons, courts and policing are concerned. Robert Gellately, in several publications dealing with the Gestapo, is one of the exceptions. Even he relies implicitly rather than explicitly on the French philosopher's thoughts. In a modern industrial society, Gellately reminds us, no agency can rely solely on compulsion or force. He goes on to cite Foucault, arguing that every regime, including that of the Nazis, requires a measure of cooperation from "acting subjects." Only then can a "disciplined" or "carceral" society emerge.[12] He then proceeds with an analysis of the functioning of the Gestapo without further references to Foucault. In an overview of the institutions and legal measures for imprisoning the regime's opponents, Gellately remarks that "if ever there was a 'great carceral network' of the sort alluded to in several well-known passages by Michel Foucault, then it existed in Hitler's dictatorship."[13]

Intriguingly, Foucault's most ardent supporters among historians of crime and justice, such as Dinges and Gellately, are found outside his native country. French historians of crime and justice have made a habit of criticizing their famous compatriot. This criticism began directly after the publication of *Surveiller et punir* and it was largely concerned with questions of detail.[14] The historians involved in it pointed at weaknesses, real or alleged, in the book's historical narrative, or the neglect of other evidence. Thus, the standard work on French prisons of the late eighteenth and nineteenth centuries by Jacques-Guy Petit (1990) has scattered references to Foucault, most of them concerned with minor criticisms. Arlette Farge, on the other hand, appears more positive toward Foucault, together with whom she published a collection of archival documents concerning private confinement.[15] Even among French sociologists of crime, as Philippe Robert notes, Foucault's influence has been less than among their colleagues in the Anglo-Saxon world.[16]

The criminal justice historians siding most conspicuously with the French philosopher were those proclaiming a "revisionist" historiography of carceral institutions. Among their foremost representatives were David Rothman and Michael Ignatieff. Essentially, they both argue that penal change, such as the introduction and spread of incarceration, was not due primarily to the conscious efforts of individual reformers; instead, penal change was a response to or part of political or economic transformations. In *The discovery of the asylum* (1971), Rothman emphasizes that the proliferation of prisons in the United States, which took place in the 1820s and 1830s, was part of a larger movement of establishing institutions, which included poorhouses and insane asylums. In a follow-up study of American prisons in a later period, Rothman (1980) focuses on the tensions within Progressive politics. In Michael Ignatieff's 1978 study of English prisons, economic change is the main explanatory factor. He focuses on the model penitentiaries, with a regime of solitary confinement, established in the first half of the nineteenth century.

Although *The discovery of the asylum* was published earlier than *Surveiller et punir*, Rothman later noted the resemblances between his work and that of Foucault and Ignatieff.[17] In a similar vein, Ignatieff (1983) proclaimed that Rothman, Foucault and he himself had pioneered a new historiography of imprisonment. One common element, according to Rothman and Ignatieff, had to do with timing: prisons emerged following the great political and economic revolutions around the turn of the eighteenth and nineteenth centuries. Although true to a certain extent for the United States, this thesis has to be rejected for most of Europe, where prisons and related penal institutions were conspicuously present throughout a large part of the early modern period.[18] More important for my discussion is that Foucault's work only partially supports the others' views. In *Surveiller et punir*, he does pay attention to the early modern precursors of penitentiaries, although most of this attention is reserved for institutions established since the 1770s. Moreover, his discussion of schools, factories and the army clearly demonstrates that the disciplinary principle far predated the great political and economic revolutions that took place around 1800. Finally, in Foucault's book on madness, "the great confinement" of the early modern period is a central theme.[19]

Another new element in Rothman's and Ignatieff's historiography – the main reason why they termed it revisionist – concerned their argument that penal change reflected, first of all, a desire for greater control over lawbreakers and similar deviants. They aimed this argument, still claiming that Foucault was with them, at the authors whose history writing they attempted to "revise." In fact, most of their predecessors were either amateur historians, students of local institutions or lawyers with an interest in the past. These authors often produced an appreciative story with an emphasis on the benevolent motives of the principal actors. One may wonder whether their view, mixing scholarship with moral judgment, needs serious attention at all. In confronting it, the revisionists created an opposite image, which, in turn, was not entirely free from moral judgment. From good guys, the reformers turned into bad guys. Their true intention was not to treat criminals more "humanely" but to subject them to tighter control. Thus, the revisionists opposed their control-oriented approach to an approach centering on benevolent intentions. In a similar vein, authors such as Andrew Scull apply the revisionist argument to the history of mental institutions, also with reference to the French philosopher: far from being treated more considerately, the insane became subject to tighter control.[20]

In my view, sentiments and the desire for control are not mutually exclusive. Although I reject "humanitarianism" as a descriptive category, I do think that sensibilities were involved in penal change. The question, again, is whether Foucault sides with the revisionists on this point. Although he makes condescending remarks once in a while about authors who applaud penal reformers, he does not bother to enter into a debate with these authors. And he concedes that punishment became less severe, implicitly acknowledging that sensibilities played a part. The "real Foucault," then, probably had more in common with Elias than some scholars, including myself, have previously thought. Although these two theorists differ in many respects, they are no irreconcilable opposites.

Admittedly, it is not the first time this conclusion has been drawn. Other scholars have noted resemblances between our two protagonists as well. Karen Halttunen (1995), who argues that the increased sensitivity toward suffering that emerged at the turn of the eighteenth and nineteenth centuries brought with it a new "pornography of pain," refers both to Foucault and to my Elias-based analysis of punishment as background works. Both a Dutch and a German historian who studied the development of hygiene and bathing argue that it reflected the disciplining process and the rise of a medical regime in Foucault's sense as well as the civilizing process as posited by Elias.[21] In a review article on Foucault's impact on German historiography, Ulrich Brieler sees parallels between Elias' portrayal of the process of civilization and the French philosopher's notion of the genealogy of the modern subject.[22] These are only a few examples of scholars linking the work of the two theorists discussed here. In the end, however, I believe that their basic agreement is to be found at a more profound level. Elias and Foucault resemble each other to the extent that they both find it imperative to analyze historical change in order to better understand our own world. Or, to put it differently, they agree that the "otherness" of past societies forms an indispensable key for the study of modern society.

That said, I maintain that the "real" Foucault can be criticized on two principal points. One, referring directly to *Surveiller et punir*, concerns the pace of historical change. The other, concerning his conception of power, equally refers to this book and much of his other work. In both cases, I will argue, a consideration of Elias' contribution to social theory takes us further.

The Penal System: An Abrupt and Total Change?

Clearly, Foucault has a tendency to see abrupt change and, consequently, to neglect gradual development taking place over the very long term. In some cases, this lack of a long-term perspective leads to inadequate conclusions. This, too, can be demonstrated by considering a few concrete examples from his book. As said earlier, he posits a total transformation of the penal system within a time span of only 80 years. With a view on Europe's long historical experience, this would be short indeed. Foucault neatly specifies the beginning and end terms: 1760–1840. He then proceeds to the explanatory level, looking for a historical background to this rapid transformation.

He finds it at the opposite end of the spectrum: the behavior of lawbreakers. The reforms of criminal justice in the second half of the eighteenth century, he says, although promoted by philosophers and politicians from Beccaria to the members of the *Constituante*, also had to do with a change in the nature of criminality. Foucault identifies three constitutive elements of this change. The first is a supposed shift in the character of criminality from a predominance of violent offenses to a predominance of property offenses. As a second element, he refers to the decline of violence in absolute terms, causing the remainder of violent criminality to be on the whole less serious. Finally, he points at the liquidation of great robber bands in the 1750s, with similar consequences. Since then, still according to Foucault, the property offenses the courts had to deal with were of a more individual and petty character. He concludes that a softening of crime preceded the softening of the law.[23]

Here I am obliged, despite my earlier reservations, to present a little criticism of detail myself. I will indicate its relevance for my overall argument though. The story of a softening of crime must be modified in the light of research appearing simultaneously with or after *Surveiller et punir*, and, in at least one case (Richard Cobb's *The police and the people*), earlier than Foucault's book. For one thing, banditry in France by no means was over after the 1750s. In fact, larger and more tightly structured bands were active in several regions toward the end of the Ancien Régime.[24] The Bande Hulin, for example, whose operations extended from 1767 to 1780, counted about 300 members.[25] The last revival of banditry occurred in the 1790s and 1800s, fostered by the unsettled conditions of the struggle between Revolutionary and counter-Revolutionary forces.[26] Second, the thesis of a shift from violent offenses to property offenses has been rejected by most historians since the early 1980s. From the seventeenth through nineteenth centuries, thefts peaked during economic crises or in the aftermath of war. This pattern has weakened much since about 1900, but the actual incidence as well as the proportion of property crime remain at unprecedented levels since the 1960s.[27]

All this suggests that a long-term perspective as advocated by Elias is better equipped to deal with shifts in property crime than Foucault's notion of sudden change. What about the development of violent crime? For one thing, we are practically ignorant about homicide rates in early modern France. When viewed on a European scale, the homicide rate indeed dropped during the eighteenth century. However, this formed part of a longer-term decline over many centuries and the timing of accelerations in this decline diverges per country and city. Nowhere can it be pinned down to a short period in the middle of the eighteenth century. So, it would be highly surprising if future research showed this to have been the case in France. These considerations cause the final pillar under Foucault's softening of crime to tumble down.

The relationship between changes in the severity of punishment and shifts in the type of crime is rather variegated. Foucault's claim that, from the late eighteenth century onward, punishment increasingly served to repress property crime is only partially true. It by no means holds for the death penalty, which after 1800 became practically reserved for murderers (see chapter 6). Foucault is right to the extent that the image of punishment increasingly came to be determined by the prison, and prisons housed mostly property offenders. But this situation was the result of a complex interplay of developments at the level of crime and that of "control." What really happened should be described not in terms of before or after but in terms of the interdependence of several long-term processes. Interdependence, of course, is a key word in Elias' work.

At this point, we can draw a preliminary conclusion: Foucault favors an ad hoc explanation for the transformation of the penal system. This would remain so even if his claim of a softening of crime had withstood later research. It is understandable to look for an ad hoc explanation, if you believe that the *explanandum* is a shift within a brief span of time. But it was not. Moreover, Foucault's argument is largely restricted to events in France, whereas the *explanandum*, the transformation of the penal system, was a Europe-wide phenomenon.

Examining a longer chain of events, we find that the entire penal system had undergone major changes in the direction of a diminution of the centrality of the public infliction of bodily harm from about 1600 onward. This casts serious doubt on the significance of the year 1760 as a marker for the onset of a quick and total transformation. So what about Foucault's end term, the year 1840? By then, he claims, all elements of our modern penal system were more or less in place; although he admits that some were introduced later, he finds these of lesser importance. Panopticism and solitary confinement, on the other hand, are unmistakably important in Foucault's analysis of penal change. Needless to say, lawyers and legislators have long abandoned the idea that complete solitude somehow benefits the mind, while the round panoptic prison is now considered a nineteenth-century architectural classic. Apparently, the penal system has continued its transformation also after 1840.[28]

This applies with equal force to another constitutive element of modern penality emphasized by Foucault: not just lawyers but a whole range of non-legal specialists are involved in the modern penal system, all contributing to the production of power-knowledge. Among them, psychiatrists and other medical experts play a crucial role, but in 1840 this role was still extremely limited. The medicalization of the criminal was a typical development of the late nineteenth century, as studies for France, England and Germany have made clear.[29] Even the classification of prisoners and their differentiated treatment, as David Garland (1985) demonstrates for England, date back no further than the end of the nineteenth century. Moreover, the professions of sociology and psychoanalysis were not yet in existence in 1840. In France, the process of the intrusion of non-legal specialisms into the treatment of crime was going on, with constant shifts of focus, well into the twentieth century.[30] For the end of that century, and possibly into the present, we can turn to another study by Garland, who speaks of a crisis in criminal justice: few people really believe in its efficacy, but the system stays in place because no one knows the road to reform.[31] Obviously, this is a far cry from the refined strategies operating in the modern penal system according to Foucault.

Elias, of course, is the theorist who has emphasized time and again that societies change continuously and that scholars should attempt to trace the interdependent long-term developments making up that change. A study of developments in penality appears to sustain his views. Interdependence is the keyword here. In Elias' and my view of historical explanation, the main task for scholars is to arrive at a better understanding of how social processes are interwoven instead of thinking in terms of cause and effect. It is highly unsatisfactory to argue in terms of straightforward causalities. Thus, we should never say that "changed sensibilities were the cause of the privatization of executions." Instead, I would say that the "privatization of executions reflected a change in sensibilities." Second, to broaden the explanatory perspective, it is important to note the more or less contemporaneous tendencies toward concealment in other spheres of social life. The concealment of the spectacle of death and suffering, apparently, was part of a more encompassing process of privatization. In this way, finally, we have arrived at a composite picture of overall historical change.

Ultimately, Elias' and my principal goal is not "to explain why corporal punishments disappeared and capital punishment came to be executed indoors." Much less is it my aim to provide a kind of overall theory of punishment. Rather, my main interest goes in the opposite direction. The aim is to explore in what way changes in punishment reflect broader, long-term developments in society; to learn, through the study of punishment, how these developments are interrelated; to find out whether all this may enhance our insight into the structure of our own society and ourselves. An examination of the concept of power serves to expound this scholarly project in greater detail.

Foucault, Elias and the Problem of Power

The theme of power obviously relates to any object of study within the human sciences; here, however, it has to be discussed in particular with reference to the history of punishment. In this case, too, we note that the views of Foucault and Elias converge on one fundamental point, while in the end they diverge in crucial ways. Their basic agreement concerns the idea that power is everywhere or, in the words of one interpreter, "the postulate of the omnipresence of phenomena of power."[32] Although this is definitely an idea that Elias and Foucault have in common, many authors appreciatively refer to it as deriving from the latter alone.[33]

In a brief, programmatic essay, Foucault clarified his position in terms of a "microphysics of power." He put forward four theses, or rather he discussed four commonly held notions that he rejected. One: power is something which certain people possess while others are excluded from possessing it. Although the phrase "they are in power" may serve as a convenient political slogan, it is unhelpful in a historical analysis. Apart from politics, power is embedded also in families, sexual relations, living conditions and neighborhood life. Consequently, a second notion he rejected was the idea that power can be localized – specifically, that it can be confined to state institutions. On the contrary, the apparatus of the state is merely an "auxiliary structure," the instrument of a system of powers far greater than the state. The police of Ancien Régime France, for example, could be effective only because of the pre-existing power structures of paternal authority and religious community. Three: power is subordinate to or a derivative of a mode of production. Rather, power is a constitutive element of the prevailing mode of production. It is only through power mechanisms that people are prepared to devote a consid- erable part of their lives to labor instead of such alternatives as taking a rest, having sex or engaging in robbery. (This thesis, obviously, serves to distance the author from orthodox Marxism.) Four: power is rooted solely in physical force. In fact, it is mistaken to draw a sharp distinction between force and ideology. Every situation in which power is exercised is also an instance of gathering knowledge. For example, especially from the nineteenth century onward, every "agent of power" routinely provided feedback to his superiors about the implementation of their commands. Thus, power is not merely repressive; it also has productive and integrative effects.[34]

According to Foucault, then, power is inextricably linked to every part of the social body. Although Elias adopts a different terminology, he would have no objections to the general idea. The notion that power is not something possessed by the mighty alone, and the acknowledgment of its relational character, are central themes in his work from the 1960s onward. Elias and Foucault, it can be concluded, developed the idea of the omnipresence of power more or less simultaneously but independently from each other. Elias' writings on the theme, however, are more sociological in tone.

His basic rule is simple: power should always be linked to people (individuals or groups), but power itself should be neither personified nor reified. Elias defines it as "a structural property of a social relationship."[35] As he said in academic lectures, "Power is not a magic substance that you carry in your pocket." Rather, it is an aspect of the interaction between two or more people, up to millions of them. On still another occasion, Elias explained: "In fact what we call 'power' is an aspect of a relationship, of *every* human relationship. It has something to do with the fact that people as groups or as individuals can withhold or monopolize what others need – food, love, meaning, protection from attack (i.e. security), as well as knowledge and some other things."[36] Consequently, power is always two-sided, operating from the top down as well as from the bottom up. Those who withhold things from others sometimes still need these other people, but usually the distribution of power is unequal. To put it differently, group A may be more powerful than group B, but that does not leave group B entirely without power. For example, we may speak of the power of a baby over its parents. Whenever the child cries, a parent is likely to devote attention to it. In a similar vein, prisoners have some measure of power over their supervisors and policy makers, even though the latter two are by far the stronger parties within this social relationship.

Moreover, these two-sided power relationships are not static. They are subject to change as new or enlarged sources of power become available to certain people in connection with broader social transformations. In the case of babies and parents, new conceptions of childhood and the value of children, related in their turn to more encompassing changes in society, may increase the readiness of mothers and fathers to respond to their offspring's calls for attention. In the penal realm, one of the most telling examples is the process of emancipation of prisoners (see chapter 6). In that process, the level of sensibility prevailing in society at large served as a source of power for a specific group. The source of power in question may be called cultural or socio-psychological, but in other situations, sources of a quite different type can be operative.

The notion of "sources of power" is closely connected with the definition of power as an aspect of all human relationships. Sources of power are no wells springing up in favorable places and empowering a person if he or she drinks from the water. According to Elias' analysis, every source of power is a function of specific social relationships, or, to put it differently, it derives from the way people's lives are organized. This applies equally to peaceful or violent social relationships. The lord of a medieval castle has power over his retinue obviously not because he is physically stronger than all his dependents together. His power is a function of the organization of the castle and the surrounding domain and the conviction of all those involved that this is legitimate. When we consider the social class of knights as a whole, on the other hand, and contrast it with the peasantry, we easily recognize that the former's power surplus rests in large part on their monopoly on bearing arms. Finally, the organization of knowledge brings forth power differences. Certain people are more powerful than others because they have valuable means of orientation at their disposal. The influential position of priests in early agrarian societies, for example, was due in large part to their expertise in timing (see chapter 9).

The last example easily brings to mind Foucault's notion of the interconnectedness of power and knowledge. In his writings, however, knowledge appears to be a product rather than a source of power. Alternatively, the two have become merged into one, as in his well-known expression of "power-knowledge" (*pouvoir-savoir*, used in the singular). Linguistic peculiarities further complicate the matter. In *Surveiller et punir* and other works, Foucault distinguishes between *savoir* and *connaissance*, which Arpád Szakolczai translates as "knowledge" and "knowledge-content."[37] *Savoir*, however, is actually a verb and in Dutch and German translations of Foucault it often is rendered as a verb. With this in mind, we might translate *savoir* and *connaissance* as "knowing" and "knowledge," respectively. *Pouvoir*, of course, is also originally a verb. Although it would be too awkward perhaps to translate the word as "can" or "being able to," it is important to realize this. Then we can take *pouvoir-savoir* to mean simply "if you are able to do something, you also know something and vice versa." Specific types of knowledge are the end result. This interpretation is concordant with a key sentence from *Surveiller et punir*: "[It is] power-knowing, [and] the processes and the struggles which traverse it and by which it is constituted, which determine the possible forms and domains of knowledge."[38] Applying this to criminal justice history, we may consider the rise of penitentiaries again: pre-existing structures of knowing and enabling were a condition for the emergence of these institutions, which subsequently produced knowledge about, among other things, the classification of criminals. However, the quoted sentence still rules out the possibility that knowledge – or control over the means of orientation – can be a source of power.

Foucault's preoccupation with the theme of power was greatest during the mid-1970s, the very period in which he published *Surveiller et punir*. Later in life he tended to deny that power was the central concern in his work, replacing it with "truth" and "the subject."[39] Because of the uncertainty in which Foucault leaves us concerning the exact relationship between power and knowledge, it is difficult to determine with precision to what extent his views diverge from Elias' notion of control over the means of orientation as one possible source of power. We can say with certainty, on the other hand, that Elias' notions of the two-sidedness of power and its relational character are largely absent from Foucault's work. This explains why scholars disagree about the question of who the power holders were in the narrative of *Surveiller et punir*. Who stood to gain from the discipline exerted on convicts; who profited from the existence of panoptic prisons? Major candidates are the bourgeoisie, the state and professional groups. It is so difficult to decide between these three because the book implicitly contains two different concepts of power. The first emphasizes its omnipresence, but it still suffers from one-sidedness. According to this concept, we might distinguish an infinite number of groups with power: A, B, C and so on. We can imagine them to confront, in a top-down process, an equally large number of objects of discipline: X, Y, Z etc. Within the framework of this concept, there is no need to answer the question of who the power holders were. Power is exercised by many people but always in a one-way direction.

Ultimately, however, the second concept prevails. It makes power much more monolithic: power still is everywhere, but this time because it is a very busy and rapid thing or person. It is "Mr. Power" himself (we must imagine him as a man, because the noun *le pouvoir* has the male gender). Toward the end of *Surveiller et punir*, Foucault formulates it thus: "The most important effect, perhaps, of the carceral system and its extension beyond the realm of legal imprisonment is that it makes the power to punish appear natural and legitimate, at least to lower the threshold of tolerance for penality."[40] In other words, Mr. Power punishes constantly, and everyone thinks it a normal thing. To conclude, Foucault severs power from real people, but at the same time it becomes an entity or even an actor who does things. Apparently, it has a will and a life of its own.[41]

Foucault's personification of power is illustrated most tellingly in a passage from his *History of Sexuality*. In that passage, Mr. Power behaves almost like a rapist: "[Power] seizes the sexual body by the waist ... no doubt [this implies] ... also a sensualization of power.... The unveiled pleasure flows back to power, who surrounds it.... [Power] attracts; he conquers the strange things he guards. Pleasure spreads over power, who pursues him."[42] This is suggestive language, as other scholars have noted, too. Herman Franke criticizes Foucault's choice of words with respect to power even without having considered the latter's *History of Sexuality*. According to Franke, Foucault's work has the effect of "reducing individuals and groups to instruments of a willful, omnipresent and all-pervading force: power. People have to comply with the wishes and desires of that power. They even do so unconsciously."[43] Significantly, Franke adds, Foucault never poses the question why some social processes proceeded more or less as influential people had imagined them while other processes did not proceed that way at all. By contrast, Elias acknowledges that social developments have a relative autonomy from the aims, plans and wishes of the people involved in them.

That observation makes it easy to see how Elias' rejection of both a personification and a reification of power reinforces the thesis that the evolution of criminal justice from a dominance of physical punishment to a reliance on incarceration took place over a longer period of time and in a less linear fashion than Foucault suggests. Because power is a two-sided aspect of all social relationships, no person or group has such a huge surplus of power as to be able to completely determine the course of historical change. Already by the early seventeenth century urban and territorial authorities in several parts of Europe were eager to impose imprisonment, on beggars in particular, but the apparatus of law enforcement was still limited and weak, so that actual numbers of imprisoned beggars remained low. Partly as a consequence of this, banishment and physical punishment stayed on the scene for another 200 years or so. If Foucault's Mr. Power really existed, he might have brought about the presumed sudden transformation of the penal system. But there was no sudden transformation and the penal system continued to change after 1840. A powerful (in Elias' sense) coalition of philanthropists and administrators, who met at successive international conferences during the nineteenth century, promoted the solitary confinement of criminals. This coalition was successful for a while, but then the power of prisoners, whose sufferings became known to the outside world, slightly increased, which was one factor in the demise of solitary confinement. These are only a few examples. In a similar vein, the massive increase in incarceration rates in recent years can be analyzed in terms of shifting balances of power (see chapter 6).

Conclusion

Summed up in one sentence, the conclusion of this essay is that Foucault and Elias converge on some points while they diverge on others. They converge to the extent that they both acknowledge the omnipresence of power and that they prefer broad historical explorations. They look for explanations at a relatively high level of generalization. In this, they contrast markedly with some works in the history of punishment published in the 1990s, notably that of Richard Evans. He dismisses both Foucault and Elias without developing an alternative theory of his own. He believes he can discredit the former's scholarly work with gossip about his personal life, and he dismisses the latter's theory of civilization by repeating the blunt and unfounded statements of a few others, fifteen years earlier, who claimed that this theory serves to uphold racism.[44]

When we examine the work of Foucault and Elias in greater detail, however, we find them diverging in their approach to the study of long-term change and their methods of sociological-historical explanation. Elias' approach, in my view, comes closer to balancing off, on the one hand, the fact that, in the human sciences, we always have to do with people of flesh and blood and, on the other hand, that these people generate processes that are beyond their control as individuals. Based on this acknowledgment, Elias' view of historical explanation centers around the interdependence of several broad processes over the long term. Applied to the history of punishment, this view of historical explanation focuses on the interwovenness of penal change and change in other social fields. Instead of having the civilizing process "explain" the transformation of punishment, Elias' and my approach, rather, takes the opposite route: a study of the development of executions and incarceration increases our understanding of the nature of civilizing processes.

5

Monkey Butt's Mate

On Informal Social Control, Standards of Violence and Notions of Privacy

The role and character of informal social control have undergone considerable changes during the last five centuries of European history. As with other subjects discussed, these changes form part of a set of interdependent long-term processes. The increasing preponderance of formal social control by state agencies, for example, has reduced the scope of informal control by local communities and private citizens. In this chapter I am primarily concerned with two transformations of a more socio-psychological nature: the increasing sensitivity toward violence and the rise of the private sphere. Let me start with violence, which perhaps comes to mind first with respect to social control. The changing standards of what is permissible and what is not can be illustrated by two contrasting cases, rendered here in reverse historical order. The cases and much, though not all, of my evidence are Dutch, but I believe that my final conclusions are valid for more than one country.

Two Contrasting Cases

It is August 27, 2002. The scene is a store of a well-known Dutch supermarket chain, kept by Simon Lindeman, the 30-year-old lease holder, and Lucas Porsius, 31 and the manager. The store is located in an ordinary Amsterdam neighborhood, not a "bad" one but certainly not wealthy. Simon and Lucas are accustomed to watching over their property, because shoplifting is not uncommon. On this day they notice a man, later identified as the 33-year-old addict Clifton H., grabbing money from the cash-box. Clifton has a knife on him, but witnesses' accounts as to the moment when he draws it are contradictory. In any case, the two store-keepers who pursue him manage to throw him to the ground and hold him there until the police arrives. They perform this task with such force that Clifton suffers a broken nose.

This incident remained largely unnoticed until October of that year, when the public prosecutor announced that he would charge the two store-keepers with excessive violence. Much commotion ensued, to which Prince Bernard, the former queen's husband, contributed with a promise to pay their fine should they be convicted. Media debates followed about the threshold of acceptable violence when the issue was the protection of one's property or a private arrest by citizens. In January 2003 Porsius was acquitted, but Lindeman was sentenced to a fine of €300. The judge explained that, although he understood the defendant's emotional reaction, he had to take his two earlier convictions for assault into account.

Another incident took place later that year, this time involving Simon Lindeman and his cousin Peter, who shared the supermarket's lease. After they had kicked an alleged thief and his accomplice from their store with some force, the specifics of which are unreported, the Amsterdam police arrived in full strength to arrest the two cousins. I was probably not the only one then who jokingly expected Prince Bernard's future bankruptcy. However, the court dropped this case, upon which one of the alleged thieves objected, which caused the case to be heard after all in 2007 and to result in acquittal. The participants in the renewed public debate in 2003 included Prime Minister Balkenende. He expressed his empathy with honest store-owners who became victims of theft more than once, but he added that citizens should not go too far in their duty of helping to stop crime.[1]

This case can be viewed from various angles. A lawyer may assess the legal merits of both trials and a historian may pose the question of whether Prince Bernard experienced even more rigorous acts of order maintenance during his time as commander of the so-called "internal forces" in 1944–5. For this chapter, the primary interest lies in the public debate: what is allowed to citizens when they exercise informal social control or allegedly assist the police? In that debate, a broad sympathy for the store-keepers in question, backed by Prince Bernard's intervention, was manifest. From this we may preliminarily conclude that many Dutch people of today condone things like kicking or fist-blows when it comes to privately combating property crime. Significantly, whereas the newspapers denoted Clifton's last name with just an initial, they always gave Simon Lindeman's full name, even though he got convicted. In doing so, the media treated him as a hero rather than a suspect.

Let us now examine a case almost 300 years earlier. The scene is another Amsterdam neighborhood and the incident likewise begins with shoplifting. It is July 5, 1719. The protagonists, men of 30 and 22, are known by aliases that approximately translate as "Big Mouth" and "Monkey Butt." They are recidivists and have already been banished but they are in town despite their sentence. They have to be, they later explain in court, "because we cannot earn a living elsewhere." This may well be true, as their primary means of living appears to be illegal activities, for which there are more opportunities in Amsterdam than in other places. On that day, between 2 and 3 p.m., they take away two pieces of cotton from a store in a cellar in the Noordermarkt. Noticing this, the saleswoman and her brother run after them, loudly yelling "Hold the thief." Their cry causes a number of passers-by to join the chase. After a few blocks the thieves decide to drop the stolen goods, but the posse continues to pursue them. In order to ward them off, Big Mouth and Monkey Butt both draw their knives, threatening those who get too close to them. One of the pursuers comes too close indeed and is stabbed fatally between the chest and the belly. This makes the posse even more furious. They overpower the two, appropriately, on the Galgebrug (Gallows Bridge).

Their trial starts on the following day. The prosecutor charges Monkey Butt with the deadly stabbing. He first denies this but confesses after hearing that the judges formally consent to torture. As a result, Monkey Butt is broken on the wheel on July 22, two and a half weeks after the crime. At the same execution ceremony, Big Mouth is hanged. These sentences are not surprising; the surprise comes from the body inspection report of the stabbing victim, named Johannes Wist. Sometimes the clerk filing the report adds a few notes about the case to the dry language of the anatomy professor and surgeons. The clerk confirms that Monkey Butt was the killer and continues: "his mate has also been apprehended. From the citizens he had received a hacked wound in his head with an axe, so that his brains lay bare."[2]

Perhaps the clerk exaggerated a little but, even so, Big Mouth's injury was far more serious than Clifton H.'s broken nose. The phrasing of the offense in Monkey Butt's sentence is significant too: "murder upon a citizen who had attempted to provide a service to justice." Thus, the court considered Johannes Wist's actions and, by implication, the posse's violence with an axe not as private retaliation but as cooperation with the judicial authorities. The sources contain no indication whatsoever of measures against the axe wielder(s) or even a discussion of their activities, which we may well interpret as revenge or private punishment for killing one of their own (assuming that in the fuss of the moment they did not know which of the two had done it). The question whether they injured

Big Mouth during or after their arrest – a key question in modern jurisprudence – was never posed. It is highly unlikely that the court blamed the posse in any way. The records denote its members consistently as *burgers* (citizens) which, in the court language of the day, means decent people, not riffraff. The arrest they performed is called a *gevangenname* (taking prisoner).

This is all very similar to comparable cases in the Amsterdam judicial archive. Throughout the early modern period the authorities appear to condone high levels of violence as long as these occur in the process of stopping and holding a suspect. When crowds severely harassed thieves or threw them into a canal, the only comment in the records is that, by arriving at the scene, the arresting constables saved their lives. It was only in the rare cases in which someone subsequently bothered the constables, that he, too, was liable for arrest.[3] A trial by the magistrates certainly was the norm, but a permissible standard of violence paved the way toward this goal.

Apart from the standards of violence used to stop criminals, the two cases contain another, implicit contrast. That contrast takes us to the second major theme in the history of informal social control, that of privacy. Note that a posse of citizens pursued Monkey Butt and Big Mouth; neighbors spontaneously offered assistance. In 2002–3, for all we know, the victims of theft acted alone. Many people sympathized with them from a distance, but bystanders did not consider it their business to help. This raises the question of long-term transformations in neighborly assistance. Has the internal cohesion of neighborhoods diminished over time? Moreover, regarding someone else's attempt at recovering his property as not your own business is but one element pointing at a changed role for the local community. Modern people's reticence with respect to corrective action also extends to the correction of neighbors, who formerly were objects of social control. Our discussion of the long-term changes in question can begin once more with relatively recent events.

Neighborhood Supervision

The annual Hein Roethof prize, existing since 1987 and awarded by a governmental agency on behalf of the Dutch Ministry of Justice, encourages activities in the sphere of neighborhood surveillance and informal social control. That is, until recently it was explicitly demanded from the candidates that they were involved in projects to prevent criminality based on solving problems within "one's own group" and cooperation between, for example, the police and a local club or neighborhood center. The 2011 call just speaks of projects "aiming at the prevention of criminality or increasing social safety."[4] Whatever lies behind this change of emphasis, the prize is rooted in a concern to revive neighborhood participation in combating crime and deviance. It was named after Hein Roethof (1921–96), Member of the Dutch Parliament for the Labor Party, who in the mid-1980s chaired the Committee for Petty Crime which issued a report called *Society and criminality*.[5] The committee's final report of 1986 offered 21 recommendations, the majority of which lay outside the sphere of justice or police action.[6]

The interim report of December 1984 ventures slightly into the domain of historical explanation with a passage describing how and why informal social control has diminished. Actually the report even says that informal social control has disappeared, but it connects that term to an anonymous "thesis" that it does not explicitly adopt. Neither do the authors present an exact chronology of the disappearance process. They do mention the alleged causes for it: (1) industrialization and, in its wake, urbanization; (2) the waning influence of traditional ties represented by family, church and private associations; (3) the de-hierarchization of society, which has made citizens more assertive and authority no longer self-evident.[7] At the time the report appeared, the media tuned in to the notion of a lost world with nostalgic reflections about a past in which neighbors were accustomed to standing in doors or to hanging out of windows, thereby exercising a permanent surveillance of the streets.

Within the framework of a historical criminology, it constitutes a challenge both to establish a more precise chronology of the alleged disappearance of neighborhood surveillance and informal control generally, and to assess whether a long-term analysis sheds new light on present-day problems of surveillance. That is a formidable task, for which this essay makes just a modest beginning. Fortunately, there is a base to work from. I am drawing on two collective volumes that contain a synthesis of our knowledge of social control in Europe since 1500, with an emphasis on informal and semi-formal types, and a few monographs.[8]

The sixteenth and seventeenth centuries can be characterized as the golden age for informal and semi-formal social control. An in-depth study by Aries van Meeteren (2006) analyzes the interplay between various institutions concerned with conflict resolution in Leiden, among which are guilds, arbitration courts and neighborhood lords. Among the three types of social control distinguished, the semi-formal level refers to supervision-exercising institutions that are relatively organized but still independent from state agencies like the judiciary or the police. In the early modern period these institutions notably belonged to the various denominations – one of the "traditional ties" mentioned in the Roethof report. In the Dutch Republic and other European countries consistories exercised discipline over church members, scrutinizing their religious beliefs and way of life. Manon van der Heijden describes this in detail for Rotterdam and Delft.[9] The consistory summoned a church member to appear as soon as it heard rumors about his or her objectionable behavior. This implies a kind of symbiosis between the gossip circuit at the neighborhood level and the ecclesiastical supervisors. For their part, the latter observed a practical division of tasks with state agencies. The consistory would handle marital conflict, for example, as long as it did not involve serious violence, which was left to the city court.

In all of Europe, Protestant as well as Catholic, ecclesiastical social control primarily upheld norms concerning marriage and sexuality. Religious institutions viewed this as their domain, even though their beliefs about right and wrong hardly differed from those of the secular authorities. The difference rather lay in the means used. Whereas the secular courts could choose from a wide array of penal options, ecclesiastical institutions usually had only censure, exclusion from communion and excommunication available. According to Heinz Schilling, church discipline aimed first of all at maintaining the purity of the community of believers, rather than at meting out punishment.[10]

In the case of informal social control within local communities, the balance between punishment and maintenance of purity was different, but another feature is even more conspicuous. Control activities brought great pleasure to the persons engaged in them and those watching them. The mocking ritual of charivari constitutes the classic example. Neighbors paraded the target person, seated backwards on a donkey or a horse, through his village or urban area, played rough music for him and his wife, or exposed him or the couple in yet another way. The performers of the ritual often wore fool's caps and everyone except the target person had great fun. This mocking ritual was a rural as well as an urban phenomenon and, once more, the reasons were almost always marriage-related. The mockers targeted a couple when one or both partners remarried, especially in the case of an older widower taking a young bride. Alternatively, the guilty person was a husband dominated by his wife, in particular when he "allowed her" to beat him.

The fact that, when a wife was dominant, the husband was considered guilty and the beating his own fault, clearly indicates that the reverse counted as the norm. The dominated husband transgressed against the patriarchal order, but other men primarily made fun of his transgression, thereby underlining that they themselves had their women under control. Charivari functioned as informal regulation in cases that were less of a concern to the authorities, even though they, too, upheld the patriarchal order. Thus, charivari should be viewed as supplementary social control, differing from formal control only in the means employed. Admittedly, Martin Ingram shows that English local courts imposed shaming punishments with comparable rituals well into the seventeenth century.[11] Within popular culture, however, mockery appears to have been used as a sanction much more frequently.

The interventions of ecclesiastical institutions, as well as those of neighbors, in the early modern period primarily concerned the regulation of private life. Social control other than that by state agencies reached only marginally into the area of crime prevention. That observation leads to a first interim conclusion. For centuries, informal controls could be effective because their legitimacy was assured by a sense of privacy different from ours. I purposely use the word "different," rather than claiming that a sense of privacy was absent. The boundaries of a home, for example, had great symbolic value, but that did not prevent neighbors from knowing what went on inside. Individual targets of a charivari might resent their treatment, but all people together were accustomed to the fact that others in their habitat actively intervened in their household and marriage situation. Consequently, the church and neighborhood controls of the early modern period offer no simple recipe for strengthening the role of extra-judicial controls today. Modern projects to that effect can only succeed if they respect modern boundaries of privacy.

The discussion up to now also points at a weakness in the model of causes presented in the Roethof report. Its authors associated the prevalence of informal social controls with a hierarchical structure of society. Although European society of the sixteenth and seventeenth centuries was saturated with hierarchy, it was precisely the exercise of neighborhood controls that took place in a context of relative equality. As shown by several authors, this exercise was largely a spontaneous affair in a bottom-up process. Hence, the weakening of informal social control after the early modern period cannot be due to the de-hierarchization of society. We must rather think of the process of individualization, which has raised people's need for privacy.

Historians dealing with early modern social control identify yet another crucial ingredient: the sense of honor. At first sight, honor seems purely personal and by consequence less relevant for problems of order maintenance. Nevertheless, the individual reputations of all respectable villagers or neighbors together constituted a kind of collective asset that was in need of protection. As discussed in several chapters, the traditional code of male honor required violence as a reaction upon encroachment. Private violence, if not too serious, used as a means to repair one's honor was acceptable for most members of local communities. This justifies calling a violent repair of honor an instrument of social control aimed at deviant behavior, as long as it did not amount to deadly revenge. Male members of a local community resorted to violence as a response to deviance in two cases in particular, a grave insult or a theft. Recovering one's property with force also meant a repair of one's honor. As the 1719 case shows, for a long time the authorities condoned the harassment of thieves, even when done collectively. On the other hand, in the course of the seventeenth and eighteenth centuries, courts and other state agencies increasingly dismissed traditional male honor, rejecting it as a ground for attacking an insulter. Gerd Schwerhoff identifies this transformation as a process in which interpersonal violence originally served as both means and object of social control, and from a certain point on only as object.[12] During the transitional period the control systems of state and community partly conflicted with each other.

With this, I arrive at my second interim conclusion. The various systems of control of deviant behavior do not always operate in symbiosis; sometimes they conflict with each other. The extent of antagonism between the various levels of social control can be considered as a variable, to be investigated both diachronically and synchronically. Systems of social control may conflict with each other in at least two ways. First, they are in conflict when certain means are used at one level – usually the lower level – that are considered unacceptable at the other – higher – level. This was the case in the 2002–3 example, in which ordinary people condoned the injury inflicted on a shoplifter but the court condemned it. Second, the very norms which the social control, exercised at the respective levels, aims to maintain may conflict with each other. That was the case, for example, when a widower was subjected to a charivari. Against this, the authorities, who had no particular concern for the marriage market anyway, occasionally emphasized the legality of remarriage. Likewise, in modern times, a neighborhood may worry about noise and filth in the streets while the city government is interested primarily in combating social security fraud.

In the long run, however, popular and state norms often transformed in the same direction. The changing appreciation of husband-on-wife violence constitutes a conspicuous example of this and, at the same time, of the transformation whereby interpersonal violence originally served as both means and object of social control and later only as object. In the sixteenth century, a husband's beating of his wife, if not too serious, could have the function of chastisement. If so, all parties would consider it as legitimate social control within the family. In a later period, beating one's wife was gradually redefined as a form of cruelty. Today, it is routinely denoted as domestic violence, rejected by almost everyone and increasingly viewed as in need of detection. During the eighteenth and nineteenth centuries, popular culture went along with this development, as evidenced by a shift in the application of the charivari ritual. Whereas it once served to mock weak men, henceforth it served to mock cruel men.

The Modern Period

The first group of historians who paid systematic attention to Europe's traditional popular culture believed that this culture disappeared around 1800. The disappearance supposedly was due to a drastic reduction in the internal cohesion of local communities. Later research, however, revealed many examples of the persistence after 1800 of internal cohesion, and with it informal controls in villages as well as urban neighborhoods. Let me briefly review some of these examples.

Vincent Sleebe's study of the Groningen Clay Area covers the years 1770–1914.[13] During this period, gossip and mockery continued to be the principal means with which villagers kept each other in line. Personal reputation was based on chastity for women and on trustworthiness for men. Admittedly, the Groningen Clay Area was predominantly rural, but it was also a region with modern labor relations where socialism became widespread. A strong internal cohesion and a concomitant exercise of mutual social control also characterized nineteenth-century urban neighborhoods, in various European countries.[14] The mobilization of participants in the Paris Commune of 1870–1, for example, was based largely on networks and solidarities at the neighborhood level.[15] In more peaceful times, the inhabitants of a neighborhood would not only correct wayward youths but also intervene in cases of simple theft, destruction of property or street fights. All this approximately amounts to the petty crime that the Roethof committee dealt with. A broad consensus prevailed that such matters were undesirable and that, if not involving too serious or large-scale activities, they could be handled in the first instance by citizens.

A study of a workers' neighborhood in Saint-Etienne by Jean-Paul Burdy (1989) is exemplary in this respect.[16] The neighborhood's name, "Le Soleil," was decidedly ironic. Saint-Etienne as a whole, its sky dark with industrial smoke, was called a black town and *Le Soleil* counted as the blackest *quartier* of all, because mostly miners lived there. In the second half of the nineteenth century, migrants flocked to this neighborhood, as evidenced by a high proportion of boarders among its population, but many of them stayed on for life. Burdy forcefully rejects the traditional image of the industrial city as containing a host of atomized individuals within its borders: "By contrast, it appeared as a place where kin and neighborly relationships constituted an essential aspect of daily life during the period studied."[17]

The interviews that Burdy held with older inhabitants about their lives in between the world wars are especially illuminating. Mutual ties play a central role in them. Many inhabitants praised the *convivialité de voisinage*, with *familiarité* as a key-word. They remembered an *entre-soi* or also *entre ouvriers* free from constraints, a kind of carefree age that had disappeared. Women in particular provided neighborly services such as mutually lending kitchen utensils or supervising each other's children. Men and women remembered mining disasters and strikes as moments of collective solidarity. Yet, the omnipresent nostalgia did not blur everyone's sight concerning the constraints and social control involved. Some interviewees explicitly said: "We helped each other but we also spied on each other." They interpreted the latter aspect, at the moment of the interview, as a lack of privacy. Burdy concludes that the strong mutual ties and the concomitant informal social control lost much of their strength after World War II.

Urban neighborhoods like Le Soleil were no exception in early twentieth-century Europe. Whereas in Saint-Etienne internal cohesion within the neighborhood was cemented by the shared mining experience, in other places it was the fact of working all in one big factory, and in still others the inhabitants' common religion or regional culture. For a final example we may return to Amsterdam. One of its neighborhoods, the Jordaan, was planned as a working-class quarter at the beginning of the seventeenth century and has preserved that character until recently. This long history was the subject of a dissertation by H.Tj. Dijkhuis (1905–38) that remained unfinished because of his untimely death. We are left with just a few data referring mostly to the first decade of the twentieth century.[18] The strong internal cohesion at that time can be deduced from the evidence about forced relocations due to the Housing Law that made possible the designation of dwellings as uninhabitable. The proportion of families who found a new home in the same neighborhood in Amsterdam was highest (90 percent) in the Jordaan. More than once, they found it in the same street. Dijkhuis provides little information about social control and his posthumous article ends in 1914, but we may hypothesize that the game of helping and spying had just become a past phenomenon by the late 1950s when popular singer Johnnie Jordaan nostalgically depicted life in his neighborhood.

On a European scale, the Second World War appears as the great divide between a long period with intensive social control within local communities and the disappearance of this intensive control. The Netherlands witnessed a relatively late industrial take-off, in the 1890s. For this country it would be possible to call the disappearance of neighborhood surveillance a belated response to industrialization. However, this is impossible in the French example. The experience of Le Soleil shows a vibrant neighborhood culture and concomitant informal controls persisting for more than a century within an industrial environment. The historical literature for England and other countries indicates a similar situation. Moreover, as various contributions to *Social control in Europe, 1800–2000* (Emsley et al. 2004, vol. II) demonstrate, the period from about 1830 to about 1930 was the heyday of industrial paternalism. This involved a large measure of social control at the workplace and even outside of it. The persistence of a strong informal social control long after the Industrial Revolution proves the thesis that the disappearance of this form of control was due to industrialization and urbanization decidedly wrong. We should rather take seriously the remarks of the older inhabitants of Le Soleil about privacy. The internal cohesion of urban neighborhoods and villages was weakened toward the middle of the twentieth century due to increasing individualization, and perhaps also due to an increased geographic mobility. This caused the strength of informal social controls to decrease correspondingly. For France, Sebastian Roché reaches a similar conclusion.[19]

It took one or two generations before scholars and policy makers noticed the disappearance of informal controls and regretted it, as in the Netherlands with the Roethof committee and the media reaction to its report. Significantly, however, this report sees informal control primarily as the first defense line in the battle against criminality, whereas in the past informal control aimed at the maintenance of a much broader set of norms. So the question remains to what extent the new awareness of the 1980s has led to a revival or reinforcement of neighborhood surveillance. Whether or not that is the case, the main tendency since then has been the reinforcement of formal controls, so that the balance between the two has probably even shifted toward the latter. For one thing, ever more police cameras spy on potential criminals and law-abiding citizens alike. And, as parts of chapter 6 discuss in greater detail, the 1990s and 2000s constitute a punitive age throughout Europe and, even more so, in the United States.

Conclusion

A historical examination of social control, in particular neighborhood surveillance, serves to correct a few easy generalizations and offer a modest suggestion for new policies. Over the last 500 years, the balance between informal and semi-formal controls on the one hand and formal controls on the other has shifted much in favor of the latter. For one thing, this is due to processes of state formation. Even though national states are said to be weakened in modern times, the scope of formal control has increased in recent decades. This has occurred in spite of an awareness that informal controls are important. Moreover, the scope of informal control has narrowed in large part to the prevention of (petty) crime and anything that may lead to unlawful activities.

Systems of social control, in particular at the popular and state levels, may be in conflict with regard to the means used or with regard to the norms upheld. Differences of opinion with respect to the level of violence among the means used persist into the present. Today's official legal restrictions on the treatment of lawbreakers are stricter than what public opinion accepts as permissible. Nevertheless, over the last few centuries, the standards of violence at both levels have moved in the direction of greater restraint. Further research is needed in order to answer the question whether the degree of variance between the norms upheld by different systems of control was greater in one period than in another. The principal suppositions that proved to be wrong concerned the idea that the decline of informal social control was due to either the de-hierarchization of society or industrialization. The first cannot be true because informal controls in the past were exercised in a context of relative equality. The second is disproved by the persistence of informal controls in an industrialized and urbanized world. Much more likely, the decline of informal controls by the mid twentieth century was due to the process of individualization which led to a heightened sense of privacy also in working-class neighborhoods.

Consequently, the stimulation of informal control in the future can only be successful when it respects the boundaries of the modern sense of privacy. All possible projects involving surveillance by citizens have to be carefully positioned between the contradictory demands of private inviolability and public security. We are looking for the perfect compromise.

6

"The Green, Green Grass of Home"

Reflections on Capital Punishment and the Penal System in Europe and America from a Long-Term Perspective

The swan has been KLM's emblem for a long time. In the late 1990s the airline ran a commercial on Dutch television which showed this bird landing on water to the sound of Tom Jones singing "The Green, Green Grass of Home."[1] I was utterly surprised. Although the difference between an execution and a plane crash is obvious, yet the association inescapably caught my mind. Didn't the people at the advertising agency know what the song was about? The combination of "a guard" and "arm in arm we'll walk at daybreak" seemed clear to me, but then I happen to know that executions are often scheduled for the early morning. The phrase in between, that I never heard quite right, turned out to speak of a "sad old padre," which suggests that the dreamer's death row is in Mexico. Perhaps the film makers had not paid sufficient attention to the text, but their ignorance also testifies to something deeper: European unfamiliarity with the death penalty, as opposed to its relative familiarity for Americans.

We know it has not always been like that. The Dutch and other Europeans have come a long way from the time that the very term "the green lawn" ("het groene zoodje") referred to the site of the scaffold, visible every day, to their present unfamiliarity. The lynching of the brothers De Witt, moreover, on The Hague's green lawn in 1672, anticipated the supposed association of US popular justice with capital punishment by two centuries. On the other hand, the United States, like Europe, has witnessed the privatization of legal executions, despite occasional pleas to show them live on television. My modest aim in this chapter is to examine the issue anew by: (1) widening the scope of the discussion by taking the penal system as a whole, in particular imprisonment, into consideration; and (2) assessing the evidence with the help of insights developed by Norbert Elias, not only his well-known theory of civilizing processes but also his notion of long-term diminutions in power differences between social groups.

The first of these strategies, a comparison between the United States and Europe from the perspective of imprisonment, forms a necessary complement to a comparison from the perspective of the death penalty, because the conclusions are radically different. Today Europe condemns the death penalty, but its incarceration rates, like those of the United States, have risen sharply during the last few decades. Although the excesses at Guantánamo Bay and Abu Ghraib have cast a shadow over the USA's image during the opening years of the twenty-first century, in Europe the battle against terrorism equally entails threats to the rule of law. In sum, while the US and Europe diverge with respect to some penal trends, they converge on others. Because the divergence is obvious, let me introduce an intriguing example of convergence. It concerns the trends in incarceration rates in my own country and the United States in the past few decades. In both countries, the number of prisoners per capita began to increase during the 1970s; by the early twenty-first century the Dutch incarceration rates had risen to six times the level of 1970.

Although the reader notes that the rates are per 100,000 and per 10,000 respectively, the steepness of the two rising curves is strikingly similar and, since the mid-1990s, even more pronounced for the Netherlands. It should be added that numbers were somewhat down again in the Netherlands in 2009, but it remains to be seen whether this indicates a permanent trend reversal.

When returning to the death penalty and its different fate in America and Europe, we note that several recent works have fueled the discussion.[2] However, although the authors concerned all draw on historical evidence, none of them goes back in time much further than about 1800. As chapter 3 argues with respect to homicide, it constitutes a crucial difference that the North American continent moved into the modern world overnight as it were, whereas European societies witnessed an extended development of some five centuries. Consequently, the pre-1800 history does count. The relatively sudden transformation to an urban-industrial society caused Americans, among other things, to remain unaccustomed to being disarmed and distrustful of a state monopoly of force. At first sight, this feature of American societal development would seem to be less consequential for the history of executions and punishment generally. Colonial Americans were certainly accustomed to capital punishment, and executions there resembled those in Europe at the time. By 1600, however, European societies had already gone through one important transformation: the sacralization of executions.

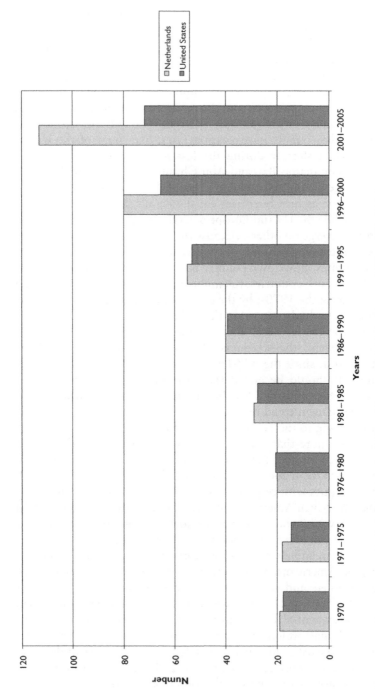

Figure 6.1 Prisoners per 100,000 inhabitants (NL) and per 10,000 inhabitants (US), 1970–2005

Source: (Netherlands) Downes and van Swaaningen 2007; (USA) www.angelfire.com/rnb/y/ratesusa.htm#years (accessed May 28, 2010)

The Appearance of Religiously Tinged Executions

The sacralization of executions is a process discovered only recently. Although James Sharpe (1985a) and Spierenburg (1984) noted a few elements, it was the art historian Mitchell Merback (1999) and the medievalist Peter Schuster (2000, 2003) who, independently from each other, brought this process to our full attention (not the term itself, which I have coined for this occasion). Their observations refer to a broad region encompassing much of Germany, Switzerland and Northern Italy. Medieval attitudes to executions, Schuster notes, were based on the prohibition for church and clergy from having their hands stained by blood. As is well known, the Inquisition handed over condemned heretics to the secular authorities to burn them at the stake. For ordinary executions, church people showed little interest. This was in line with the attitudes of urban and territorial rulers, who viewed them as completely profane events. The message that the authorities wished to convey was that capital convicts were totally worthless and less than human. As they would surely face damnation, it was futile to give them the opportunity to confess to a priest.

Gradually, however, church people started to object. They insisted that everyone, even the most hardened criminals, deserved to receive the sacrament of confession. As early as 1312, at the Council of Vienne, Pope Clement V threatened ecclesiastical sanctions for those magistrates who prevented this from happening, but they were still unimpressed. The Konstanz authorities did not grant the opportunity for priestly absolution to capital convicts until 1434 and the council of Strasbourg complied with the wishes of its bishop as late as 1485. There is some evidence that, by the mid fifteenth century, the ecclesiastical views in this respect found an echo in popular sentiment. The introduction of an elaborate religious ritual at the scaffold by the authorities, however, did not come about until the early sixteenth century. Schuster fixes the breakthrough of the religious embeddedness of executions at 1525. This precise date originates from a detour in his argument, that of the failed hanging. Because the medieval method of hanging was by strangulation, it was not uncommon to find the convict still breathing after the rope had been cut. Other failed hangings resulted from the breaking of the rope; also some criminals sentenced to be drowned did not do so. The spectators as well as the authorities considered such a failure as a sign from above, which induced the magistrates to pardon the convict. Schuster interprets this as a magical custom reminiscent of the earlier ordeals. He connects the new religious view of executions with Lutheranism. This new view symbolically broke through in Nürnberg in 1525, when a convict whose rope broke was hanged anew. Magical beliefs and practices surrounding executions, it should be added, remained alive in popular culture throughout the early modern period, especially in Germany.[3]

A recent study confirms the shift to religiously tinged executions for England, fixing its breakthrough at the mid sixteenth century. In the middle ages English convicts received no spiritual comfort whatsoever.[4] Esther Cohen's (1993) study of punishment in late-medieval France does not explicitly refer to the sacralization of executions, but she confirms that they still included various magical elements. Methods of capital punishment that involved total annihilation, for example, were meant to ensure that the convicts in question would not become revenants.

Merback provides evidence for the sacralization of executions from the viewpoint of art history. In particular, he studied the genre of the calvary, a crucifixion in a landscape with a number of people, around 1500. While painters were theologically restricted in the way they could depict Jesus, they gave free rein to their fantasies in representing his companions, the "Two Thieves." Many artists modeled the representation of their tormented bodies on the contemporary punishment of breaking on the wheel. This reveals that they associated the crucifixion of Christ with contemporary executions of criminals – a parallel that had already been drawn by medieval theologians like Jean Gerson. This parallel, Merback concludes, ensured that from the late fifteenth century onward – and hence before the Reformation – executions were infused with religious symbolism. The capitally condemned, if they were penitent and acted solemnly, became kinds of martyrs and the execution turned into an act of expiation.[5]

Merback's use of the word "martyr" is perhaps exaggerated, but his observations provide a clue to the argument about the status of convicts and changing power differentials that I wish to unfold in this chapter. The sacralization of executions meant a slight rise in the status of capital convicts. From undeserving wretches, bound for hell, they turned into penitent Christians, reflecting Jesus' death on the Cross. They were still mostly poor and outside the domain of earthly honor, but God potentially forgave them in heaven. Significantly, in the German-speaking countries, *Armesünder* (poor sinner) became the standard term for a convict bound for and dying on the scaffold. It is highly unlikely that the authorities or the church consciously wished to raise the status of the condemned. It was an unintended consequence of the interplay between secular customs and ecclesiastical demands, or, in Elias' words, the outcome of a blind process. In this process, the condemned lost something too. They were deprived of their small chance of getting away with it through a failed hanging or drowning, and their raised status only applied if they cooperated, acknowledging their sentence. The condemned were certainly not allowed to deny their guilt. However, exactly this provided them with a measure of power. They were able to (threaten to) spoil the show by being obstinate, announcing their intention to display defiance instead of penitence. This would mean sabotaging the moral play that the authorities intended the spectacle of the scaffold to be. Indeed, when an Amsterdam convict showed this kind of obstinacy, the court dispatched a special deputy-minister to him who exerted every effort to convince him to comply.[6]

This implies that early modern authorities were content with the religious element in executions and the morality show that it entailed. Why did the secular rulers and courts of the seventeenth century relish something that their predecessors had tried to avoid? Neither Schuster nor Merback provides a plausible explanation. To arrive at one, we must take account of the various changes in penal practice at the end of the middle ages and the beginning of the early modern period and the state-formation processes lying behind them. Medieval criminal justice was, for the large part, a justice of arbitration. Most cases were conducted according to the accusatory procedure, in which accuser and accused faced each other as equal parties and the judges acted largely as media-tors. In the rare cases that a trial resulted in a death sentence, the accuser usually had the right to execute it. Few jurisdictions had a professional executioner. Death sentences were infrequent, mainly imposed on rebels or robbers or any other outsiders without a network of support within the community. The infrequency of executions did not stem from any kind of sensitivity against physical retaliation. At times citizens them-selves retaliated, because vengeance and feuding were common too and relatively accepted. The coexistence of arbitration justice, private revenge and a low incidence of executions reflected the relatively low level of monopolization of force during most of the middle ages. In this situation it made perfect sense to stigmatize the tiny minority of capital convicts as a subhuman set. Unlike vengeance victims they lacked honor, so why would even God care about them?

By 1500, change was visible in various ways. The inquisitorial pro-cedure, which had already existed for some time, became the one most frequently applied in criminal cases. In this procedure, the public pros-ecutor and the suspect were the principal parties facing each other, with a highly unequal power ratio. Meanwhile, almost all jurisdictions kept a paid executioner, who symbolized the expropriation of private revenge and inherited the infamy of medieval capital convicts. The inquisitor-ial procedure was not necessarily concomitant of legal change, since it remained absent from England. In England as well as Continental Europe, however, the incidence of executions markedly increased during the sixteenth century and they remained at a high level during most of the seventeenth. Monopolies of force had been established and those who disposed of these monopolies showed that they had them. Reformation and Counter-Reformation, moreover, brought a heightened moral concern. Despite Schuster's emphasis on Lutheranism, the religious underpinning of the death penalty appears to have been prepared before the Reformation and subsequently strengthened in Protestant as well as Catholic countries. From the mid sixteenth century, the representatives of church and state usually cooperated, sharing the same moral outlook and upholding a patriarchal social order that mixed benevolence with sternness. Within this climate, religiously tinged executions easily found their place. As several scholars have noted, early modern executions not only were aimed at deterrence and prevention, but reached out to the whole population by telling them that their own sins might be early symptoms of a career in crime.

It is difficult to determine what it meant for the development of criminal justice in America that this continent never went through a phase of completely profane executions. Perhaps it did not matter at all. The ritual of capital punishment was exported to the colonies on the Atlantic coast from England and a few other countries at a time when religiously tinged executions were the rule everywhere. Stuart Banner (2002) discusses the religious element as an integral part of the ceremony in Colonial America. One conclusion about the different trajectories of European and American criminal justice is obvious. Whereas, in Europe, execution ritual with its religious flavor underpinned both the power and patriarchalism of the elites in developing states, the white settler communities on the Atlantic coast practiced the same ritual in the absence of a monopoly of force. Significantly, Colonial America knew no professional executioners and this continued to be the case until the invention of the electric chair.[7] This meant that Americans held on to a feature of execution practice that in Europe was characteristic of the middle ages with its arbitration justice and private retaliation.

In early modern Europe religiously embedded executions were common, whatever the dominant faith. In Geneva their ritual extended to the penalty of drowning.[8] Executions in France included the *amende honorable*, in which the condemned knelt down in front of a church with a torch in his hand and asked forgiveness from God and Justice. This could also be required from non-capital convicts. Throughout the eighteenth century the *amende* was a frequent feature of capital punishment in Paris. In the French capital, too, the status of the condemned as a penitent sinner did not preclude his infamy. The ceremony of capital or corporal punishment began with the reading of the final sentence. At that point, not only did the criminal become infamous, because the executioner came into play, but also, when the sentence was capital, a priest immediately arrived to hear confession. One of the executioner's first tasks was to dress the convict in a white shirt, so that he could perform the *amende honorable*. He did this during the procession, in front of a church or at the spot of the crime. The ritual opened with the court clerk summarizing the sentence with emphasis on the convict's evil intentions, which the latter had to repeat on his knees, torch in hand and the executioner standing behind him. At other stops the clerk read the sentence anew. The cart taking the convict from jail to the place of execution was one of those normally used for the disposal of the city's trash.[9]

Not surprisingly, modern values such as freedom of religion were absent from the Christian executions of the early modern period. As a rule, the spiritual consolation offered came exclusively from the officially recognized church, whichever it was in the place where the trial was held. The monopoly of the dominant religion in enacting the Christian ritual of executions made sense. While in theory its function implied spiritual consolation for the condemned, in practice its primary aim was the edification of the multitude. As late as 1767, the prosecutor's speech to an Amsterdam criminal broken on the wheel exemplified the profoundly Christian overtones of capital punishment. Nathaniel Donker and his mistress had murdered his wife to escape from her unwanted attention. Preceding the execution the prosecutor reminded Donker that no sins were too grave to be pardoned, if only he would earnestly beg forgiveness. Even if his wife's blood cried for vengeance before God's throne, this sinner should realize that the sacrificial blood of Jesus carried greater weight with his Father.[10] It was a moving speech, but things were about to change.

The Enlightenment and the Death Penalty

Around the time of Donker's trial, the Enlightenment caused the first breaches in the religious edifice built around capital punishment. As part of his critique of the death penalty, Cesare Beccaria rejected the Christian element in executions. The promise of heaven, he argued, merely eased the convict's fear of death and consequently diminished the audience's fear of committing crimes. Thus, the religious drama subverted capital punishment's ostensible goal of general prevention. Beccaria's argument that prevention was best served by maximizing a criminal's chances of getting caught and tried is well known. His book was no plea to return to the medieval situation. Although abolitionism remained a minority opinion for quite some time, sensitivity about public physical punishment was clearly visible toward the end of the eighteenth century. It foreshadowed the marginalization of the death penalty and the increasing enthusiasm among lawyers and politicians for the prison.

The end of the Ancien Régime constitutes the chronological starting point for James Q. Whitman (2003). He does not dwell on the sacralization of executions, even though the status accorded to convicts is the central element in his thesis.[11] That thesis is relevant, nevertheless, if only because it puts the differential developments in Europe and America at center stage. Essentially, he argues that on both continents punishment became more democratic but in entirely opposite ways. Whereas democratization in Europe meant the extension of dignity to all offenders, in the United States it meant degradation for all. As status differences mattered less in America to begin with, all forms of privileged treatment of individual prisoners were increasingly viewed as unfair. This comparison has definite geographic limits. Europe actually meant France and Germany, but Whitman believes that his thesis holds for more countries than just these two. America at first is the Anglo-Saxon world, with the breakdown of status differences in punishment anticipated in eighteenth-century England. After 1776 England disappears from the picture and it remains unclear whether or not it is supposed to have returned to the European path later. In Continental Europe at least, the central theme is the gradual extension to all offenders of privileges in punishment that originally applied only to high-status offenders.

The first phase of this development is a very French story. In Ancien Régime France, beheading was the honorable mode of capital punishment, reserved for aristocrats; so the Revolution extended the privilege of being beheaded to all capital convicts. This shift is peculiarly French because, in pre-Revolutionary France, hanging, breaking on the wheel and burning were almost the only modes of capital punishment practiced. Elsewhere, although high-status offenders sentenced to death were indeed beheaded, it was not true that beheading was solely reserved for them. In early modern Amsterdam, for example, this was the standard punishment for manslaughter, unless the condemned faced additional charges such as street robbery. Most decapitated killers were of very humble origin. It is true that the relative honorability of beheading owed much to its noble association, but this honorability simply made it a lighter punishment than hanging. It allowed judges to attune the mode of the death penalty to the type of offense, regardless of the offender's social status. Decapitation, moreover, was not totally honorable. The condemned had to mount a scaffold, an infamous act by itself. The hangman led him there and blindfolded him, unless the condemned had received the privilege of walking alone untouched by the hated official. The honorableness of decapitation was only relative.

In March 1792 the French legislature adopted the guillotine as the exclusive mode of capital punishment for all, but did this mean a dignified death for all? Significantly, Whitman hardly pays attention to the question why, in the Western world, decapitation counts as the most honorable form of capital punishment. He notes that the Chinese have a reversed appreciation, implying that it is just a matter of culture. A brief remark about decapitation's positive "military associations" in European history is tucked away in an endnote.[12] I believe there is more to it and that the sword is the crucial element. This weapon was the aristocratic attribute par excellence and a symbol of nobility. In the early modern period carrying a rapier – a lighter type of sword – was a mark of status (see chapter 2). Even hangmen tried to raise their infamous status by styling themselves with fancy names such as "master of the sharp sword." Successful executioners were proud of their skills in handling the sword, leaving other tasks as much as possible to their servants. The relative honorableness of the penalty of decapitation, then, does not lie in the act of losing one's head but in the instrument used. The guillotine was developed not so much as a machine of honor but as a remedy because many executioners were clumsy rather than skillful. Whitman rightly concludes from the 1789 drawing meant to promote the machine that the executioner was to avert his eyes, but he fails to notice that the drawing has him activate the machine by cutting the rope that holds up the blade with a sword. The sword makes the whole scene honorable, because the guillotine itself is less than honorable. The falling blade is actually an axe, as its German and Dutch names confirm. Moreover, the introduction of the guillotine in Paris did not end the infamous parade of the convict from jail to the place of execution on a dung cart, which lasted until 1832.[13]

To conclude, it is doubtful whether the introduction of the guillotine had much to do with the reduction of the infamy inherent to punishment. Although, as Arasse already showed, this was certainly one of Guillotin's goals, the primary motive was to make capital punishment as painless as possible. That was equally a concern for the machine's opponents, who believed hanging to be most painless.[14] Although France kept the guillotine for nearly two centuries, it was severely compromised during the Terror. In countries occupied by the French, this machine soon became a symbol of the hated foreign invaders. William, within two weeks after his return to the Netherlands as sovereign prince, decided that the death penalty would henceforth be executed with either sword or rope.[15] Although some German states kept the guillotine after the Napoleonic period, the populace as a rule hated it. At about the same time, the majority of German states introduced a new custom: they replaced the sword with a big axe. Obviously, this was a shift from lesser to greater infamy, and the only difference from the guillotine was its handling by a human agent. The introduction of the axe, too, was to prevent unhandy strokes and hence to ensure the convict's painless death. Despite popular sentiment, Hamburg decided in 1842 to re-introduce the guillotine, and when the next person was on trial for a capital crime 12 years later, it was additionally decided to move the death penalty indoors.[16] Throughout Europe, the main feature of the death penalty's history in the nineteenth century would be its privatization. Although France postponed this shift, from 1872 onward the guillotine was placed flatly on the ground, so that only the front rows of spectators could actually see the spectacle.[17]

While Whitman's interpretation of the introduction of the guillotine is one-sided, the death penalty as such plays only a minor role in his account of degradation in the Anglo-Saxon world. For eighteenth-century England, he relies partly on Douglas Hay's (1975) classic essay, but he reverses his conclusions. Where Hay saw a hierarchical society in which the criminal law served to maintain the dominance of the ruling classes, Whitman sees the beginnings of an egalitarian disregard for status. Hay considered minor concessions to fair trial or the occasional hanging of an aristocrat such as Lord Ferrers as mere tokens, meant to divert the people's eyes from criminal justice's real purpose of keeping the lower orders in line. For Whitman, Ferrers' execution is a triumph of egalitarian degradation. Neither does the death penalty play a major role in Whitman's account of Colonial and Revolutionary America, except for the fact that, as in England, hanging was the standard mode. In fact, the death penalty is largely absent from his entire account until its abolition in various European countries after the Second World War.

In the 1789 drawing of the guillotine the only person near the convict looking him right in the eyes is a priest. For the artist, apparently, the confessor's presence still was self-evident. Religion remained an important element in nineteenth-century solitary confinement and, with or without it, in women's prisons, in Catholic countries often run by nuns. Religion's role in punishment diminished with the overall decline of its influence in society. In democratic countries, consulting a clergyman of any persuasion is merely one of the services available to prisoners. The principal contribution of religion to the long-term history of punishment consisted of the sacralization of executions, which led to the first slight increase in the status of convicts. This status surely is a crucial factor in the long-term history of punishment, but as I just argued, changes concerning the death penalty during the Revolutionary period can hardly be viewed as an extension of dignity. After this period the status of convicts increasingly came to mean that of prisoners.

The Emancipation of Prisoners

We must return to Whitman once more. His account, from 1815 to 1933, revolves around imprisonment. Throughout the nineteenth century both France and Germany knew separate régimes for privileged inmates. In the German case, this was part of a formal system that comprised three types of imprisonment, "fortress confinement" being the most comfortable. Whereas France extended the privilege of comfortable treatment to political prisoners in particular, in Germany persons of great moral worth, who included some political activists but also duelists, came to enjoy fortress confinement. The most notorious among these morally high-standing persons was Adolf Hitler after his beer-hall putsch. This modest extension of privileged treatment to persons outside the aristocracy, as long as they were considered no real criminals, paved the way, still according to Whitman, for its generalization after World War II.

When it comes to the United States, Whitman considers forced labor and the prevalence of corporal punishment in nineteenth-century penitentiaries as prime symptoms of degradation. He attaches great significance to the fact that the Thirteenth Amendment, abolishing slavery, explicitly excluded convicts when properly tried. Not every scholar shares his interpretation that this clause made prisoners into slaves of a kind. Moreover, a major weakness of Whitman's book, for Europe no less than for the United States, concerns its prime focus on legislation and legal opinion. There is much less attention for changes in the actual prison conditions of the non-privileged majority. Prison conditions since 1800 are a central issue in the work of Herman Franke.[18] Although this is mainly confined to the Netherlands, his theory, based on Elias, is preferable to Whitman's. He introduces the concept of the emancipation of prisoners, of which I will first give a few empirical examples.

On a European scale, Franke traces the emancipation process back to the rise of professional criminology in the late nineteenth century. According to him, criminologists of various schools, even when they only measured skulls, were the first to show a scientific interest in individual prisoners. More specifically for the Netherlands, around 1900, several socialist leaders served a term in prison, an experience which shocked them. They turned the diffuse interest in convicts into an active movement, bent on ameliorating carceral conditions.[19] In the interwar period though, it was mainly the sensitivities outside that increased, rather than the benefits on the inside. The Dutch were exceptional in long preferring the cellular system, which continued to be imposed on the majority of inmates until just after World War II. In other European countries, where research is still scarce for this period, the alleviation of prison conditions probably began earlier. When the Netherlands replaced solitary confinement with a régime of communal resocialization, privileges for inmates soon expanded. They were allowed to play sports, watch films or television and make telephone calls. Some open and half-open prisons were established and, in the closed ones, too, the possibilities of obtaining leave or interruption of a sentence increased. At the beginning of the 1970s the first prisoner newspaper appeared. A few years later, inmates were allowed unsupervised visits by their partners for sexual purposes. This is only a selection from the many examples of emancipation. During the 1980s the pace of the emancipation process began to slacken, but most of the privileges acquired in the preceding decades survived.[20]

Intriguingly and despite Whitman's claim of increasing degradation, such a process of emancipation also took place in the United States. Its outline was already known to scholars, but the process is more amply documented in a recent book by Rebecca McLennan (2008). The bulk of her evidence is from New York, but she stresses that the Empire state served as a model for many other Northern and Western states. The Old South went its own way. Chronologically, the American emancipation process did not lag behind Europe and it certainly predated the Dutch reform period. In the USA changes in prison conditions were introduced just after the abolition of large-scale labor, with reform concentrated in the so-called "Progressive era." One of its early markers was an interstate phenomenon, the convict newspaper *Star of Hope*, whose first issue appeared in 1899. Among other things, the *Star* published letters from prisoners, signed with their number rather than with their name. In New York in the same year, humiliating practices such as the shaving of heads and the obligation to wear striped uniforms and to march in an excruciating fashion, were abolished. Prison libraries were set up and inmates, most of whom were literate by then, were allowed to write letters. In the 1910s Thomas Mott Osborne even introduced prisoners' councils in Auburn and Sing Sing, but these were discontinued later. More lasting was the introduction of films and sports. All these privileges first applied to white inmates only, but they were later extended to African Americans. Osborne's successors expanded the sports program and introduced occasional performances by singers and comedians.

Admittedly, cells often continued to be dirty and infested with vermin. Riots broke out repeatedly, as in the 1950s. Solitary confinement in dark cells still existed as a disciplinary punishment and Alcatraz was opened as an institution devoid of privileges for the most hardcore federal convicts in 1934. These observations do not diminish the importance of the emancipation process. McLennan does not take her story much further than the 1920s, but Edgardo Rotman concludes that "the concession of benefits and privileges during the Progressive Era had become accepted social practices that ultimately gave substance to the nascent prisoners' rights movement [in the 1960s]. Those concessions were largely the result of the policy of patterning the prison on the community."[21] This book's author, moreover, possesses material evidence for the continuation of the emancipation process until the end of the 1960s in the form of two CDs of Johnny Cash's concerts in Folsom and San Quentin, California, in 1968 and 1969. As is well known, Cash was allowed to sing "San Quentin I hate every inch of you." The evidence for the process of emancipation of prisoners in the United States constitutes the clearest refutation of Whitman's thesis that degradation was the central element in this country's criminal justice history.

In order to explain the process of emancipation of prisoners, Franke draws on the work of Norbert Elias. Elias identifies several long-term developments in European societies that are broadly interrelated. These include civilization processes and the diminution of differences in power between social groups. To describe the interaction between two social groups with rather unequal power chances, Elias uses the conceptual pair of established and outsiders. In that connection, the term "emancipation" appears. The power relationship between the two groups may become (but does not necessarily always become) less unequal. This means that the outsiders emancipate. In order to fully understand the structure of such an emancipation process we must be aware of Elias' concept of power. As explained in chapter 4, Elias maintains that power is always two-sided. There cannot be differences in power if only one group "possesses" it. Power, moreover, can have various sources. When new or enlarged sources of power become available to an outsider group, it starts to emancipate.

Prisoners clearly constitute a bunch of outsiders. They are much less powerful than the various groups interacting with them, who include politicians, lawyers, bureaucrats and guards. Nevertheless, according to the theory that power is always two-sided, prisoners have a measure of power. Consequently, we must identify their sources of power. Franke mentions two types of sources: sensitivity in the outside world to their suffering, and obstruction by themselves. The first appears to me as the most important. When sensitivity in the outside world to the suffering of inmates increases, this means that their source of power is enhanced. Consequently, they are able to negotiate an extension of their privileges. Conversely, when sensitivity in society at large diminishes, the life of inmates will tend to become harder. Is this what has happened in the Western world since about 1980? In order to preserve the more or less chronological structure of this chapter, I must first return to the death penalty.

The Death Penalty: Re-Introduction, Abolition and Near-Abolition

Few possibilities for emancipation are available to capital convicts, who have to die per definition. For them, the two principal forms of alleviation were the acceptance of the principle of making death as painless as possible and the change that spared them onlookers, except for a decreasing set of invited persons. The other major development with respect to capital punishment in the nineteenth and twentieth centuries was that ever fewer criminals met that fate. In France the annual number of executions per million inhabitants, documented since 1825, was just over 2 then, but it quickly dropped to about 1. Averaged per five-year period, the number declined to about 0.2 in 1865–70, after which it fluctuated between 0.1 and 0.4 until it peaked at nearly 0.5 after World War II. Note, however, that the French graph is interrupted during both world wars. The execution rate in France decreased to nearly zero in the 1970s.[22] In the United States the decline set in somewhat later: per capita since the 1880s and in absolute numbers since 1935. The Northern states, which had privatized executions already between 1830 and 1860, made the principal contribution to this decline.[23]

The world wars had no significant effect on execution rates in the US, but in Europe this was clearly different. In Germany the annual number of death sentences in 1942–4 was about 50 times as high as the average in both the Weimar and the early Nazi years. There is no information on the number of executions in these war years, but for 1939 Evans lists 139 death sentences – and 219 executions![24] Obviously, he has included a number of judicial killings that were less than legal. The problem of which ones to count as legal and which as illegal is even greater for the occupied countries. There, World War II certainly brought an increase in execution rates, but as the interruptions in the French graph indicate, there is no consensus about the numbers.

To more fully grasp both the secular decline of capital punishment and its return in relation to WW II, it is instructive to examine developments in the Netherlands, the second European country in abolition's chronology.[25] In fact, the abolition in 1870 was neither total nor definitive. It was probably preceded by a decline in execution rates, but this is hard to determine with precision from the figures provided by Sibo van Ruller. In the whole country (Belgium, which belonged to it until 1830, excluded) 442 death sentences were pronounced between 1814 and 1870, of which 75 were executed. Because the pardon rate progressively increased, the number of executions probably declined correspondingly.[26] Following the last public execution in 1860 all capital convicts were pardoned.

Between 1814 and 1860 executions thus averaged 1.6 per year, which amounts to an average execution rate of about 0.5 per million. The legal change in 1870 caused the Netherlands to skip a phase with indoor executions, but the abolition of capital punishment applied only to civilian law. The death penalty remained part of military penal law, listing 15 capital offenses and ordering execution by a firing squad without an audience. A separate clause, however, allowed capital punishment to be imposed only when the defendant's act had caused danger to the security of the state and most lawyers agreed that this required a state of war.[27] Thus, even in the absence of research into court-martial archives, it is likely that the alleged deserter Chris Meijer, shot at the military compound in Doorn on May 12, 1940, was the first person legally executed in the Netherlands since 1860.[28]

Meijer's death sentence foreshadowed things to come. A lessened respect for life was present not only among Nazis and fascists but also among many of their opponents. This manifested itself in various ways, but for this book I must confine myself to legal executions. As early as 1941, clandestine newspapers in the Netherlands called for the execution of the leaders of the Dutch National Socialist Movement (NSB), and the next year Queen Wilhelmina's radio message from London assured that no traitor would escape his deserved punishment. The exiled government made legal provisions for this in a series of decisions in 1943–4, all called special or extraordinary. That designation referred to the absence of a legislature that could authorize them (directly after the war, most lawyers thought this procedure acceptable). The decisions included the creation of new punishable acts, for example by extending the range of the offense "assistance to the enemy." Nowadays, many lawyers consider this a violation of the *nulla poena sine lege* principle. Most fatefully, the special decisions included the re-introduction of capital punishment into civilian criminal law, for the most serious wartime offenses. All this was decided without much debate. The cabinet and its advisors believed that it would be dangerous not to give in to some extent to the lust for revenge that was widespread in the country. The primary aim of capital punishment's re-introduction was to prevent lynchings and other forms of extralegal justice directly after liberation, and to ensure immediate control for the returning authorities.[29]

These events make it clear that, even when a country has reached a certain level of civilization, exceptional circumstances may lead to heightened feelings of revenge and an increase in judicial harshness. In the Netherlands from 1940 the long-forgotten death penalty was re-introduced with the hope of satisfying feelings of revenge. In all, the Special Justice after the war (including a court-martial in the liberated region before the war's end) led to 159 death sentences and 42 executions, the last one in March 1952. Those put to death included a few Germans and one woman.[30] Until the end of 1947 the press and public opinion in majority favored quick executions and the rejection of pardons. Since then, the call for revenge has disappeared, while the government usually preferred clemency. For decades the death penalty was retained in military law, but the new constitution of 1983 included an article that proscribed it. Thus, scholars consider 1983 as the legal end of the death penalty in the Netherlands, although a few laws had to be adapted afterward to make them conform to the new constitution.

The major Western and Central European countries abolished the death penalty between 1949 (West Germany) and 1981 (France), while the United States witnessed an abortive abolition between *Furman* v. *Georgia* in 1972 and *Gregg* v. *Georgia* in 1976. There is no need to discuss these episodes in detail.[31] For my argument it suffices to emphasize the paradox inherent in the comparison between the American and European experiences: a legal change under political pressure vs. a political change in the absence of pressure.[32] In the USA the death penalty is primarily a legal issue, with the Supreme Court deciding about its constitutionality, whereas in European countries it is a political issue with the legislature deciding whether to retain or abolish it. Nevertheless, in several European parliaments the abolition of the death penalty came about as a project of the political elite, who were able to ignore majority opinion. By contrast, American officials, political and legal, are much more sensitive to public opinion, which applies even to the non-elected justices of the Supreme Court. In Europe, it appears, the majority of the population eventually accepted the values of their political leaders, which sealed the fate of the death penalty.

The Modern Return to Punitiveness

With the death penalty absent in Europe, the modern return to punitiveness revolves around imprisonment. At least two issues are important in this respect. One refers to the statistical question of incarceration rates and the general harshness of the criminal law, as reflected in such rulings as "three strikes and you're out." The evidence regarding this issue is relatively easy to ascertain, even though there are methodological problems even here, such as which types of institutions qualify to have their inmates counted as prisoners. The other is the question to which extent the process of emancipation has been discontinued or even reversed. For an answer we need data about prison conditions and inmates' rights from a number of countries, and this over several decades. Collection of these data requires an elaborate comparative investigation that cannot be performed within the framework of this book. I restrict myself to referring to a few authors whose work touches on the question of whether the US is unique with respect to the new punitiveness or merely ahead of Europe. In terms of the graph presented at the beginning of this chapter, do we attach primary importance to the steepness of the curve or to the absolute numbers?

Authors with such divergent backgrounds as the sociologist Loïc Wacquant (2010) and the journalist Anne-Marie Cusac (2009) appear to support the position of uniqueness. Wacquant speaks of the penal or neoliberal state that has totally replaced the welfare state. Notably, the abolition of the Aid to Families with Dependent Children program in the late 1990s constituted a landmark. The social profile of today's prisoners, Wacquant continues, is strikingly similar to that of (former) welfare recipients (this applies much less, however, to the gender profile). He furthermore stresses that penal administrators have given up every pretense of resocialization, prisons just being places for neutralizing and storing people. Although he maintains that the penal state has made intrusions into some European countries – and that under socialist governments – his analysis is perfectly attuned to the United States. For her part, Cusac opens with commenting on America's elevated incarceration rates, but she quickly leaves that subject for a historical and qualitative analysis. Her most original chapters deal with the increasing and often illegal use of devices such as restraint chairs and stun belts on prisoners, as well as tasers by the police, and she finds evidence of torture and sexual humiliation in American prisons akin to the practices at Abu Ghraib. Cusac further reports that the producers of several of the repressive devices export them, but mainly to countries with dictatorial régimes, thereby underscoring the USA's uniqueness among Western nations.[33]

David Garland's *The culture of control* (2001) can be considered as a study maintaining that the US is merely ahead of other nations with respect to a trend that is nearly universal in the Western world. Garland identifies several factors that all imply a shift away from "penal welfarism." Although he takes his evidence from the USA and Britain, he considers the rise of the culture of control as characteristic for most of Continental Europe too. Indeed, even his critics are able to come up with only a few counter-examples, and some of them not valid.[34] If we also take into consideration Wacquant's remarks that the penal state is on the rise in the major European countries, it would seem that the argument that the United States is merely ahead of the others is persuasive. Amidst the modern trend toward punitiveness and control, the increase in incarceration rates stands out as the most tangible element. There are just a few partial counter-examples, such as the German Federal

Republic during the 1980s where the rates declined.[35] In the Netherlands, on the other hand, the post-1970 rise was even more marked because it followed several decades of per capita decline. During a period of which the 1960s formed the nucleus, Dutch incarceration rates were among the lowest in the Western world. This was a period of great social optimism that Downes and van Swaaningen call the Second Golden Age.[36] Does the return to punitiveness, then, imply the resurgence of pessimism?

Perhaps pessimism sounds too negative, since modern punitiveness also has a positive side. The idea that it has to do with an increasing compassion for crime victims plays a part in Garland's analysis and it is central to the work of Marie Gottschalk (2006) and Jonathan Simon (2007). It would be incorrect, therefore, to state that the sensitivity in society at large, which in an earlier period was the motor behind the process of emancipation of prisoners, has vanished. Rather, a shift in the public's sensitivity has taken place, from having prisoners as its objects to crime victims as its objects. Around the 1960s victims received scant attention, while perpetrators were often seen as themselves victims of unfavorable social circumstances. Viewed from one angle, this modern shift should be regarded as a de-civilizing trend because, if it continues, its ultimate consequence would be to allow widespread physical retaliation in response to victims' anxieties. In any case the evidence so far seems to indicate that the power of prisoners has somewhat diminished again. Viewed from another angle, the concern for victims involves more of a civilizing trend, because it is not simply a return to the age of feuding. Medieval concern for a victim was restricted to his or her family's right of private vengeance. Third parties did not particularly care. By contrast, the modern concern for victims involves sympathy for them from larger groups, often unrelated, within society. The movement against "senseless violence" that gained momentum during the 1990s stems from a rather diffuse anxiety about lethal incidents that should not happen.[37]

From the observation that modern punitiveness implies a shift away from the rehabilitative attitudes prevalent from the 1950s to the mid-1970s, it is a small step to an explanation in terms of a backlash at the sixties. In this view, the modern culture of repression and control constitutes a reversal of the permissive and progressive culture that had its heyday in the 1960s. This is one of the conclusions emerging from Cusac's historical exposition. The argument is present even more forcefully, though still semi-implicitly, in the work of Wacquant. For one thing, he speaks of a re-masculinization of the state in reaction to the women's movement. This revived masculinity has powerful political managers posing as virile protectors against troublemakers. Second, Wacquant sees a re-activation of the stigma of blackness, in this case of course as a reaction to the civil rights movement. Once more nowadays, African Americans are viewed primarily as dangerous persons. The first factor in his argument, unlike the second, is universal rather than peculiarly American, but it is also flawed. The modern compassion with crime victims actually has its roots in the second feminist movement! This movement began with a focus on the issue of abortion, but toward the end of the 1970s its concerns extended to sexual and domestic violence. For the first time the more or less progressive attitudes of the sixties led to a preference for criminalization, presented as the only solution favorable to the victims.[38] This suggests that an explanation in terms of alternating spirits of the age is too simple and that, again, we have to take the longer term into consideration. I will come back to this in the conclusion.

First, I should relate the preceding discussion to the subject of the death penalty. One way of doing this would be to state that attitudes toward capital punishment simply evolve with the flow. On neither of the two continents, for example, has the return to punitiveness extended to public tortures on a scaffold, which all but a few people consider as a phenomenon of the past that should remain so. Clearly visible from the early 1980s onward, the return to punitiveness proceeded within the framework of each continent's penal spectrum at that point in time. For the United States this meant including the death penalty, which had just been declared constitutional again, whereas for Europe this meant, with the populace just having accepted the political elite's position, that capital punishment was outside the moral value system. Consequently, in Europe the subsequent increase in punitiveness referred to imprisonment alone and in the US it referred to both imprisonment and executions. The corollary of this argument would be that abolition of the death penalty in the US is only possible after a drastic trend reversal.

But I am not content with such an easy answer, since, after all, I believe that a broader historical-sociological theory is required. We can base it on Stephen Mennell's (2007) analysis of the American civilizing process. He observes that, unlike European countries, America never knew a single model-setting elite (as a reference group for what constitutes polite behavior and what, generally, are civilized values). Instead, there has been a succession of partially model-setting groups. Today, for example, a jet set of television and movie stars plus some popular singers that lives around Los Angeles sets the model for some people, but not for everyone. As discussed above, in European countries the model-setting elite – by that time, the political establishment – took the lead in abolishing the death penalty. Hence, Mennell partly attributes its retention in the USA to the absence of such an elite.

In addition, Mennell adduces my democracy-came-too-early thesis about the persistence of high homicide rates in the United States (see chapter 3) and extends this thesis to the death penalty. In doing so, he relies heavily on the association of capital punishment and popular justice, first posited by Franklin Zimring (2003). Like Zimring, Mennell emphasizes that lynchings then and executions now concentrate in the South but he adds that the weakness of the monopoly of force has always been greatest in the South. Moreover, he interprets the ethic of self-help and the distrust of state agencies as a brake on civilizing developments, while considering abolition of the death penalty as reflecting such developments. Thus, he concludes that "the political structures of American democracy have subtly constrained the workings of an underlying civilizing process that would not otherwise have been radically different from that seen in Europe."[39] I agree with his analysis to a large extent, but I wish to give the argument a different twist.

Returning to Europe, I observe that an important historical development involves the gradual intensification of the demands made from below upon the representatives of the state to moderate the practical uses of their monopoly of force. The disappearance of the scaffold and the emancipation of prisoners form part of this moderation process, along with other changes not discussed here, such as increasing restrictions on police action. The crucial point is that the moderation in the uses of a monopoly of force is a function not only of civilizing processes but also of the diminution of power differences within society. This last factor ensures that we can view the sacralization of executions as a very early phase in the moderation process. While it was no particularly civilizing change, it did involve a slight raise in the status and hence the power of convicts. This long history of moderation characterized American society to a much lesser extent. Prisoners did emancipate there during a large part of the twentieth century, but capital convicts had fewer power chances. The relative weakness of the moderation process in American history can be connected to the democracy-came-too-early thesis. This connection results in the following paradox: as Americans are inclined to a lesser recognition of the existence of a monopoly of force, they have a lesser inclination to make demands for restraint on it.

Conclusion

The principal analysts referred to in this chapter all contributed pieces of the puzzle, which I have tried perhaps not to solve but to rearrange. In all societies and throughout history the criminally condemned have in common that they feel the state's monopoly of force striking at their person in one way or another. Hence, every change in the treatment of the condemned is also a change in the way in which the monopoly of force is used. When successful demands are made on state agents for moderation of the uses of their monopoly, the power of the condemned increases. This is a manifestation of the overall diminution of power differences that Norbert Elias views as one of the principal aspects of long-term change. In Europe, the sacralization of executions, involving a slight rise in the status and power of capital convicts, constitutes an early example of the moderation process. Subsequently, the ritual of religiously tinged executions was exported to Colonial America, which is one indication of this continent's more compressed long-term development. Crucial in this compressed development was the "too early" advent of democracy, which led Americans to remain particularly distrustful of a state monopoly of force and, paradoxically, inclined to make fewer demands for moderation in its uses. Nevertheless, some examples of moderation, in particular a phase of emancipation of prisoners, took place also in the United States.

In the last three decades or so, the power of the criminally condemned appears to have somewhat diminished again, but further research is needed to determine its extent with greater precision. For one thing, average prison terms have increased and the supermax régime has spread. The extent of ordinary inmates' privileges and rights, on the other hand, has certainly not been reduced to the nineteenth-century level. Moreover, these recent developments are coupled with a partially civilizing trend of increasing compassion with crime victims that balances between vindictiveness and solidarity. Taken together, these developments are to a large extent common to Europe and America. In European countries, however, where the determination of the political elites to reject the death penalty meets with no serious opposition, this punishment remains out of the picture. In the United States, in addition to prisoners being even worse off than their European counterparts, the popularity of the death penalty has markedly increased. Thus, the modern return toward punitiveness is a trend common to most Western nations, but in the USA it is exacerbated due to the lesser inclination of its citizens to make demands of moderation on the use of the monopoly of force.

The principal conclusion of my thesis for Elias' theory runs like this: in the long run, civilizing processes and the decrease of power differentials between social groups go together and reinforce each other. In the short run, however, they sometimes proceed in opposite directions. The history of violence offers another example. In recent decades, respect for authority figures such as teachers or public transport officials has decreased, which led to an increase in aggression directed at them. Recent developments in punishment and control are even more complex. They involve a less moderate use of the monopoly of force and a concomitant decrease in the power of the criminally condemned but also a civilizing trend toward compassion with crime victims. An analysis of these partially contradictory developments helps us in better understanding present-day society, but it cannot tell us how things will continue.

PART THREE

CIVILIZING THE BODY IN HUMAN HISTORY

7

Elites and Etiquette

Changing Standards of Personal Conduct in the Netherlands until 1800

As a corollary to the long-term decline of violence and the spiritualization of honor, discussed in several chapters of this book, standards of personal conduct moved in the direction of greater refinement. The early modern period, which witnessed the steepest decline in homicide rates, also was the age with the most rapid changes in rules of etiquette. Whereas in 1500 everyone ate with their hands and drank from a common cup, by 1800 elite groups observed a strict set of table manners. This is of course a major theme in Norbert Elias' classic work on the civilizing process. As primary sources he examined manner books written in French, German and English. For the concomitant study of processes of state formation, Elias concentrated, as is well known, on France. Along with the refinement in rules of conduct, French aristocrats transformed from a class of warriors into a class of courtiers.

Given this, an inquiry into standards of conduct in the Netherlands is especially worthwhile. At the most mundane level, such an inquiry enhances our knowledge about manner books by examining specimens of this genre in the Dutch language. But it offers more than just that. The investigation extends to an analysis of the position of the elites of the Dutch Republic, whose origins were bourgeois rather than aristocratic. Chapter 2 showed their indifference to dueling, quite unlike the habit of the elites in most other European countries. Did the Dutch also adopt a distinct set of etiquette rules or was there a refinement of manners similar to that in France? And if the development was similar, what accounts for this? After all, the social identity of the Dutch elites did not depend, as it did for the French, on spending their days in the vicinity of a king.

Several scholars have turned to manner books as a major source for the study of changes in personal conduct. Cas Wouters (2007) focuses on standards of etiquette in the late nineteenth and twentieth centuries in the Netherlands, Germany, England and the United States. The period he studied was characterized by democratization and informalization, which caused rules of conduct to increasingly reflect the decrease in power differences between social classes and the genders. By contrast, I am focusing on the period before 1800. Books of etiquette from this period often do not deal explicitly with issues of gender, although in many instances it is possible to determine whether they speak implicitly to men or to women. They do deal with issues of social class. This is the period when the political structure of the Netherlands was much different from that of most of its neighbors. While some of the manner books examined date from the late middle ages, my study of the elites focuses on the Republican period.

The principal sources consist of conduct books published in the sixteenth through eighteenth centuries. I collected their titles in the systematic catalogues – at the time of the research, in the form of card-boxes – of the University Library in Amsterdam and the Royal Library in The Hague. In both libraries the catalogue included a category labeled with a term like moralistic lessons, which encompassed more than just books of etiquette. It included moralist works of a more philosophical nature, such as Coornhert's *Zedekunst*. Coornhert denounced cruelty, for example, without specifying which acts he considered cruel and which not. I defined as manner books only those works which did provide concrete rules of conduct and hence made it possible to inquire into changes over time. The titles collected in this way in the Amsterdam and The Hague libraries were supplemented with references found in historical literature, including medieval manuscripts published in modern editions.[1]

One more introductory note concerns proper terminology. In Dutch historiography it is customary to refer to the ruling class of the Republican period as the *regenten*, which becomes "regents" in English. Contemporaries, however, used *regenten* merely as a general term for administrators or governors, such as the boards that supervised a prison or an orphanage. Urban leaders, most commonly called the *heren* (gentlemen), certainly did not view themselves as members of a "class of regents." Therefore, I will alternately denote them with the more technical term of "patricians" or as "the gentlemen." The second terminological question concerns the translation of the word *Staten* (Estates). Seventeenth-century English visitors to the Dutch Republic, who only knew a Parliament, translated *Staten* as "states," but it is unwise to repeat their mistake. Throughout early modern Europe, meetings of

Estates differed in composition, and their rights and duties varied per region and country. There is no reason at all to single out the Estates of one country as so totally different from the rest that they deserve another name.[2]

Changing Rules of Etiquette: Texts

Elias grouped the rules of conduct dealt with in manner books under five headings: table manners, bodily functions, nose blowing, spitting and behavior in the bedroom. These themes also figure prominently in the Dutch manner books I studied. Indeed, some of these books were translations or adaptations of works published in other languages. Hence, I will group my texts under the same rubrics. In each case, chronologically ordered quotations are followed by a brief discussion. I translated the texts into English as literally as possible, in order not to introduce biases.

Table Manners

Fourteenth century

Where great people are at the table, pour out the wine or drink from it; and cool the cup and put it back on the table when it has been cooled. . . . When you eat, don't scratch your head or hand, if someone can see it. . . . Give the food first to the highest-ranking person at the table. You shall pour out the wine into the cup, from which the people will drink.[3]

Fifteenth century

You shall not cut your nails at the table, neither in front of the people; you shall do it when you are alone. When you arrive at the table, then you shall not sit down above other people; where you are told to sit down, there sit down. . . . You shall learn to eat with both hands. If the dish is on the left, then you shall eat with your right hand; if it is on the right, then eat with your left hand. Then you don't nudge your comrade who is eating with you. You shall take whatever lies in front of you in the dish; you shall not reach to the other side and take what lies in front of your comrade.[4]

1546

Shall a boy reach for the dish with his hands, directly when he has arrived at the table? Pigs do that and those who consume the gifts of God without saying grace before. Why shall the boy not reach for the dish first? In order that he learns to tame his own will and desires and gets used to being obedient to older people; also to prevent him from eating the food too hot, so that he burns his mouth and people laugh at him. . . . What shall you do, if a spoon full of soft food is given to you? You shall take the spoon and eat what is in it and then you shall clean the spoon with the napkin and give it back.[5]

1591

Young man, if you want to sit down at the table, wash your hands. You shall not have long nails; you shall cut them in secrecy. . . . You shall not smack like a pig and don't lick your thumb or finger. . . . You shall part from the dish quickly and not reach for the food too long. . . . Close your mouth when you eat and don't show your tongue like a dog. Let the food sink well and wipe your mouth, when you want to drink. . . . You shall not pick your nose or your teeth or scratch your head with your hands. . . . You shall not clean your hands or mouth with the table-cloth.[6]

1664

Many people who are practicing the art of carving [a whole animal], are first swinging and twisting with their arms and carving-knives and forks so much, that they rather look like experienced fencers than graceful dissectors. . . . There should always be a clean plate on either side. You shall keep your fingers as free from grease as possible and don't wipe them off, except each time after the carving of every piece of food; and especially don't lick them, like some do, without thinking. Such a thing makes people despise you and makes them think you are a rude person. But in order to neatly wipe your fingers, the custom among carvers is to have a clean napkin hanging over their left shoulder.[7]

1677

While you are eating, you have to hold your lips together, in order not to smack like the pigs. Much less should you make a noise or scrape the dishes or wipe your plate until the last drop is gone. It is like a click-clack of weapons that shows, like with a sign of war, our lust for eating to the one who, without that, wouldn't notice it.[8]

1793

I think one can describe delicacy as a kind of aversion one feels against
some food or drink, originating from direct observation, or only imagination, that something is in it, which one is not used to finding there
and which could produce an awful taste in us, or something dirty, which
might produce disgust in us. For instance, as soon as a dish looks different from what one is used to, or as one notices a fly or a fiber in the food,
many people will exhibit this caprice. Thus, I have often seen, that one
rather threw away a bowl of nice-smelling cinnamon or meat-sauce, than
put one's mouth to it, after one had found a small hair in it. And likewise
a drop of tallow, fallen on a plate with partridges, not seldom has been
the ridiculous reason that the servants enjoyed the things, for which their
masters had longed and on which they had spent much money.[9]

Discussion

While some texts are directed specifically to boys, we also hear of women
at the table especially when the social milieu appears to be high. The
texts from the fourteenth and fifteenth centuries are comparable to the
medieval table manners in other European countries, as reported by
Elias. Behavioral rules are little differentiated. Forks are not mentioned
and spoons hardly. Frits van Oostrom's detailed study of the court of the
Counts of Holland confirms this.[10] Everyone drinks from the same cup.
Interesting is the technique, mentioned in the second fragment, of eating
from the common dish without nudging your neighbor. A probate inventory of the castle at Wijk bij Duurstede, owned by the Bishop of Utrecht,
confirms the rarity of forks, even around 1500. Among the table-silver,
it lists only one fork.[11]

The text of 1546 is actually an adaptation of Erasmus' *De civilitate
morum puerilium*, which plays a prominent role in Elias' discussion of
sources. The Dutch book essentially presents Erasmus' rules in abbreviated form. The quotations from the second half of the sixteenth century
reflect similar standards of behavior. That of 1664 comes from a specialized book about the carving of game (whole animals) served at the table.
Apparently, this job had not yet been removed to the kitchen; sensitivities
are limited to the sight of greasy fingers. Indeed, two Dutch noblemen
had carved the game at a dinner in The Hague in 1660 which the Estates
of Holland offered to Charles II on his way to be restored to the English
throne.[12]

The 1677 treatise once more is based on a foreign example; most
chapters are a translation of the influential French manner book by
Antoine de Courtin. The additional chapters, revealing about the Dutch

situation, are discussed below. I restricted the quotations about table manners to passages that also are new in this Dutch edition. Perhaps significantly, making too much noise with the plates is compared to the sound of weapons.

I found no original texts dealing with table manners from the eighteenth century. The last quotation, over 100 years later than the preceding one, is from an encyclopedia. The author describes what he considers a caprice of delicate persons, who nevertheless represent "many people." Actually, it appears, they are the masters rather than the servants. Given the author's surprise about rejecting food on which you have spent much money, he may have been of middle-class origin. That is also suggested by his emphasis on cleanliness: "If one could see how everything is prepared, especially in the houses of the Great, how bread, cheese, wine and beer are made and through how many dirty hands most things pass, before they are served at the best tables with an inviting look of charming cleanliness, then delicate persons will starve, as they are unable to find absolutely clean food."[13]

Bodily Functions

1526

One has to take care for the cleanliness of the teeth, but to make them shine with some powder is for girls; to rub them with salt or alum is pernicious for your gums. To do this with urine is a habit of the Spaniards.[14]

1531

From now on no one, be it a man or a woman, shall go out and pray or beg for alms . . . with the exception of the Religious Mendicants . . . and the Lazaruses and lepers, who will be allowed to beg for alms as they are used to, if the above-mentioned Lazaruses wear their hats, gloves, coats and other required signs, on the condition that, when they want to make their water, they will go away from the crowd, on penalty of being sent to prison on bread and water, as mentioned before.[15]

1546

Shall you also hold your water, if you feel an urge? That is bad for your health, but in any place you shall do it in secrecy, if you feel the urge. . . . Are you also allowed to fart among the people? That would be rustic, but it is more honorable to leave your company, when you're not able to stop it.[16]

1626

There are those, who order a child to retain the winds from the belly with compressed buttocks. And indeed, it is boorish and shameless to fart at the people around you.[17]

1778

The Spaniards make much use of their own piss, to keep their teeth white and to wash their mouth, which is also a custom among some of our countrymen yet, although it is very detestable. . . . We call it detestable, because no animal can be found, which does not have a visible aversion against its own droppings; why then shall a human being use them?[18]

Discussion

The quotations contain three remarkable points. The first is the habit of whitening the teeth with urine, known to Erasmus (a passage not quoted by Elias) and the author of an eighteenth-century encyclopedia (under the plain heading of "piss"). Both ascribe this habit to the Spanish, the latter condemning it with greater vehemence. He adds that Leiden workers use urine also for whitening cloth.

From the 1531 quotation, from Charles V's decree against begging, we may conclude that it was normal for healthy men not to leave the crowd, when they had to urinate. In line with texts quoted by Elias, we must assume that the references to "making your water" concern men only. Moreover, this is one of the few examples in the sixteenth century of a "civilizing" restraint being prescribed probably for hygienic reasons only. According to Elias, the tightening of rules of conduct was motivated originally by sensitivity; only later did manner books mention health as an additional argument in favor of stricter behavior. In the sixteenth century, by contrast, health was used more often as an argument against too many restraints, as with Erasmus' permission to fart.[19]

That observation leads to the third point: the bowdlerization of manner books. The 1626 quotation is from the official edition of Erasmus' little book of etiquette for use in Dutch schools. A hundred years later, the translator simply turns the humanist's permission into a prohibition. I found one similar example, involving mitigation rather than outright reversal. Giovanni della Casa's *Galateo* (1558), like other sixteenth-century texts, elaborately instructs its noble readers not to urinate in the presence of others from the noble company and to wash their hands in secrecy, so that others won't ask why they do this. The 1715 Dutch translation of *Galateo* simply omits this passage. It was followed by an injunction not to point at, much less to poke with a stick into and invite others to smell something which is recognizably described as a piece of excrement lying in the street. In a decidedly more veiled manner, the Dutch translator speaks of "something that stinks."[20]

Nose-blowing

1546

Are you also allowed to blow your nose into your sleeve? No, but you shall do it with a handkerchief; and if you stand in front of somebody, then you shall turn your face. Shall one also smear the snot into one's clothes? No, but blowing the nose with two fingers, one shall throw it aside on the earth and wipe it away with one's foot, so that nobody loathes it.[21]

1591

All the schoolboys who don't instantly wipe away the saliva from their nose or mouth with their feet, who walk along the city walls when they have to go home, who throw snot, fleas and lice at each other, they all will have two ferules or will cane each other.[22]

1677

You shall neither pick your nose, nor scratch yourself on any other place. You have to prevent yourself from yawning, blowing your nose and expectorating. And if you can't avoid it, there on the spot or in any other place where it is clean, you shall do it into your handkerchief, turning away your face and covering it with your left hand and when you are finished, don't look into your handkerchief.[23]

Discussion

We know that the use of handkerchiefs still was uncommon in the first half of the sixteenth century. The author who adapted Erasmus simply lets two different rules follow each other without deciding which method is the better one. Neither were the schoolboys of master Valcoogh obliged to use a handkerchief, but they were forbidden to aim the snot at a fellow pupil on purpose. De Courtin's translator made no changes in the Frenchman's rules on this subject. For the Dutch, too, by now a handkerchief was obviously a normal attribute. This can also be inferred from another source: a contemporary observer talks about the quack medicines that were sold at The Hague fair in 1679. People carried them home in their handkerchiefs.[24]

Spitting

1546

How shall a young man behave, when he wants to spit out his saliva? He shall turn away from the people and take care to make nobody unclean. And when he has spit it out on the ground, he shall wipe it away with his foot, so that nobody loathes it. But if there is no room to spit between the people, then he shall do it into his handkerchief.[25]

1591

All the schoolboys who spit into the drinks of others, or step on their food, who cannot keep a secret, who don't directly wipe away the saliva from their nose or mouth with their feet . . . they all will have two ferules or will cane each other.[26]

1677

If one sits by the fire, one has to avoid expectorating into it, or spitting on the logs or against the mantlepiece. . . . Another example of bad manners is that of those who believe they are not heard unless they speak mouth to mouth, spitting the people into their face and making them dirty, if they have a strong breath.[27]

Discussion

Erasmus' adaptor retains the humanist's rule unchanged. Standards in the country schools in Holland at the end of the sixteenth century are more or less similar, or a little less refined if we consider the prohibition against spitting into someone else's drink. The translation of De Courtin's work obviously represents a more refined standard. The passage about strong breath anticipates modern norms of polite social intercourse.

Behavior in the Bedroom

Fourteenth century

And does it happen, that you go to sleep along with your comrade or a better person, first ask him, loudly or silently, on which side he wants to lie down.[28]

1546

How shall you lie in the bed? Not on your back or belly, but on your right side. You also shall not draw in or bend your legs, not turn around here and there or draw the bedclothes from the one to the other, if somebody else is sleeping in the bed.[29]

1677

If it happened, because of the bad inn, that you had to sleep in the room of the person whom you owe respect, propriety requires you to let him undress and go to bed first and to undress yourself after that in a corner and near the bed in which you will sleep, and go to bed without making noise, remaining silent and quiet the whole night through. As you went to bed the last, propriety requires you to stand up first, in order that the distinguished person in any case finds us dressed in the morning. For propriety does not permit that a person, to whom we owe respect, sees us naked and undressed.[30]

Discussion

The first quotation is in line with what we know about medieval customs throughout Europe. Friends and strangers often shared beds, in particular when travelling. Politeness simply required leaving the choice of sides to the highest-ranking person. Sharing beds was still common in Erasmus' times, but he and his adaptor required all persons not to disturb each other. Probably, these two texts refer implicitly to men only. When a woman and a man shared a bed, this was usually for sexual purposes, although in a few cases in Dutch seventeenth-century taverns this appears to have happened for practical reasons.[31]

The third quotation is from a chapter translated literally from De Courtin's work (not quoted by Elias). The chapter is about hunting and the passage has a great lord and his companion drifted so far away that there is only a rustic inn. Even there they are not obliged to share beds but a single bedroom. The rule is in line with Elias' observations about nudity in early modern Europe: it is shameful for a person to show up naked in front of a social superior, but conversely the superior would not mind being seen in the nude. In this respect, he viewed the social inferior like we view a pet today.

The Spread of Models of Behavior: A Closer Analysis

The preliminary conclusion to be drawn from the quotations above is perhaps surprising. Despite the distinct political and social developments in the territory which became the Netherlands, the succession of Dutch manner books points at a process of refinement of behavioral standards not unlike that in France and other European countries. Of course the expression "the Netherlands" is historically ambiguous. In the sixteenth century it primarily referred to the seventeen provinces under Habsburg rule, including present-day Belgium in whose Southern provinces French was the language spoken.[32] When Habsburg attempts at centralization failed and the Dutch Republic was established in the North, *Nederland* gradually came to refer to this polity alone. The texts from the seventeenth and eighteenth centuries that I found were all from the Dutch Republic. Even then, it is important to try to determine their reading public with greater precision. That question is even more complicated for the texts from the sixteenth century.

As Elias noted, the publication of Erasmus' *De civilitate morum puerilium* marked a new spurt in the refinement of manners away from medieval standards. The first edition appeared in Antwerp in 1526 and the book was an immediate international success. Editions soon followed in France, England and Germany, and already in 1540 in a distant place such as Cracow. At least 18 editions of the Latin text and 3 Dutch translations or adaptations, from one of which I quoted, appeared in Antwerp until the 1580s. Subsequently, there was a Europe-wide lull in publications until the Leiden edition of 1626, the first one in the Northern Netherlands.[33] Hence, no editions of *De civilitate* were published in the sixteenth century in the territory which would become the Dutch Republic. This is not surprising given the fact that Antwerp was the commercial center of the Low Countries until the Northerners closed off the river Scheldt in 1585. In the sixteenth century, few printers operated in the North, but books published in Antwerp found their way there. We know, for example, that Northerners read heretical works printed in Antwerp.[34] But does this mean that Northerners were equally keen to learn about the new standards of behavior?

In spite of his relatively independent stance vis-à-vis princely power,

Erasmus had begun *De civilitate* praising courtiers. In his dedication to the young Henry of Burgundy he explained that the boy himself had no need for these rules since he already knew them. The rules were meant for those eager to learn how courtiers behaved. Henry's father, Adolf of Burgundy, was one of the *Grands Seigneurs* of the time, holding a high office in Charles V's administration in Brussels. As Antwerp was the commercial center, Brussels was the political center of the Habsburg dominions in the Low Countries. Aspiring nobles and wealthy entrepreneurs – the sort of people who would read books of etiquette – all looked toward the South. If they did not live there, they would at least try to spend much of their time there. It seems reasonable, therefore, to assume some delay in the spread of the new behavioral standards to the Northern Netherlands. Expressions of resentment at Southerners and their "Spanish" manners in the North, even at the turn of the sixteenth and seventeenth centuries, lend further credence to this supposition. We find such expressions in the work of the poets Roemer Visscher and Bredero.[35]

The edition of *De civilitate* in Leiden in 1626 comes as no surprise. In the previous year a decree issued by the Estates of Holland aimed at standardizing the reading in the province's Latin schools. The decree prescribed which books the schools were to use and the Estates requested the Leiden professors to prepare new editions. *De civilitate* served as reading for the lowest class. We don't know whether all Latin schools obeyed the decree, but an extant book list of 1677 from Amsterdam mentions that the work was in use.[36] As we saw, a Dutch translation, with a new standard of always abstaining from farting in company, appeared also in 1626. Presumably, it was in use in the Dutch schools. The last edition of *De civilitate* in the Republic was a rhymed version in Dutch by the village schoolmaster Michiel Komans, printed in Amsterdam in 1693 and Rotterdam in 1695. He provides one more adaptation to changed standards. Where Erasmus had written "to your right is the knife, to your left the bread," Komans adds a fork. He ascribes the habit of blowing the nose into the sleeve to fish-selling women.[37] No new editions of Erasmus' booklet appeared in the Republic during the eighteenth century, save for its inclusion in the *Opera omnia* (1703–6).

We can conclude that Erasmus' standards of conduct slowly descended down the social ladder. The pupils of the Latin schools reading his work from 1626 on were mostly sons of patricians and wealthy merchants. The rhymed version at the end of the seventeenth century was meant for another type of school, frequented by the children of prosperous farmers and townspeople from the lower-middle class: about the same groups to whom Valcoogh had directed himself 100 years earlier. Elias describes the spread of models of behavior down the social ladder as a process characteristic for France in the seventeenth and eighteenth centuries. Its corollary was the adoption of more refined standards by the country's top groups. Can we observe this in the Dutch Republic as well?

In France, Antoine de Courtin's *Nouveau traité de civilité* marked a new spurt in the refinement of standards of conduct. It informed elite groups without access to court what counted as well-mannered in Versailles. We saw that a Dutch translation was prepared soon. The original version, however, had already appeared in Holland six years earlier. The publisher omitted De Courtin's name from the title page but added "sur la copie imprimée à Paris." We can contrast this with the title page of the Dutch version which reads, also without De Courtin's name: "New treatise on the courtly civility and laudable well-manneredness, practiced in The Hague at the court and furthermore throughout the Netherlands among distinguished persons." Of necessity, the original version was meant for persons well-versed in the French language and, as explained below, these mainly included Dutch and international circles in The Hague and patricians of the larger towns, especially in the leading province of Holland. As the title page suggests, Paris was their focus of orientation. The Dutch version probably appealed to people just below the elites. The publisher included foci of orientation for both Orangists (the Stadholder's court) and non-Orangists (the patrician elite). One passage in the Dutch version, moreover, constitutes a remnant from earlier standards. Whereas De Courtin had stated that a section on carving whole animals was unnecessary and that a polite man need not be ashamed if he did not master this art, the Dutch translator/adaptor includes such a section, simply copying it from the 1664 treatise quoted above.

The French edition of De Courtin, identical to that published in Paris, was printed four times in Holland between 1671 and 1731. This suggests that the Dutch elites felt an immediate and continuous need to acquaint themselves with French standards of conduct. This need kept them in line with the elites of other countries. In a 1702 review of a new book by De Courtin, the reviewer mentions that the *Nouveau traité de civilité* is well known throughout Europe.[38] After 1731 no new etiquette books which can be identified as meant for the elites appeared in the Dutch Republic. They apparently learned about new standards of conduct through personal contact, which is in line with Elias' observations for France. Dutch patricians could also learn the rules of etiquette during the Grand Tour with which they completed their studies.[39]

The Dutch version of De Courtin of 1677, on the other hand, was not printed anew until 1733.[40] This edition, appropriately omitting the words "new treatise," also lacked a reference to the court in The Hague, understandably since there was no Stadholder then. It was published again in 1737, 1742 and 1768. The publisher's preface of 1737 says that the book has been received very favorably by *het gemeen*. Although this term most commonly referred to the lowest stratum in the cities, it is more likely that we must understand it here in the sense of the general public, primarily the middle classes. This is also suggested by the publisher's capitalization on the name of Erasmus: the book contains a letter ascribed to the great humanist, announced in large characters on the title page and expressing a skeptical attitude toward furthering one's interest at a court. In the 1768 edition, this letter has become anonymous. Together, the four editions can be considered as the Dutch counterpart to the work of the Jesuit Jean-Baptiste de la Salle, which taught new manners to the French middle classes in the eighteenth century.

The Process of Aristocratization

All our primary sources point in one direction: the process of refinement of manners in the Netherlands in the early modern period hardly deviated from that observed by Elias for France, especially as far as the elites were concerned. Elias attached great importance to the simultaneous development of the French state, with the court as a center of prestige, and bureaucratic centralization at the administrative level. Both of these factors were relatively weak in the Dutch context. The court of the Stadholder, when one was in office, was far less magnificent than that of Louis XIV. Politically, the Republic remained decentralized, although legal uniformity in particular increased over time.[41]

Yet some measure of state formation took place in the Dutch Republic. For one thing, The Hague usually was its center. The Estates of Holland as well as the Estates General met there and the town was the residence of the Stadholder of Holland (until 1702 there were two branches of the house of Orange, one claiming the Stadholdership of five provinces and the other that of the two Northern provinces). Only during the second Stadholderless period (1702–47) did Amsterdam enjoy factual preeminence over The Hague. During the first Stadholderless period (1650–72), the Grand Pensionary Johan de Witt, residing in The Hague as well, was the strong man. Apart from the question of the geographic center, a crucial transformation came about in the mid eighteenth century. First, William IV became Stadholder for all seven provinces in 1747, and his office was declared hereditary. The latter privilege had already been bestowed on William III, but it had been undone directly after his death. When William IV died in 1751 leaving a minor son, the Estates appointed a regent, which sealed the heredity of the office of Stadholder.

In between these years, the Tax Farmers' Rebellion swept over the country. As a reaction to this uprising, a new tax system, replacing tax farmers with collectors, was introduced. Whereas patricians at the local and provincial level had dominated the tax farming system, the Prince of Orange supervised the nomination of the new tax collectors.[42] This means that, for the first time, a monopoly of taxation was in the Stadholder's hands. As supreme commander of the army, he had enjoyed a military monopoly for a long time. Thus, before the mid eighteenth century, the military monopoly and the monopoly of taxation were in different hands; thereafter the Stadholder, as a semi-monarch, disposed of a dual monopoly of force.[43] Revolutionaries and the French deprived the House of Orange of its recently acquired monopoly between 1795 and 1813, but they introduced further administrative centralization. This enabled the last Stadholder's son to return as king and to rule the country (for a time including Belgium, but that was no success) as an enlightened despot. Finally, the 1848 constitution marked the start of a new phase in which representatives of the people would gradually co-possess the monopoly of force.

The crucial steps within this process of state formation obviously postdate the refinement of manners among the elites as observed here. Consequently, the first cannot explain the second. We must identify the motors behind the early modern refinement of manners within the figuration that emerged from the Dutch revolt. For France, Elias attributes the rapid succession of new models of conduct among the elites mainly to pressure from below. This pressure resulted from imitation. When townspeople and provincial nobles imitated the refined manners practiced at the court, these manners devaluated as a means of distinction for the top aristocracy. This obliged them to develop ever more elaborate standards of conduct in order to continue to distinguish themselves from the rest. The Dutch elites probably also experienced some pressure from below, but there was pressure from above as well. "Above" primarily meant the aristocracies of other countries. The Dutch elites wanted to be taken seriously on the European scene. They had never been warriors and they would not become full-time courtiers. Their continuing rejection of the duel actually helped them to become the fully pacified elite that the French aristocracy never completely was. Instead of a transformation from warriors to courtiers, the ruling class of the Dutch Republic transformed from peaceful bourgeois to peaceful semi-aristocrats.

It was Daniel Roorda (1961, 1964) who coined the term "process of aristocratization," but he used it primarily to refer to the establishment of an increasingly oligarchic régime in the Republic. According to Roorda, "the people," as represented by the guilds, the civil militia and the Reformed consistories, had acquired a measure of influence on political affairs, in particular in the cities, during and just after the revolt.

Subsequently, the patrician leadership, who had always filled their ranks through cooptation anyway, was able to gradually reduce this popular influence again. With it the patrician elite established itself as a semi-aristocratic ruling class. Modern historiography, however, has nuanced the notion of a strictly oligarchic régime. Already, ten years after Roorda, van Deursen (1974) denied that the Reformed consistories can be considered as representatives of the (lower) middle class. More recently, Jan Luiten van Zanden and Maarten Prak (2006) argued that, throughout the Republican period, and particularly at recurring moments of crisis, the patriciate was obliged to take the wishes of the broad middle class into account. This "citizenship model" of state formation ensured that the inhabitants of the Dutch Republic were prepared to pay higher taxes per capita than those of France did.[44] In my thesis, however, aristocratization refers first of all to habitus and life-style. I am arguing that it was precisely the less-than-absolute rule which the patriciate exercised according to modern historiography, that prompted patricians to look for other means of distinction. They found these in an aristocratic life-style and a French orientation.[45]

The evidence for this process comes from primary sources such as contemporary treatises as well as references in older historical literature. Courtly influences were first visible among real aristocrats, Dutch and foreign, in and around The Hague in the second quarter of the seventeenth century. By that time France still was an ally. Many officers in the Dutch army were French, which obliged the Stadholder to speak their language. In 1625 Frederic Henry succeeded his half-brother Maurice as Stadholder. Maurice had been on campaign during nearly all his years of office and, moreover, he was unmarried – a severe handicap when it came to building up a court. Frederic Henry married Amalia of Solms, one of the ladies from the aristocratic suite of the "Winter King" (the deposed King of Bohemia) who had arrived in The Hague a few years earlier. This was a boost to court life, where French equally became the *lingua franca*. In 1634 the Elector of Brandenburg considered The Hague an appropriate place for the education of his son.[46] The marriage of the Stadholder's young son William to the even younger Mary Stuart in 1640 formed an occasion for extending the court. Frederic Henry acted as a lavish patron of painting, preferring the courtly and baroque style of Flemish and Italian painters and the Utrecht school.[47]

Urban patricians, by contrast, were the main patrons of Rembrandt and the Dutch school. Very likely, they were not influenced by aristocratic and French manners before mid-century. When two young Dutch noblemen visited the Dutch ambassador in Paris in the winter of 1657–8, they were annoyed because the ambassador's wife, whom they typified as a simple mother from Amsterdam, spoke no French and didn't know how to entertain her guests.[48] Urban patricians probably started having aristocratic pretensions without a French orientation at first. Gentry titles were the key. Sixteenth-century town governments had already bought manors in the surrounding countryside, and in the early seventeenth century individual patricians started to do so. From mid-century onwards, it became common for them to add the manor's name to their family name, styling themselves as Lord of Purmerland and the like.[49] The urban elites equally coveted knighthood conferred on them by a foreign prince. The source of a noble title mattered little, since no legally sanctioned system of formal ranks existed. In the 1660s Coenraad Droste counted as a nobleman because the officials of the West India Company had referred to his father as a *jonker* when he arrived from the Rhineland to serve them.[50] A foreigner cynically remarked in 1678 that the people of Holland were all gentlemen.[51]

We find the first signs of a French aristocratic orientation among the patriciate with the man whom nineteenth-century historians considered as the embodiment of the ancient Dutch civic spirit. The future Grand Pensionary Johan de Witt and his brother Cornelis first learned to dance fashionably during their Grand Tour through France and England from 1645 to 1647. After his return Johan became a well-received guest in The Hague salons. His membership card in the Ordre de l'Union de la Joye, founded by Amélie, Baroness of Slavata, daughter of a Dutch nobleman and married to one of the Winter King's courtiers, dated from February 23, 1653. Johan wrote affectionate letters to the *grande maistresse* and later, when his office preoccupied him, he continued to attach importance to society life. He reproached his daughter, who studied in Leiden, for failing to inform him about the courting of two distinguished young ladies, thereby making a fool of him. When he walked through The Hague with an important guest, he would observe a rule of civility by insisting that his companion take the "upper hand." Conversely, he obliged his first clerk to speak to him bare-headed.[52]

De Witt was not alone in valuing rank, civility and social life. For an overall judgment of the patricians of the first Stadholderless age, we depend on an admittedly partisan source. Just after William III's takeover, the Amsterdam lawyer Petrus Valkenier published 't Verwerd Europa (Europe confused), an anti-French and pro-Orangist analysis of contemporary events. According to Valkenier, it was precisely the patriciate's French orientation which had contributed indirectly to the success of Louis XIV's army: if an artist had to depict a man from Holland in his typical costume, he would depict him naked with a pair of scissors in front of the latest French design. With the income from foreign sales, the French king financed the war. More generally, the effeminateness of the patricians and their rejection of sobriety had weakened the country. In the old days, Valkenier continued, the representatives went to the Estates meetings on foot in ordinary burgher-clothes, taking their food with them from home. Nowadays they went in costly carriages, accompanied by servants, messengers and their wives and children.

> Instead of behaving humbly and without external pomp in public and solemn activities, according to old and proper habit and the common custom of all Republican Governments, they started to raise the sail higher and higher and to *regard themselves as the equals of Crowned Heads*, to whom they would not concede an inch.[53]

No doubt, Valkenier exaggerated, but we may still conclude that his preference for republican egalitarianism and sobriety was no longer the norm. Under William III, aristocratization would continue. Our witness is the 1677 translation/adaptation of De Courtin. The most revealing passage comes from a new chapter, not present in the French edition, on various ceremonial occasions. The passage is concerned with the proper way of addressing oneself to a social superior. The author instructs the social inferior to say or write "My Lord" ("Mijn Heer") and denounces those who insist on "master" or just "you."

> These and other words of deference have lost a great deal of their bitterness and they no longer have such a harsh meaning, having become softer in the mouths of the people. Therefore, one must not have such a reprehension against them, like some rude and blunt people who would want that the letters that one is allowed to write to the Princes or Gentlemen (*Heren*), would begin in such a manner: If you and your family are well, I am glad; as far as I am concerned, I am in good health: because the ancient Romans were used to write in this way. If one wanted to believe these people, one would soon let the age return in which people lived on nothing but acorns.[54]

The appeal to the ancient Romans is significant. In modern Europe the image of the Roman republic was often dear to revolutionaries. Here it is simply rejected as invalid. Familiarity with the *Heren*, which word primarily refers to the patricians, belongs to an uncivilized dark age in which people ate acorns. Deference is the proper attitude.

The very patricians whose ancestors had become "sovereigns against their will" (having first offered sovereignty to the French and English monarchs) now aspired to be the equals of crowned heads. They struggled for a recognition as such at the international level as well. The struggle revolved around a particular custom during the first reception of an ambassador by the prince of the country to which he was sent. At a certain moment the prince would invite his visitor to put his hat back on. The idea was that, since the ambassador represented his sovereign

a light encyclopedia, not meant as a reference work but to read once in a while in order to better partake of conversations at social gatherings. The preface says: "We know that some scholars, whose pronouncements no less than those of the Popes we regard as infallible however, look down on this kind of works . . . because they would like to see the sources from which they have acquired and are acquiring their erudition being concealed, because they want people to be obliged to lock themselves up in their caves, which deprives them of the most useful gift of humanity which is sociability."[62]

Most eighteenth-century commentators, however, remained skeptical about sociability and elegant manners. Thus, P. van der Schelling, who continued a work describing distinguished banquets of the past, begun by his father-in-law, gave it a different twist. He focused on the abuse of banquets, in particular in the form of drunkenness. Along the way he contrasted good morals, following from Christianity, reason and law, with good manners, merely deriving from the constraint to please others.[63] At the end of the century Jan Hendrik Swildens was milder in his critique. He wrote a preface, anonymously, to the translation of a contemplative work on social life by the Baron Von Knigge, taking this as an occasion to comment on Dutch society. I quoted his views about merchants and the Great World above. Swildens lays value on civility because rudeness in social intercourse is unpleasant. However, there are too many and complex rules of etiquette. He recommends dropping these but preserving the true and loveable state of being civilized. Thus, his attitude resembles that of the Count of Mirabeau in France, as analyzed by Elias.[64] Nevertheless, Swildens acknowledges that, ultimately, standards of conduct derive from courts, in particular that of France:

> The Courts, as they are the center to which everything flows, are also the center or general source from which the modes of thought and the way of life of all nations continually spring and receive their modifications. This takes place in particular with respect to the civilized World, not only in the monarchical countries, but from these everything moves from nation to nation, at least in Europe, where one knows the Court and the People who have set the general tone of Society for over a hundred years, to which before and after most other Nations, even into the distant and barren North, have tuned in.[65]

Conclusion

The process of aristocratization constituted the primary motor behind the adoption of refined standards of conduct by the Dutch elites in the seventeenth and eighteenth centuries. In its turn, this process was rooted in the peculiar figuration which emerged in the North from the revolt against Habsburg domination. Although the degree of participation of "the people" in politics had been greatest during that revolt, the "citizenship" model of government remained a potent force. This situation induced Dutch patricians to distinguish themselves from the middle classes in other ways, in particular by their life-style. They started to behave partially as aristocrats, took France and the French language as a cultural model and adopted the new standards of personal conduct first developed at the French court. Simultaneously, they demanded deference from the very groups to whom they sometimes had to listen in affairs of state.

All this can be considered as pressure from below, resulting from the dynamics of the interdependence between patriciate and middle class. Pressure from above, however, was important too. "Above" meant the leading groups in the entire European network of states. They exerted social pressure upon the Dutch elites, because the Republic, despite its hybrid structure, was a powerful player on the European scene at least until the end of the War of the Spanish Succession. As leaders of a powerful country, the Dutch elites wished to be taken seriously. This involved gaining respect as sovereigns as well as being recognized more or less as social equals. Pressure from above, too, induced patricians of Holland and later those of the other provinces to behave like aristocrats and to adopt refined manners. Aristocratization and the civilizing of manners were intertwined. Both resulted not so much from a home-grown process of state formation, but from increasing interdependence within the European network of states.

8

Civilizing Celebrations

An Exploration of the Festive Universe

Next to the refinement of manners, another corollary to the decline of violence involved the emergence of new forms of celebration and festival. Festivities became more benign, gradually losing their association with recreational fighting, excessive consumption of food and drink and sexual adventure. This story belongs to the last 200 years or so. In addition, this chapter explores the very long term, discussing the merits of various theories along the way. Note that for French and German theorists, one word (*fête*, *Fest*) is central, which refers to festivals but also to occasions that in English would be called parties. English also knows the word "holiday," which helps us to further delineate the subject.

Both parts of the word "holiday" are significant. The first refers to the religious roots of festivals, to which I return below. The second refers to a characteristic of many celebrations: they recur annually on a particular day or at least within a brief period of the year. It may happen that because of adverse circumstances people skip a year, while some celebrations may even be discontinued over a somewhat longer period, but that leaves the annual principle intact. This typology fits the well-studied tradition of preindustrial popular festivals. We may take this tradition as our point of departure, from where we can search for parallels in earlier and later ages. A festivity, then, takes place on a specified day (or days) of the year; something special must happen (an ordinary Sunday doesn't count; most languages distinguish between Sundays and holidays); and the participants must have fun. However, there is a second type of festivity which lacks the element of annual recurrence: we also speak of the celebration of a wedding or someone's first communion. Consequently, important days for individual persons have to be taken into account, especially when we are examining preindustrial societies. Many inhabitants of a preindustrial village or neighborhood joined in the celebration of a wedding or, for example, at the occasion of the return of a member of their community whom they had considered lost. National events like the birth of a royal child or a crown prince's marriage also were celebrated locally.

Liminality and Status Reversal

Before historians turned to the study of such special days, a number of anthropologists and a few sociologists subjected them to a theoretical analysis. These scholars concentrated on the ritual elements inherent in festivities. The French ethnologist Arnold van Gennep was one of the first, in a book that originally appeared in 1909. His starting-point consisted of an inventory of rituals in situations that he defined as transitional: geographic and spatial transitions, encounters between strangers and natives, encounters between travelers, pregnancy, labors, birth, infancy, various initiations, betrothal, marriage, funeral and a residual category of various events. Hence, the celebrations among these situations were largely of the second type just identified.

Van Gennep took most of his examples from non-European societies of his day, and secondarily from past societies, especially ancient Greece. In a second book he made an inventory of French folklore. Because people felt connected to the cosmos, still according to van Gennep, transitions from one year to another, as well as between the phases of life, required some kind of ritual. In all those *rites de passage* he observed a similar sequence of three phases: *séparation* (farewell to the old situation), *marge* (a period of ambiguity) and *agrégation* (integration into the new situation). Each of these three phases had its own rituals, which he called *préliminaires*, *liminaires* and *postliminaires*, respectively.[1] Moreover, the three phases could be distinguished at various levels. Being betrothed, for example constituted a period of *marge* between adolescence and marriage, but the transition from adolescent to betrothed person in its turn involved a ritual sequence of three phases. This theory obviously refers to more than just festivities, but its application extends to celebrations of an important event in a person's life as well as to those marking the transition from one season to another.

The anthropologist Victor Turner built on van Gennep's theory.[2] For Turner, too, transitional situations were essential, but he shifted the focus to Africa. For various nations of this continent, he investigated the rituals performed during such special events as giving birth to twins or the installation of a new leader. It was the very ritual, according to Turner, that generated the participants' joy. Their surrender to the rite resulted in collective extasy, causing an intensified sense of community. When everything was over, a sober return to the normal social order followed. During the period of extasy, the participants' condition was one of "liminality": they lived neither in the old, nor in the new era. To this concept Turner connected two new elements. First, he observed that "liminal" situations often involved rituals of status reversal: men wore women's clothes or youths commanded older people. According to Turner, this phenomenon actually strengthened the established order, which appeared unshaken afterwards. The temporary elevation of baseness as well as the degradation of highness reconfirmed the principle of hierarchy. The second new element involved the extension of the notion of liminality to persons and social groups. Moments of special significance led to a temporary liminality of an entire community. Conversely, the status of some persons or groups caused them to be permanently liminal; or rather, their status was unclear, because they forever lived in a border area.

Historians took up the second element in particular. The notion of liminality appeared a perfect tool for the analysis of processes of inclusion and exclusion. According to this view, the discrimination of ethnic minorities, for example, can be explained by their liminal status: they belong neither to their country of residence nor to the country of their roots, so that they live in a kind of twilight zone. This condition makes them "contaminated." Since this aspect takes us too far away from our festive theme, I am leaving it undiscussed.

There is another reason for not dwelling too long on the notion of liminality: this concept has been buried in its own success. Liminality can be applied everywhere at any time, because nearly every social group lives in one twilight zone or another and with some imagination we can say of every person that he or she belongs neither to one group nor to the other. Hans de Waardt, for example, even though skeptical himself about this concept, yet applies it to a theme recurrent in this book: honor. An early modern man or woman who stood to gain or lose a measure of honor, De Waardt maintains, first went through a phase in which it was not exactly clear yet what his or her new status would be. During this ambivalent phase, such a person was liminal.[3] It looks like the perfect recipe: you just call the situation or the social group that you are studying liminal and you have made a discovery. But the discovery has been made too often, which has largely deprived the concept of liminality of its perceived explanatory power.

The other new element, that of status reversal, appears more promising for further theorizing and, even more importantly, it has a direct relationship with festivals. Historians have studied various types of status reversal, which often formed part of a holiday or a festive period of the year. During the Saturnalia in the Roman Empire, for example, slaves gave orders to their masters. In fifteenth-century France and Spain a child was allowed to act as bishop for one day. The festival of fools and carnival, each a manifestation of the world upside-down, were celebrated throughout preindustrial Europe. The world upside-down recurred as a motif on popular prints, showing funny images like fish in the air, pigs slaughtering the butcher or women in men's clothes.[4] Thus, festivals, merriment and the reversal of hierarchy belonged together.

This observation again leads to a theoretical question. Should we take the world upside-down literally? Was its celebration threatening for the established elites or did they purposely allow it to their subordinates as a pastime, which caused the latter to be content with their subordination afterwards? Along with Turner, many historians tend toward the second interpretation, which Peter Burke summarizes as follows: "It looks as if they [the upper classes] were aware that the society they lived in, with all its inequalities of wealth, status and power, could not survive without a safety-valve, a means for the subordinates to purge their resentments and to compensate for their frustrations."[5] Such an interpretation, Burke continues, finds support in the views of various contemporaries, who indeed described carnival and similar festivals in terms of built-up energy that occasionally needed to erupt. At the end of Mardi Gras, however, when the participants burned "Lord Carnival," they indicated that from now on the sober routine of reality reigned again. Hence, the celebration of the world upside-down meant a re-confirmation of the existing social order.

Subsequently, however, Burke calls this interpretation one-sided. He emphasizes that, although festivals often functioned as a safety-valve, a return to the established order did not always follow automatically. On the contrary, the association of festive ritual with social protest was recurrent in preindustrial Europe. Festivals sometimes got out of hand. What began as a merry procession, for example, ended as a political demonstration. Or a large-scale revolt ensued. Carnival in the North Italian town of Udine in 1511 and Mardi Gras in the Southern French town of Romans in 1580 constitute two well-documented examples of a festival ending in a blood bath.[6] When a festival assumed the character of protest, the rebels sometimes had planned this in advance. Moreover, the participants in revolts not begun as a celebration often employed festive play to make their grievances known. For France, Yves-Marie Bercé (1976) studied this phenomenon in detail.

It appears that we can take our pick. Whereas Burke closes the case in terms of on the one hand and on the other, Mikhail Bakhtin appears to stress the revolutionary potential of festive rituals like the world upside-down.[7] He labels the popular humor of the European past as "grotesque realism." This included facial grimaces and obscene gestures as well as everything connected with the body below the waist. According to Bakhtin, the "popular-festive mentality" contained a regenerative and creative force that was absent from the fossilized world view of the establishment. The motif of the world upside-down in particular was reminiscent of a primitive equality which had once been around. The festival of fools and other ritual celebrations constituted a potential danger for the social hierarchy, which the elites had no option but to tolerate. Or perhaps we should not speak of the elites. As Gabor Klaniczay points out, Bakhtin associated "official culture" not so much with the ruling class as with institutions such as the state, the church, civil service and the law. The opposite "culture of popular humor" was open to everyone, as long as they momentarily did not represent these institutions.[8] Klaniczay's interpretation of Bakhtin's theory assumes an ambivalence among festival participants with an official function. During the celebration they mocked the very institution which they upheld on routine days. This is far from strange. We find a parallel in the attitude of medieval city governors toward feuding. These patricians represented authority, but as members of influential families they often were a party to a vendetta. That situation caused them to be ambivalent in combating the feud.

We can conclude that social stratification is a crucial factor in the theoretical reflection on the world upside-down. Festivals constitute a threat to or a confirmation of the established order, or sometimes the first and sometimes the second. There is another type of theory, however, in which the celebrating crowd represents a single, undivided community. In this view, festivals belong to everyone. Their celebration strengthens the collective sense of unity, by recalling a mythical past or simply because of the strong appeal to all members of the community. In this way, festivals make a significant contribution to the survival of a social group. We find this thesis in the work of Emile Durkheim and Marcel Mauss. Durkheim considers festivals as a typical manifestation of the "mechanic solidarity" which in his view characterizes traditional societies. In addition, he stresses the religious dimension. According to Durkheim, every important religious ceremony resembles a festival, and every festival, even the most secular one, contains religious elements. In both cases the result is that individuals come together, crowds are on the move and everyone gets excited. However, Durkheim also notes that festivals often lead to excesses and the transgression of norms.[9]

The idea that festivals foster collective solidarity is equally one-sided. By de-emphasizing the existence of social inequalities, this type of theory tends to overlook conflicts and violence. Essentially, it is a functionalist theory, which explains the recurrence of festivals by attributing a useful function to them. Admittedly, a historian who studies past social phenomena may ascribe functions to them of which contemporaries were hardly aware, but some scholars view the people as totally ignorant, performing festive rituals without any knowledge of their ancient meaning. Authors writing about various pastimes with bulls in Spain, for example, have attributed a magical–religious significance to them, which they traced back to animal sacrifices in Antiquity and even further back to the drawings of bulls in Neolithic caves. The anthropologist Timothy Mitchell rightly criticizes such views: "The interpretations of the fiesta de toros that we have discussed so far share an assumption common to many folkloristic or anthropological theories: that is, they take for granted that the people involved do not really know why they do what they do."[10]

Change over Time

Mitchell's warning introduces the second part of my exploration of the festive universe. We can conclude that theories about festivals are concerned primarily with the attribution of functions and general explanations. The leading question is "Why do people celebrate?" From the participants' perspective, however, this question is largely superfluous. Mitchell's respondents did not care whether other scholars insisted that they were continuing an ancestral tradition of animal sacrifice. They just had fun. That equally applies to historical actors celebrating, whether in a recent or distant past. Only a group completely preoccupied with the struggle for survival lacks time for a party. In all other cases people occasionally celebrate, because it provides joy, because it is fantastic, because it makes life worthwhile. If we accept this simple explanation, evident to the participants themselves, we can move on to a second question: how did festivals change over time and what does the change tell us about transformations in the encompassing society?

Hypothetically, we may assume that festivals originated in the common dances performed among the earliest human groups. William McNeill writes about this custom in a book that contains speculative passages in its turn. According to McNeill, dancing as well as marching and rhythmically singing or screaming together are all typically human achievements, along with language: "... learning to move and give voice in this fashion, and the strengthened emotional bonds associated with that sort of behavior, were critical prerequisites for the emergence of humanity."[11] Language emerged c.40,000 years ago, but McNeill believes that dance preceded it. Learning and continuing to dance together reinforced mutual solidarity and enabled a better coordination of activities in a slightly longer chain of events than before. In its turn, this enhanced coordination increased the efficiency of hunting as well as the quality of child care, which made it possible for groups of over 100 humans to survive.

It is likely, then, that, during the earliest history of humanity, festivities indeed had the community-building function attributed to them by theoreticians like Durkheim. That is understandable, since the human groups involved were hardly stratified. We lack concrete details about the dance parties in question, which must have been recurrent in two types of societies: that of gatherers only, and that of female gatherers and male hunters. We know for sure that the members of these societies had plenty of time for partying, because, as discussed in chapter 9, hunting and gathering took only a part of the day. Agriculture, on the other hand, required full working days during large parts of the year. With it arose a fundamental contrast between festival and labor. Major celebrations took place during those periods of the year when the work load was modest.

The earliest documented festivals were intimately connected with the agrarian cycle. The change of the seasons, varying according to region, determined the rhythm of partying and working. For the larger part of the Eurasian continent this meant two festive periods in which holidays concentrated: in wintertime just before sowing, and in summertime when the grain was ripening but could not yet be harvested. Just a few holidays, for example to celebrate the completion of the harvest, fell outside these two periods. For communities situated to the very North, understandably, the summer cycle of holidays was more important than the winter cycle. Julio Caro Baroja (1979) notes that the alternation between partying and work implied an "order of passions." To contemporaries the rhythm of the seasons symbolized the alternation between joy and seriousness, sobriety and passion, anger and acquiescence, and more. In Eliasian terms we might say that the life of extremes, which characterized the affect economy of most individuals, was reproduced at the level of the calendar. Nevertheless, people had to achieve a certain measure of self-control by observing the alternation between holiday and labor, which was a collective and unchangeable reality. The external constraints that they exerted upon each other made this measure of self-control possible.

As also discussed in chapter 9, religions led by priests appeared at a moment in time when the process of agrarianization was already under way. Consequently, the religious dimension which Durkheim attributed to all festive rituals cannot have been inherent to the holidays of the agrarian cycle until that moment. Because priests originated as specialists in measuring time, such as determining when the day for sowing had come, it is understandable that seasonal festivals received a religious tenor. Very quickly, this happened to all aspects of life. When discussing the order of passions, Baroja notes that in Europe the Christian and the agrarian calendar came to overlap each other. However, the agrarian calendar already had acquired a religious dimension, a Roman or Germanic one, in pre-Christian times. In branding winter festivals and the like as pagan, Christian leaders actually were right.

As is well known, the new shepherds solved their problem by transforming Roman or Germanic festivals into Christian festivals, for which the large supply of biblical stories served as a base. Subsequently, the spread of the cult of saints facilitated further regional differentiation in the festive cycle. The transformation of pagan into Christian festivals was no total innovation, because the broader principle of their agrarian embeddedness implied continuity. To this principle, however, Christianity – and other world religions like Judaism and Islam – added one new element: the weekly day of rest, which I will call, with a general term, "the sabbath." That it falls on a different day of the week in each of the three religions matters little. We can consider the sabbath as an intermediate category between holiday and labor: you don't work but you spend the day in a contemplative mood without exuberance. In this way, the world religions managed to create some distance from the pre-existing festival culture after all. With the sabbath, the principle of sobriety entered upon the scene, which in due course became increasingly characteristic of religions, including Christianity, to which most of this chapter's evidence refers. This principle also led to (demands for) a less exuberant celebration of religious holidays.[12]

In view of the abundance of stories to build on, it is remarkable that not every pagan-agrarian festival was integrated smoothly into the Christian order of the year. For one thing, church leaders rejected this when they found that the exact date of a celebration depended on a pre-Christian calendar. Thus, they forbade celebrating the *idus* of a month. Carnival was the most conspicuous festival that lacked an official position on the Christian calendar, but it was unofficially tolerated in due course because of its implicit association with the subsequent period of Lent. The representation of a struggle between Carnival and Lent during the evening of Mardi Gras marked this period of toleration, especially if Lent won the fight. With the coming of the Reformation and Counter-Reformation, however, unofficial toleration soon was over again. And when carnival was revived in the Dutch province of Limburg, first in the 1930s and more fully in the 1950s, the clergy once more was not amused.

The motif of the world upside-down, it appears, was especially characteristic for the "classical" festivals in late-agrarian societies. It presupposes a measure of hierarchy and social differentiation. The Saturnalia disappeared with the Roman Empire and no enactments of the world upside-down are reported from the early middle ages. In European history, this motif returned with urbanization. Status reversal implicated the ecclesiastical hierarchy as well as city governments. The subdeacons' festival, celebrated annually in the chapters of urban cathedrals, was the oldest manifestation of the world upside-down in Europe.[13] In Egypt this motif is documented from the ninth century on, in the form of the festival of Nawruz.

Nawruz, originally a Persian spring festival, came to Egypt in the Coptic variant, in which it coincided with the flooding of the Nile beginning on September 11. The world upside-down manifested itself, among other things, in throwing eggs at high officials, who subsequently were obliged to pay a "ransom." It further included cross-dressing, masquerades and walking in the (nearly) nude. The people elected an emir of Nawruz, who wore a long fake beard and rode a donkey, collecting "debts" from various high-ranking persons. The parallel with the European festivals of fools of the twelfth through fifteenth centuries is obvious. Despite recurrent prohibitions by the authorities, the festival of Nawruz continued to be celebrated in Cairo until about 1400 and in the provinces it even survived until the beginning of the twentieth century.[14]

The success of this Egyptian celebration demonstrates that the embeddedness of festivals in the agrarian cycle was widespread geographically. Moreover, it lasted for centuries, also in Europe. As Alain Corbin notes, the French celebrated lots of political festivals in the nineteenth century, but only those taking place from May to August, in particular July 14, survived into the twentieth. The season still is the determinant factor, Corbin concludes.[15] In a de-agrarianizing world, however, it is likely that the season primarily refers to the weather rather than the agricultural work load. Quite probably, the weather also was a consideration for the Dutch Queen Beatrix when she decided that Queen's Day would continue to be on her mother's birthday (April 30) and not on her own (January 31).

During the last two centuries or so festivals underwent various changes, due to the gradual marginalization of the agrarian régime and other social developments. Within the confines of this essay these changes can be noted just briefly. The stratification of society, reflected earlier in the celebration of the world upside-down, became more complex, and processes of state-building brought various political festivities with them. These tendencies were already manifest during the Ancien Régime. Until well into the seventeenth century French citizens celebrated, each for their town, the day on which it had been liberated from the English during the Hundred Years War, but Louis XIV replaced these local celebrations by uniform national ones. The motif of status reversal lost prominence due to further social differentiation, which divided communities into more groups than just elites and the people. Instead of enacting the world upside-down, every social group held a celebration of its own. In Rome this was visible already by the end of the fifteenth century. On the Sunday preceding Ash Wednesday, the common people celebrated the Testaccio, named after a hill just outside town where it was held. The aristocracy and the higher clergy preferred the processions and tournaments at the Piazza Navona, where, in 1492, they celebrated the taking of Granada.[16]

The French Revolution marked the definitive breakthrough of political festivals. The leaders of each of the successive régimes considered them a perfect means of propaganda. Paris, as well as smaller places, was the scene of Revolutionary celebrations. There was the festival of Reason, the Supreme Being, Federation, the Republic, People's Sovereignty, Victory, Youth, Old Age, Spouses and Agriculture. The common element was their secular character. The festive calendar of the Revolution was meant to replace that of the Ancien Régime and the church, but its imagery remained quasi-religious. Thus, Paris became "the true Rome, the Vatican of Reason."[17] Slogans like these provided ammunition to Durkheim's belief that purely secular festivals also contain religious elements. The "Vendredi dit Saint," popular among French anticlericals during the period 1870–1930, was perhaps the most irreligious celebration. The participants mocked Good Friday during copious meals where all sorts of meat abounded.[18]

Despite the persistence of quasi-religious elements, the secularization of the festive universe progressed during the nineteenth and twentieth centuries. For one thing, the introduction of political and other non-religious celebrations was not matched by new saints' days, save for the somewhat unorthodox "Saint Napoléon" (August 15) during the First and Second Empire in France.[19] The importance of the agrarian-religious festive cycle further declined because of industrialization. With it, the age-old pattern of an alternation between periods of merriment and periods of labor gradually disappeared. Ever more celebrations and manifestations took place on an ordinary Sunday or in the evening after work. Commercialization reinforced this trend, which also led to a blurring of the distinction between the festival as a holiday and "ordinary" leisure time.

In the political realm national celebrations faced competition from party celebrations, the most prominent of which was the socialist First of May.[20] Next to political parties, in the recent past various social groups, such as homosexuals, have introduced festivities of their own. Thus, Amsterdam and other European cities witness an annual gay parade. We can conclude that social differentiation is accompanied by festive differentiation. Nevertheless, the celebrations of distinct social groups retain a general and public character. The organizers of the Amsterdam gay parade, for example, expect heterosexual spectators to enjoy themselves, while politicians of various persuasions show up in one of the boats. The distinction between public and private parties, in its turn, is relatively modern. In the preindustrial period nearly every celebration, even a personal one like a wedding, involved an entire community. Nowadays, weddings or birthday parties are considered private. Even if the host invites, say, 200 guests, the invitation counts as their right to join the party.

Finally, the long-term development of festivals during the last four or five centuries reflects processes of civilization in Elias' sense. "Grotesque realism" retreated. The trinity of sex, food and violence, which was so characteristic of festivals in preindustrial villages and neighborhoods, gave way to orderly merriment, often carefully programmed. Paradoxically, we find this reflected in the reintroduction of carnival during the nineteenth century. The organizers envisaged a celebration by decent citizens, who enjoyed themselves in a civilized way in predetermined localities at set times. This novelty originated in Cologne in 1823. Respectable citizens introduced a procession of carriages as an alternative to "foolishly cruising the streets," which apparently preceded it. So-called "Sitzungen" confined merriment inside localities. The people of Cologne also invented the Council of Eleven, although their number varied at first; its chair originally bore the title of Hero, later that of Prince. The most daring things to be seen or heard consisted of veiled jokes about Prussian censorship. Throughout the Rhineland, regional speech and the Catholic tradition were sources of cultural resistance to the Prussian régime.

In the second half of the nineteenth century this new-style carnival spread over the entire region, including the Dutch towns of Maastricht and Venlo.[21] In the Netherlands this festival further spread over the provinces of Limburg and Brabant, beginning in the 1930s and especially after the Second World War. Limburg even knew its "carnival ideologists," who explained to the people that they were in fact practicing age old rituals. Change between 1945 and 1995 involved a shift of focus from the local context to the formation of a regional identity. The carnival ideologists created a standard Limburg dialect which had never existed before.[22]

In this case the festive trend appears to move in a regional direction. In today's world, however, regionalization and localization are intimately connected with enlargement of scale and globalization. We find the latter process reflected in the rise of multi-cultural manifestations and festivals of migrants and minorities like the Antillian summer carnival in Rotterdam.[23] Enlargement of scale is manifest in the geographic mobility that accompanies present-day festivities. For at least three decades, crowds have flocked to Amsterdam by train on Queen's Day. Recently, this author also spotted British youths of both sexes, appropriately dressed in orange. International visitors have been present for a somewhat longer time at the celebration of the New Year, especially in and around the Nieuwmarkt. This area has seen the Chinese joining in with the Dutch for a long time, but presently Germans, Italians, the French and still others drink and watch the fireworks, usually along with this author.

9

The Body's End

Death and Paradise in Human History

Genesis, the first book of the Jewish and Christian Bible, opens with two incompatible tales of creation. Chapter 1 has God making the earth, populating it with animals and creating, on the sixth day, humans, both male and female. In chapters 2 and 3, the creator first shapes a man, then all animals and concludes on the sixth day by giving a woman to the man.[1] The second story, dating from *c.*1000 BC, is some 600 years older than the first. The tale continues with the vicissitudes of the man and the woman, named Adam and Eve, in the garden of Eden. Readers who grew up in a Christian culture will be familiar with this myth and its unhappy end. Because of their disobedience to God, Adam and Eve must leave the garden, or Paradise, forever. After their expulsion they are worse off in at least three respects: they have forfeited their immortality; they are obliged to earn a living in the sweat of their brows; the people (and the animals) no longer live in peace.[2]

The tale of Adam, Eve and Paradise forms a convenient starting-point for an essay dealing with the long-term history of humanity, in which religion, magic and death figure prominently. The essay is inspired by Johan Goudsblom's work on the history of humanity, as expounded in his book *Fire and Civilization* and his contributions to the collective volume *The Course of Human History*.[3] In particular, five of Goudsblom's sweeping theses play a role in this chapter: (1) one of the earliest collective experiences of mankind involved the very long competitive struggle with (other) animals, from which humans finally emerged as the most powerful species on earth; (2) the domestication of fire was the first important ecological transformation brought about by humans; (3) in the course of the process of agrarianization, labor pressure increased, which enabled human communities as a whole to enlarge their production;[4] (4) each ecological transformation brought new problems of living together and orientation, which in their turn led to new demands posed on the self-control of individual people; (5) the idea that religion "has always been around" is incorrect; religion emerged as a corollary of agrarianization in connection with the appearance of a caste of problem solvers who came to be called priests.

The first and last theses combined produce another, more speculative one: the custom of burying or cremating human bodies has no religious origin; it originates from the very real danger that predatory animals, having tasted human flesh, will hunt humans.[5] Here Goudsblom touches on themes, such as funerary rituals, that have long been dear to socio-cultural historians. Nevertheless, his studies covering prehistoric eras concentrate on inter-human relationships and the relations of humans with organic and inorganic nature. His excursions into the cultural sphere mainly concern the rise of religion and the belief in gods. He depicts this rise as rather abrupt. In a dual amendment, I aim to trace the belief in gods and the supernatural further back in (pre)history and to connect it with the problem of death.

The Ubiquity of Paradise

One of the privileges Adam and Eve lost concerned their ease of life. In the garden of Eden, hard work had been unnecessary. There was an abundance of nice fruits and water to quench their thirst. They could do whatever they pleased. No other creature troubled them, except the snake on that fateful day. Adam and Eve shared this easy life with the protagonists of the myths of other peoples, among whom the ancient Iranians. The word "Paradise" originates from the Hebrew *pardès*, which in its turn is a corruption of the Persian word for garden. In between Palestine and Persia, there is Mesopotamia. The Sumerian tale of Enki opens with the state of peace in Dilmun: animals did not fight each other and people knew no diseases. The epos of Gilgamesh, too, contains stories about the miraculous gardens of the gods and extremely fertile mountains. In India the holy books, as well as the Mahâbhârata epos, praise the golden mountain of Meru, from where four rivers irrigate Elysian fields. The notion of a primordial Golden Age, associated with Saturn or another deity, was widespread in the Greco-Roman world. According to Hesiod, the people of that wonderful era lived like gods: they feasted, remained forever young, and when they died, nevertheless, it was like falling asleep; each year the harvest was abundant.[6] Already in the late nineteenth century, the Italian literary historian Arturo Graf made a comparative study of paradisiacal myths from the Middle East to China and Hawaii, and exactly 100 years later Jean Delumeau stated that, until the formulation of the theory of evolution, the people of many civilizations believed in a primordial paradise, where peace, happiness and abundance reigned and humans and animals lived harmoniously together.[7]

To conclude, the myth of a blissful initial era is a constitutive element within various religious traditions. If we accept Goudsblom's thesis that religions led by priests emerged during the process of agrarianization, it follows that a link between agrarianization and Paradise becomes likely as well. Productivity is the key. Although production (per human community) increased in the course of the process of agrarianization, productivity (per man-hour) decreased. The production of a community could increase because of a new element: labor. It remains to be investigated when exactly hard labor became a necessity. Goudsblom speaks both more generally, of the transition from a society of gatherers and hunters to an agrarian society, and more specifically, for regions where this applies, of the transition from slash-and-burn agriculture to sedentary farming. With slashing and burning, in the words of Esther Boserup, "the fire did most of the work."[8] In any case, the productivity of hunting and gathering was relatively high too. As a result, peasants had to work harder than their ancestors had done.

The link is evident: the myth of Paradise represents the collective memory of the time when everyone had less work to do.[9] The words "the sweat of the brow" from Genesis say it almost literally. Conversely, later Christians drew an analogy between the garden of Eden and life in primitive societies. Both Columbus and Vespucci, for example, believed that their voyages had brought them near Paradise. Vespucci described the coasts of Suriname and Brazil as a happy country with tall trees keeping their leaves, the singing of all kind of birds, lovely scents of flowers and plants, delicious fruits and healthy herbs; the people, moreover, lived to be no less than 130 years.[10] The link between the myth of Paradise and agrarianization on the one hand and the fact that many religions know such a myth on the other, firmly support Goudsblom's thesis that organized religion emerged during the process of agrarianization. I will come back to less organized religion below.

In addition to an absence of labor, most stories of Paradise assume a state of peace. Perhaps the myth of a Golden Age also represents collective memory of a world without warriors, but something else is relevant here. Peace also meant relaxed animals. In the Christian tradition, the wildness of animals was due to the Fall of Man. Significantly, wildness referred foremost to the behavior of animals amongst each other. A major continuity before and after the Fall lay in human primacy over animals. Directly after creation, God had made humans the masters of all other creatures, and in Paradise Adam had given all species their names. When animals became wild and men started to wage wars, human–animal relations remained on the same footing. Although the Bible sometimes refers to man as the brother of animals, he is more often designated as lord over them. This attitude remained characteristic for Christian thought well into the seventeenth century.[11]

Scholars as well as popular authors often stress the exceptionality of the Christian view of a hierarchical relationship between humans and animals. In many other cultures and their corresponding religions, this relationship is rather one of symbiosis, in which humans have to respect other species. In Buddhist thought, humans, animals and plants all form part of a continuing cycle of reincarnations. In the legend of Nigrodha it is the Bodhisattva himself who assumes the shape of a gazelle in order to negotiate immunity for all animals in the park of the prince of Benares. The Bodhisattva succeeds, albeit after the prince, for a time, has drawn lots each year to pick out one gazelle for his cook.[12] Note that, although kindness to animals is the outcome of the story, it starts with the prince's mastership. A similar ambiguity is inherent to the keeping of pets, in particular dogs, by gatherers and hunters some 13,000 years ago. According to James Serpell, this habit paved the way toward the rise of cattle-breeding.[13] In recent societies where gathering and hunting still play a role, respect for animals is said to be the norm also. In the view of American Indians as well as Australian Aboriginals, all living creatures belong to mother nature.[14]

However, whether the prevalent beliefs in a culture or religion consider man as the master of animals or as an equal in the chain of being, no story depicts humans and other species as competitors. That is the basic similarity between the views of human–animal relations in all religions and their paradisiacal myths. Every form of competition is totally foreign to Paradise. The widely shared view of original peace and harmony among all creatures is totally at odds with the actual earliest history of mankind. As mentioned above, for more than 100,000 years humans and other large mammals were each other's rivals. Eventually, humans "won" this struggle, emerging as the most powerful species on earth. For the people who composed stories of Paradise, this power of humans was a fact of nature that prompted no reflection. The very long episode of a competitive struggle for "ecological power" had simply faded from memory. It left no traces in the myths of religions led by priests. This is in line with William McNeill's conclusion that, already in Paleolithic times, man was the chief predator.[15] All this lends further support to the thesis that the rise of religions was a relatively recent phenomenon in humanity's overall history – that is, as far as organized religion led by priests is concerned.

The story becomes a little more complicated when we turn to a third privilege forfeited by Adam and Eve. For their disobedience God imposed a stern penalty: mortality. This motif introduces the problem of death, largely ignored by Goudsblom. This lack of attention is remarkable in view of the central role of the rise of religions for his argument. Many scholars and philosophers consider the neutralization of the fear of death as one of the essential functions of religion. Elias formulates it like this: time and again people have believed that the observation of certain rituals guaranteed them eternal life, and almost as often this caused them to bloodily persecute those who sought another way to salvation.[16] The intimate link between religious faith and the promise of eternal life raises the question of whether or not pre-religious people calmly accepted the prospect of their own demise.[17] Or perhaps the story of the rise of religious faiths is more complicated, after all, than that of the sociogenesis of a caste of priests in agrarianizing societies.

In Goudsblom's scenario, the origin of the notion of a god appears as a very sudden and contingent event. Priests predate the belief in gods; they are experts in the timing of agriculture and the handling of its products. In order to teach the community not to consume every slaughtered animal immediately, they punish transgressions by publicly destroying the meat. One day, when a priest directs a ceremony in which he ritually burns the meat for this reason, some of the spectators have second thoughts. A rebellious person among them cries out "For whom, then, is this costly food?" The clever priest invents a destination on the spot: "For a supreme being." In this way the ritual destruction becomes a sacrifice and the belief in gods emerges. This is a slightly popularized rendering of Goudsblom's exposition, but the abruptness is his.[18] Could it be possible, however, that religious beliefs, if only notions about the supernatural, predated the appearance of priests? And, if so, would these notions about the supernatural have something to do with the problem of death? In a parallel argument, Goudsblom does maintain that wars predated the appearance of a caste of warriors, although he rejects the idea that wars have always been waged.[19]

We might give a negative answer to the two questions just raised. In that case, Adam and Eve's immortality represented the collective memory of a pre-religious age in which people were unafraid to die. Similar themes are present in related myths. The protagonist and a second hero of the Gilgamesh epos, for example, almost manage to steal immortality from the gods.[20] In Chinese stories of Paradise, it contains the yellow source of immortality.[21] Yet it is unlikely that such themes originated from the recollection of an era in which people were unaware of the problem of death. On the contrary, for immortality to become imaginable as an ideal, you first need to be aware that you will die. It is more likely that we must interpret the theme of immortality in Paradise simply as one of the elements contributing to the state of bliss reigning in this holy garden. This suggests a positive answer to the two questions raised above: even before agrarianization set in, people entertained beliefs about the supernatural, and death played a prominent role in these beliefs.

As noted several times, Goudsblom usually defines organized religion as cults led by priests. This leaves open the possibility of pre-existing unorganized, or at least less-organized, cults. Fred Spier, another scholar examining the very long term, unquestioningly assumes the presence of religion in societies of gatherers and hunters. He uses the concept of religious specialist as a general term for, among others, priests, monks, wizards and fortune tellers.[22] The word "wizard" is remarkable; historians would associate it with magic rather than religion. The analytical distinction between magic and religion has haunted scholars for generations.[23] Today, few people will posit a neat succession from a magical phase to a religious phase in the history of humanity. In fact the two coexisted for a long time, but coexistence still implies distinction. That distinction is rooted in real long-term developments. According to Max Weber, the rise of world religions with a systematic doctrine formed part of the process of rationalization. Before this process set in, people's image of the universe resembled a "magic garden." Subsequently, theologians and church leaders combated a number of magical beliefs and customs.[24] I am using magic and religion as sensitizing concepts: magic belongs for the larger part to the field of concrete objectives in life, for which cleverness is more important than veneration; religion has to do first of all with the veneration of a supernatural being and the concomitant moral rules. This definition implies a gradual rather than an absolute distinction: magic and religion often mingle with each other.

Magic and Death

When considering past societies lacking a caste of priests, we should imagine the prevalent view of life and the cosmos as influenced by magic and unorganized, or local, religion. Long before people cultivated crops and kept cattle, death was a problem for them and magical specialists were there to neutralize it. One historian, perhaps more than others, has attempted to unravel the riddle of death in human culture: Carlo Ginzburg.

Ginzburg first encountered the subject in his study of the so-called *Benandanti*, people in sixteenth-century Friuli who were convinced they were waging a nightly battle against sorcerers. Female *Benan-*

danti claimed to possess the gift of communicating between the living and the dead.[25] Ginzburg's most encompassing study of the subject is *Storia notturna*, better-known under the English title of *Ecstasies* (1990). Nominally, this book tries to uncover the origins of the idea of the witches' sabbath, but death is the motif lurking in the background.[26] Ginzburg has his own peculiar method. His aim is to trace popular beliefs as far back as possible, but before the fourteenth century the historical documentation lets him down. To compensate for this, Ginzburg performs a morphological analysis, as he calls it. Step by step he looks for elements in myths, fairy tales and rituals that resemble each other. Beginning in European regions where he expects to find remnants of Celtic culture, Ginzburg takes the reader to ever more remote parts of the Eurasian continent. Along the way we hear about the wild horde of those who died prematurely, shamans in trance, fairy tales about lost shoes and stories of children raised by wolves. It is a fascinating tour of discovery, with just one conclusion though. Ultimately, Ginzburg maintains, all myths can be traced back to the mother-story of a voyage to the world of the dead.

Ginzburg's morphological method leaves little room for a developmental approach. His method is based on the following principle: if A has ever been referred to together with B and B with C and C with D, then we can safely throw A, B, C and D in the melting-pot of explanations. This method differs from the approach to human history advocated here, in which the continually changing versions of popular beliefs, stories, myths and rituals – and the patterns to be found in those changes – would be more interesting than the common original source which they possibly share. Nevertheless, the impressive mass of data collected by Ginzburg is convincing. We cannot get around the conclusion that death plays a central role in the myths and magical beliefs of many societies – and probably for a few hundred generations. This does not mean that humans have had an "animistic" awareness from the earliest phase in their history. The position of animals in the magical universe is suggestive. Like other scholars, Ginzburg pays ample attention to the folklore of metamorphoses, masquerades, werewolves and beasts with human traits. Such stories reflect a world in which people live near the animals, but there is no indication whatsoever that these stories contain reminiscences of the competitive struggle between humans and other species that roughly coincided with the domestication of fire. This suggests that, as with organized religion, a magical or animistic view of the world has not always been around.

To conclude, the problem of death is a central element in the mythical tales and the magical world view of many peoples. At the same time, the awareness of one's mortality constitutes an essential difference between humans and all other animals. That is a static pronouncement, but it can be made dynamic within a sociogenetic approach.

That only humans are aware that they themselves will die is a truism. Nevertheless, few scholars, as far as I know, have drawn the inescapable conclusion for human history: once this awareness must have dawned for the first time! William McNeill comes close with his remark that when humans had acquired language, they learned to see death approaching.[27] It is unclear whether this remark refers to an individual awareness of one's own inevitable demise. Whether this is the case or not, it is my thesis that, in the earliest phase of human history, no one realized that, just like other living creatures around, he himself or she herself would die. It is difficult to determine when exactly people began to realize this, but the problem can be formulated in terms of Goudsblom's "there-was-a-time" propositions. He developed this conceptual tool as a means to overcome the objections to traditional stage theories. Each transformation in human history, he argues, can be represented in the form of a sequence of there-was-a-time's. Subsequently, the when, where, how and why can be established in principle.[28] For death, it goes like this: (1) there was a time when there were only groups who were unaware of their own mortality; (2) then there was a time when there were both groups with and ones without an awareness of their own mortality; (3) we have now reached a time in which all people, except those robbed of their senses, know that they will die.

The second of these periods raises several questions. How did the awareness of one's mortality spread over humanity as a whole? One option is to view this spread as an inevitable process. As soon as one group knew it, it was impossible again not to know it, even though people would have liked to forget it. One group passed on the horrible news to the other, until everyone on earth was aware of their own mortality. Alternatively, we may view the spread of the news as analogous to that of the control over fire. This control provided certain advantages for survival, which in the long run caused the groups possessing fire to supersede the have-nots.[29] In a similar vein, groups who knew they would die may have superseded those who did not. A possible advantage of the awareness of mortality lies in greater carefulness in the face of danger. In other words, the advantage had to do with the flight/fight reaction, which humans share with animals. Elias refers to this reaction in his essay on emotions.[30] Only among humans, he says, have learned ways become dominant over unlearned ways in their emotional behavior. The emotional component of the flight/fight reaction, called fear and anger respectively, is not expressed according to a genetically determined pattern; it has undergone changes in the course of human history. It is highly probable that an awareness of mortality raised a person's chances of choosing the most adequate reaction in the face of various types of danger. Hence, this awareness had survival value.

As discussed in chapter 8, dancing and celebrating are ancient customs, carried over from groups of gatherers and hunters to agrarian villages. Festivals contributed to the mutual solidarity within communities. Solidarity operates for better or for worse. When a group acquired knowledge of individual mortality, this is likely to have soon become a collective problem. We may suppose that the historically oldest form of neutralizing death consisted of comforting oneself with the thought that one's own troupe or tribe, the collectivity, lives on.[31] This assumption is implicit in Ginzburg's work. The problem of death, he argues, was central to the magical universe, which established a link between individual well-being and the survival of the collectivity. We may add that in this phase of human history people were conscious of the fact that the survival of one's community depended on successful procreation and the availability of food. It is no coincidence that fertility – of the women and the fields – also is a central theme in magical views of the world. A permanent fertility, which people hoped to conjure up with magic rituals, would guarantee collective immortality. With the word "field," moreover, we have arrived in agrarianizing societies, in which organized religion emerged.

Historically, the belief in gods constitutes the second form of neutralizing death. Compared to the idea of the survival of the collectivity, this involves a much more individual solution: every single person may achieve a kind of immortality because there is life after death. Although these two forms of neutralization differ markedly, they are not incompatible. Their coexistence, however, may well have led to tensions between specialists in the "old" type and the "new" type of neutralization: those who knew the way to the world of the dead of their community vs. mediators between people and the gods. From such tensions, the Weberian process whereby religions gradually pushed back magic – in spite of mutual interpenetration – must have originated. At its root lay competition with respect to the neutralization of death. In this competition, specialists in mediation between people and gods eventually acquired an advantage because of their greater reach. Religious doctrines promised an afterlife to an essentially unlimited group of individuals, instead of the earthly survival of one community. This open character was a precondition for the rise of universal faiths, which gradually superseded cults tied to one tribe or nation. It is also understandable that these universal faiths tended toward monotheism. The moral appeal to an unlimited set of believers was far more persuasive when made in the name of one God than with an eye on a pantheon of (tribal) gods.

The Origins of Organized Religion Revisited

Up to now I have identified two different roots of the belief in a deity: the "second neutralization" of the problem of death and, as argued by Goudsblom, the justification of the priestly regulation of cattle slaughtering. These two can be reconciled by introducing a nuance in my rough sketch of the process in question. Once more, this involves a hypothesis which can be tested empirically: when priests and organized cults had just appeared on the scene, the eternal life of the faithful was hardly their business. Primarily, they were specialists in disciplining and providing orientation. According to Goudsblom, peasants eventually learned to solve the problems of sowing, harvesting and storing food themselves. He says little about the consequences for the role of priests, just embracing Max Weber's thesis that priests acquired new functions in the realm of individual salvation. The term "individual salvation" is a little ambiguous and sounds too much like the theological reasoning which Goudsblom rejects.[32] In a sociological-historical terminology, we should say: priests became the experts pointing out to the faithful the road to the hoped-for eternal life. My hypothesis implies that priests usurped this function, because before them the neutralization of death had been a task for magical specialists only, or any "lay" person who knew the correct rituals. Within the Christian tradition, the story of the three magicians coming to pay homage to baby Jesus symbolizes this usurpation by priests.

This argument constitutes a specification of my thesis. The roots of the problematic relationship between magical and religious specialists lay, not only in mere competition with respect to the neutralization of death, but also in the latter's usurpation of this role.[33] For a long time, however, the inherent structural conflict remained submerged. As a further hypothesis, we may suppose that the rise of "salvationary faiths" first resulted in a relative division of tasks: magical specialists were occupied primarily with problems of material survival in the present (fertility and averting disasters); religious specialists were occupied primarily with the problem of conquering death (the expectation of an afterlife).[34] This original division of tasks caused the conflict between religion and magic not to erupt seriously until a later phase in the development of world religions.

There may be another reason for this delay. In many older faiths, access to heaven was the privilege of a minority, in particular warriors and, of course, the priests themselves. This applies, among others, to the Germanic peoples with their notion of the Walhalla.[35] When exclusiveness is the dominant belief, priests' knowledge of the right road to heaven is of limited applicability. Salvationary faiths, by contrast, offered them new chances. Heaven became accessible for all believers, no matter what their rank. Obviously, this new emphasis on the survival of individual souls implied a measure of democratization, but it also became harder to reach heaven. The faithful had to live a good life or, in some cases, to be slain in a holy war. Priests, of course, determined the criteria for a good life.[36] Once more, the myth of Paradise contains a suggestive metaphor: Adam and Eve were forbidden to eat from the tree of the knowledge of good and evil because, if they did, they would become God's equals. Priests knew the difference between good and evil; they were "a little equal to God." They provided orientation on how to reach heaven and disciplined the unwilling. Christians often designated the "democratized" heaven as a new Paradise; within Christian thought, the garden of Eden had been transferred from the beginning to the end of time.[37]

As alleged mediators between humans and god(s), priests acquired a new source of power.[38] It is understandable that, as long as the idea prevailed that heaven is only for warriors and a few other fortunate people, priests worried less about the activities of magicians and the specialists of local religion. They provided orientation mostly to peasants, unfit for heaven. It was the universal claims of the world religions that exacerbated the tensions between priests and locally based specialists. The conflict between them raged most intensely within Latin Christianity, especially from the Reformation and the Counter-Reformation onwards.[39]

The conflict between priests and magical specialists continues in many parts of the world until today. When the author of this book visited the Jade Buddha Temple in Shanghai in the summer of 2011, there was a sign on the outer wall prohibiting all kind of "superstitious" practices, including traditional Chinese divination, inside. On the other hand, secularization and the concomitant decline of the belief in an afterlife have made the role of specialists redundant for many people. They have to find other strategies, if they want to acquiesce in the inevitability of their own physical demise. Writers of the Enlightenment and the French Revolution were the first to formulate the idea that the prospect of admiration by future generations constituted an alternative for the expectation of a life after death. Philosophers, in particular, through the products of their intellectual labor, would earn the admiration of those coming after them. As a parallel to Max Weber's analysis of asceticism, this idea has been termed *innerweltliche Unsterblichkeit* (inner-worldly immortality), in contrast to the *ausserweltliche Unsterblichkeit* (other-worldly immortality) of the belief in an afterlife.[40] Consequently, we may ask whether the workaholic attitude of many modern scholars is actually a sublimation of ancient magical and religious conjurations.

Epilogue

A Personal Recollection of Norbert Elias and How I Became a Crime Historian

My reminiscence of Norbert Elias is inextricably wound up with my own intellectual history. These are two sides of one coin and an attempt to separate them would be futile. Human memory, I realize, is selective and biased, but the events must have occurred more or less as depicted here. I remember Norbert most intensely from a period beginning in 1969 until about the mid-1970s, when I was a history student in Amsterdam and he frequently lectured at the university there. In particular, I recall his first Amsterdam seminar. More than anything else, Norbert was the teacher who had a decisive influence on my scholarly development. In those years he definitely was Professor Elias to me. Later, however, when he lived in Bielefeld, we corresponded a couple of times, calling each other by our first names. So, I will refer to him as just Norbert.

Related to this, a minor misunderstanding occurred the very first time that I encountered his name in writing. At the end of the 1960s teacher–student relations at Dutch universities still were rather formal. Often, you did not even know your teacher's first name. In his publications, as a rule, only his initials were indicated, often with "Dr." or "Drs." preceding (we were instructed, however, to omit academic or noble titles from our bibliographies). The implicit idea was that, once a student had seen his teacher's first name in writing, the next day he would pat him on the shoulder and say something like "Hey, old boy, let's get a beer." The curriculum guide in particular would always list academic title, initials, last name. When I noticed a "Professor Norbert Elias" in the curriculum guide for the academic year 1969–70, I thought that this professor, unknown to me, had a double-barreled name.

By coincidence, I soon discovered I was wrong. As well as my major subject, modern history, I had to take two minors, and I had opted for sociology and social psychology. A few days later, I had an appointment with the psychology professor, Duijker, who was happily surprised that a history student had interest in his discipline. He said he knew an interesting book, which he found too exotic for his own students, but which I, as a historian, was allowed to read, along with others, for the exam. It was *Über den Prozess der Zivilisation* by Elias. Since the history guide had also recommended the book, I recognized its title and, somewhat puzzled, I asked "Do you mean Norbert Elias?" Finally, I realized that the mysterious visiting professor's last name was just Elias. Maybe the history staff had thought him to be too famous to be patted on the shoulder. Teacher–student relations soon changed when the department hired younger staff members who had been fellow students of mine.

The old university curriculum comprised two principal stages, respectively ending with the *kandidaats* and the *doctoraal* exam. Officially both stages lasted three years, but it was common and acceptable to spend four on the first. Students who could reasonably be expected to pass their *kandidaats* exam before Christmas of their fourth year were entitled to start with *doctoraal* classes in September. I was one of them. It was a year of transition. Presser, the highly popular professor of modern history, had retired that summer. No new professor had been appointed yet and the available funds were used to have Norbert come over to give a course. A choice was offered – perhaps because it was considered unwise to list only an English-language course – between Norbert and one of the regular staff members. I do not recall the exact title by which Norbert's seminar was announced, but it must have been suggestive of the major issues which had prompted me to study history in the first place. Besides, I did not get along well with the teacher who gave the alternative course. Sometimes things are as simple as that.

There was this short man, who indeed looked like the person I would have expected when thinking of an intellectual whose formative years lay before the war. His lectures were lively and clear. It was not uncommon at that time to hear an occasional (optional) lecture in English, or even another foreign language. We were expected to read text-books in Dutch, English, German or French, with only the teacher's judgment about the quality of the content determining which one. Once, Norbert announced that he was going to quote Leopold von Ranke, adding "if you allow me to read a quotation from Ranke to you in German." I was surprised. None of our regular teachers would have found it necessary to give such a warning or ask for permission. Now I am aware that every guest lecturer apologizes for his ignorance of the local customs; I have often done so myself. At the time, it struck me as an especially polite remark.

Of course, my primary interest was in the seminar's content. It was dealing with major issues, indeed. One of Norbert's first questions was "When historians say they are writing history, whose history is it that they write?" He found one student's answer "of mankind" not quite satisfying. "No one writes the history of a dog," he continued, which provoked some debate about whether this might be an interesting endeavor after all. The right answer turned out to be "of societies." Whether historians were conscious of it or not, they were always, in fact, dealing with human societies. Later, when I read the introduction to *Die höfische Gesellschaft* (1969), I realized that the seminar's hidden agenda had been to keep track of its argument.

Well-taken as that argument was, I have never accepted the implicit idea that all historians are traditional craftsmen, eschewing a broader view. Neither did most of the participants in the seminar agree, but whenever someone made a remark to that effect, Norbert replied: "Don't confuse what ought to be with what is." The matter remained undecided, since neither of the parties had made a quantitative analysis of, say, all major historical journals over the past five years. According to Norbert, each historian arbitrarily chose a frame of reference for his book or article. It might be his political beliefs, a personal preoccupation or yet another source. Much was to gain, he continued, if historians would henceforth take the social structure prevailing in the period about which they were writing as their frame of reference. (The word "figuration" came up only once; I am quite sure that he spoke of "social structure.") Meanwhile, I was trying to get to grips with this concept. According to my thoughts at the time, to refer to "the social structure" was just as arbitrary, because who was to determine the criteria for establishing what the social structure was? And wouldn't there be different criteria for different periods? I wanted to make this point in one of Norbert's classes. I had prepared it carefully, since it included a summary of his argument, as I grasped it, so far. Maybe because of my lengthy introduction, the final point got lost for Norbert, who just replied "Thank you for summarizing what we have discussed up to now."

No one failed to see how different Norbert's approach to history was from that of the retired professor. Although politically radical, as a historian Presser was the traditional type. A year earlier, he had rejected a paper proposal of mine. I had wanted to follow up on a remark by a high school teacher that Rousseau was the first to define puberty, saying it lasted six months, while modern psychologists define it as a period of several years. To Presser, this was venturing into another discipline, which would inevitably lead to grossly and uncontrollably false statements. At the time I did not yet know Ariès' book on childhood, and maybe Presser was unfamiliar with it too. Such books were not put on reading lists at the Historical Institute in Amsterdam in the late 1960s. Yet the institute had known a short-lived tradition of experimentation with a theoretical and interdisciplinary approach. That tradition had started with Jan Romein (another member of the minority group who often had their first name listed) and it was kept alive more or less by M. C. Brands. The latter had invited Norbert to be a visiting professor. Romein's introductory essay on "theoretical history" was the crucial publication. In it, Romein had advocated an "integral historiography" and mentioned *Über den Prozess der Zivilisation* (1939) as one of its few specimens.

Half-way through Norbert's Fall 1969 seminar I started reading his book on the civilizing process. Although I cannot have grasped its full theoretical significance right away, I found it fascinating. I told Norbert so, adding that I read it as the work of a historian – a good historian. He just smiled. Now I realize that his insistence on being called a sociologist was a tactical ploy. If he failed to be identified as one of them, no sociologist would ever adopt his approach. Historians, on the other hand, would be influenced by him, no matter how he was labeled. In his seminar Norbert loved to admit: "As far as history is concerned, I am completely an autodidact." When he said that, his eyes always twinkled.

The late 1960s and early 1970s are memorable for more things than just Norbert coming to Amsterdam. It was a period of political ferment: the student movement aimed to overthrow the hierarchical structure of the universities and, within and outside academia, many people had high hopes for a better world. Rock music, including the "protest songs" of singers like Bob Dylan, was central to the flourishing youth culture. In those years, I tended to draw a sharp line between my involvement in the youth culture and my academic activities; between my personal life and my life as a beginning scholar. In the latter case – to mention a crucial distinction – I found it self-evident that I needed to take lessons from people belonging to an older generation, whereas in the former case I felt autonomous. The line threatened to get blurred when a lecture by Norbert on the youth culture was announced. Of course I was curious what he had to say, but I was afraid that someone whom I admired as a scholar, might denounce persons or events I cherished for other reasons.

As it turned out, the lecture was a little flat. Norbert had no provocative statements about the youth culture, only some critical remarks. Among other things, he commented on the posters hanging all over Amsterdam which had to do with John Lennon and Yoko Ono; perhaps they were to promote their single.[1] Anyway, they said, "War is over, if you want it." Norbert stressed that an anti-war sentiment expressed only on one side (of the Iron Curtain) was ineffectual. People in, say, Czechoslovakia had to organize demonstrations or other such activities as well. I explained to him that, as a pacifist, I refused to wait for them to act: "I am demonstrating here, where I live, and I can only hope that they do the same over there." Norbert did not seem entirely satisfied with the answer, but he left it at that.

While Marxism, as an academic paradigm, became ever more prominent among students and young teachers, in the world of political activism it faced strong competition from other currents. The Dutch Provo tradition represented a more playful kind of leftism, intimately connected to the youth culture. In the spring of 1970, the Kabouter movement emerged, an offshoot of Provo. For a time, Amsterdam and the whole country seemed to buzz with creative excitement. For me, this culminated in a nationwide meeting of the movement in the summer of 1970. Enthusiasm was high. We really felt we could change the world, that a Europe-wide revolutionary but peaceful movement could gain strength in the near future. Soon, however, the enthusiasm and the movement faded away. This sequence of events made it quite clear to me that change seldom comes overnight. At that point I realized that it was necessary first to acquire more knowledge about how society worked. That, of course, was Norbert's approach.

Meanwhile, the Historical Institute had hired a "house sociologist," which the students who opposed the traditional curriculum had demanded. In her classes Norbert showed up at times. A group of students emerged who had a special interest in his work and agreed with its basic tenets. It was a mixed group, in which Cas Wouters was the most outspoken of the sociologists, and I of the historians. Occasionally, we would continue a discussion with Norbert at some place over a beer or another drink. I remember us sitting outside at Hoppe's: an old man and four or five long-haired youths. It struck me as an unusual event at the time, but to Norbert it seemed quite natural. Later I realized that he had already been accustomed to such informal gatherings in his Frankfurt years. In Amsterdam Norbert gradually became well known. Suddenly, one of the editors of *Propria Cures*, a student paper which was progressive but critical of the Marxist current in the student movement, wrote an article about him. The issue was passed around in the Historical Institute's coffee room. Norbert's appearance in the student paper, even though the article – entitled "the new prophet" – had a skeptical tone, in a sense elevated him to greater notoriety: he was someone worth commenting on, not just another academic. Incidentally, the author of this skeptical piece later became an established scholar identified with the Eliasian approach.

During the following years, Norbert kept coming back to the Historical Institute for occasional lectures. I recall the atmosphere of those years especially from the lectures I was not able to attend. The discussion went on anyway; information was always exchanged. When I was absent, my fellow student, Mark van Galen Last, would be present and vice versa. In our minds, the Eliasian approach was developing into a discipline by itself, transcending history and sociology. When I graduated in March 1973, Mark commented that I had now taken Cas Wouters' place as the youngest "Elias-*doctorandus*."

About two years earlier, I had told Norbert that I wanted to work further on his theory of civilization. He had chided me then: "I am against further work on a theory which still needs to be tested." My master's thesis on the process of civilization in the Netherlands, I believe, counts as a test. It was Norbert himself who thought of some further implications. He suggested that the Dutch urban patriciate during the revolt could be considered as a *Zweifrontenschicht*. I am still in the possession of an unfinished drawing with which he had wanted to represent the situation of a *Zweifrontenschicht* schematically. Eventually, I became a historian of crime and punishment, more or less by coincidence. It turned out to be a rewarding subject, offering the opportunity to expand creatively on Norbert's work. This also meant that I largely went my own way. I discussed the subject thoroughly with Norbert once, when I had completed the first draft of my dissertation. He was staying in an apartment at the Royal Institute for the Tropics and I lived in the area then, so I picked him up from there. Walking to my home, I had to try very hard to slow down and match my steps with his.

In retrospect, it is hard to tell what exactly was Norbert's influence upon my becoming a historian of crime and punishment. As far as I recall, this particular subject never came up in our discussions during my student years. *Über den Prozess der Zivilisation* contains just a brief passage about medieval knights dining while servants are disciplined physically. One chapter, of course, is devoted to changes in people's propensity for violence and aggression. Violence was the overall theme when I made my first plans for a dissertation and it was my supervisor who suggested bringing this theme down to manageable proportions by concentrating on physical judicial sanctions. You did not have to be a specialist to know that brandings and public hangings were once common and accepted and not so today. Obviously, this could be analyzed in terms of civilizing processes. There turned out to be lots of books about executions and torture in the past, but they were all purely descriptive, or, worse, written from a perspective of applauding human progress. Foucault's book on the subject did not appear until a few years later. It was a challenge, then, to write about changes in punishment in the idiom of historical sociology.

Indirectly, Norbert's influence on my work in this field has been considerable. Listening to his lectures, I first learned what it meant to have an open, inquiring attitude, even in matters relating to life and death. He insisted that historical developments are complex and that they cannot be captured in a tale of losses or gains for some political goal. To the opponents of his idea that the Nazi régime contributed to "functional democratization," he replied that they thought the Nazis were bad and democracy was good and so the two cannot have been connected. He also emphasized that any persons at any time who had a "civilized" habitus had no reason to take pride in it as if it were their personal accomplishment. Such insights are helpful, too, when it comes to the study of physical punishment. Self-congratulatory remarks, about having done away with former cruelties, abound, especially in nineteenth-century literature. You have to see through them and realize that these remarks are themselves part of an unplanned, longer-term process. Even today, such an approach is still not quite understood by certain scholars. They cannot get loose from the idea that the historical study of executions, torture or murder must involve assigning praise or blame to individual people. Without claiming that I have reached complete detachment, I am sure that Norbert's open attitude has been of much help.

A notorious episode of misunderstanding Norbert's work occurred in 1982. The second volume of *The Civilizing Process* had finally appeared in English and the historian Geoffrey Barraclough reviewed it in the *New York Review of Books*. Dutch critics of Elias' work, among others, were content with what they considered a devastating attack. The review called for a corrective reaction and I wanted to seize the opportunity, but eventually the editors decided to publish just one reaction they had received. This was unfortunate, because the published letter came from a sociologist and Barraclough had claimed with some emphasis that Elias' work was of no use to historians. In my letter I had pointed out, after clarifying several misunderstandings, that socio-cultural historians like Peter Burke and Robert Muchembled referred to Elias' work. I had concluded with expressing my indignation at Barraclough's suggestion that in 1939 a man whose mother was to perish in Auschwitz expressed a longing for a Nazi world empire.[2]

In the mid-1980s I visited Norbert when he was in a hospital in Rotterdam, my university's town, for an eye operation. It was a memorable visit again. A nurse directed me to his room, where I found him talking over the phone to someone he called Renate (Rubinstein, no doubt). Since he had not noticed me coming in, I waited in the window. When he had finished his conversation, I walked toward him, but because of his bad sight only at the last moment did he see a large figure coming toward him. He learned it was no foe and we had a long discussion about state formation in Africa. Except for briefly congratulating him on his ninetieth birthday in 1987, this turned out to be the last time I saw Norbert.

Notes

I would like to thank Jonathan Skerrett, editor at Polity, and Leigh Mueller, copy-editor, for their assistance.

Introduction: Violence and Punishment within Civilizing Processes

This introduction incorporates a section from the introduction to Pieter Spierenburg (ed.), *Men and violence: gender, honor and rituals in modern Europe and America*. Columbus OH (Ohio State University Press) 1998. Copyright by Ohio State University Press; used with permission. It also incorporates a section that originally belonged to chapter 1 in this volume (see credits there).

1 For a more elaborate justification of this definition, see my contribution to Body-Gendrot and Spierenburg 2008.

2 Major studies include: Bourdieu 1972; Bennassar 1975 (esp. 167–84); Wyatt-Brown 1982; Peristiany and Pitt-Rivers 1992; Muir 1993; Dinges 1994; Schreiner and Schwerhoff 1995; Barton 2001; Blok 2001.

3 This tripartite scheme, in various wordings, is recurrent in the literature on honor. See, however, Stewart 1994, who argues that honor must be viewed primarily as a right.

4 Thoden van Velzen 1982. He calls the maroons "Djuka," which today is considered a pejorative term.

5 Stewart 1994 (esp. p. 142). The word "contemporary" is essential, since Stewart presents no historical data for the Bedouins, as he does for Europe.

6 Blok 2001: 173–209. See also Bourdieu 1980, esp. the chapter "La croyance et le corps" (111–34).

7 Law cited in Salisbury 1994: 40–1. The law was probably never put into practice, but the idea matters.

8 Quoted in Schick 1999: 135 (here with grammatical correction).

9 Kalof and Bynum 2010. Earlier publications that offer a long-term perspective on the history of the body include Feher et al. 1989 and Culianu 1991.

10 Bynum 1987, 1991, 1995; Camporesi 1988; Cadden 1993; and, though less with reference to gender, Pouchelle 1983.

11 "Medieval" mainly stands for the period from about 1100 to around 1500. In fact, the ambiguity about sex and gender may have arisen with the increased emphasis on clerical celibacy in the early twelfth century. Cf. McNamara's contribution to Lees 1994.

12 Cadden 1993: 201–2.

13 Bynum 1991: 102–14.

14 Monica H. Green in Kalof and Bynum 2010, vol. II: 155. Nowhere in her entire passage about sex differences (146–56) does she refer to Cadden.

15 Crawford 2007: 105–11.

16 Laqueur 1990. See also Laqueur's and Schiebinger's contributions to Gallagher and Laqueur 1987. Laqueur's approach differs from that of Foucault (1976b) to the extent that the former is concerned with views of what it is to be a man or a woman, rather than with sexuality and the discourse about it. It is intriguing to realize that the medieval view, that not all bodies can be classified as either male or female, is closer to modern biological knowledge than the view originating in the eighteenth century. Cf. Shilling 1993: 52–3.

17 See, for example, Foyster 1999: 28–9.

18 In Kalof and Bynum 2010, only Green rejects Laqueur's thesis, but unconvincingly (see above and note 15 to this chapter). In the same book series, Katherine Crawford (vol. III: 61), Lisa Forman Cody (vol. IV: 19) and Kevin Siena (vol. IV: 40) largely support his thesis, while George Rousseau (vol. IV: 53–71) accepts it entirely.

19 Nye in Spierenburg 1998a: 87.

20 Cohen (Thomas V.) and Cohen (1993) consider women's role as slightly more active than other scholars do: "by her beauty, clothing, industry, wit, modesty and social grace, a woman could win honour for herself and for her menfolk" (24). On different conceptions of male and female honor, see also Spierenburg 2008 (esp. chs. 3 and 4).

21 See Ingram 1987: 125–67, and chapter 5 here.

22 Nye 1993: 13 and *passim*.

23 Compare Stewart 1994: 41–7, who further distinguishes between a naturally internal and a morally internal type of honor.

24 See, for example, Sabean 1984: 144–73; Farr 1988: 180; Muchembled 1989: 260–8; Gauvard 1991: 724–6. The most recent synthesis is in Spierenburg 2008: chs. 1 and 3.

25 Wiener in Spierenburg 1998a: 197–212.

26 Spierenburg 2004: 136–7.

27 See, among others, Godfrey (Barry) 2003 and Simon Stevenson, The international decline of violence, 1860–1930: if there was one, did it come from a new masculinity? Paper presented at the 19th meeting of the Social Science History Association, Atlanta 1994. The historical literature on masculinity *per se* has expanded greatly since the 1990s. A recent, interesting monograph looks at the subject from the perspective of crime literature: Godfrey (Emelyne) 2011. See also Hughes 2007.

28 Elias 1971 [1970]: 176–7.

29 Sharpe 1985b: 213–15; Stone 1985: 222–3. The debate began with Stone 1983.

30 See the discussion by several contributors to the special issue of De Sociologische Gids about Elias' theory, 1982.

31 This distinction of two axes, it seems to me, is better suited to grasp the complexities of violence, historically and cross-culturally, than a mere dichotomy. The contributors to the special issue of the *Amsterdams Sociologisch Tijdschrift* on Dutch violence adhere to a dichotomy in one way or another: Franke (1991: 36) distinguishes instrumental from impulsive violence; Wilterdink (1991: 9) adheres to the same distinction, but he equates impulsive with expressive; Blok (1991: 194) contrasts violence called "instrumental" or "technical" with violence called "expressive," "ritual," "symbolic" or "communicative." Blok is the only one who emphasizes that these are different aspects (rather than types) of violence, which can be combined in one and the same act. Incidentally, Wilterdink's equation is the opposite of the equally erroneous assumption of a number of historians that ritual requires control of impulses.

32 Argued in greater detail in Spierenburg 2001.

33 Cockburn 1991: 93–6.

1   Long-Term Trends in Homicide: Amsterdam, Fifteenth–Twentieth Centuries

From *The civilization of crime: violence in town and country since the Middle Ages.* Copyright 1996 by the Board of Trustees of the University of Illinois. Used with permission of the University of Illinois Press. The 1667–1816 homicide rates presented here deviate slightly from those in the original article due to new population estimates; the same is true for the figures in the contextual evidence section, because I found a few more supplementary cases. The theoretical section has been integrated into this book's introduction and a few passages now outdated have been suppressed. For a specification of some of the calculations from others' data, the reader should turn to the original article.

1 Stone 1983: 22.

2 Spierenburg 1978: 84; Jüngen 1979: 41, and 1990: 84; Faber 1983: 71; Boomgaard 1991: 111–12.

3 Faber 1983: 94–5, 98; Gijswijt-Hofstra 1984: 156. The former performed the research, but the latter presents the exact figures.

4 Both projects remained unfinished. The data are preliminarily analyzed in Gijswijt-Hofstra 1984: 151–7.

5 van der Hoeven 1982: 40–1.

6 Berents 1976: 57–66 and 1985: 136, 210 (note 103).

7 Graafhuis et al. 1976: 41. Possibly, other cases of homicide in the city were prosecuted by the (provincial) Court of Utrecht.

8 Compare Cameron 1981: 192; Cockburn 1991: 87.

9 See the argumentation in Spierenburg 2008: 128–31.

10 See the discussion in Franke 1991.

11 Boomgaard 1992: 92–3 (table 4.1; I discarded the data for the years 1426–30, because they did not refer to fiscal years and most killers were unidentified). I am grateful to Jan Boomgaard for making the data available to me before he published his book.

12 de Vries 1984: 271 counts 14,000 inhabitants in 1500. Bairoch et al. 1988: 53 count 3,000 in 1400 and 15,000 in 1500.

13 Jüngen in Fijnaut and Spierenburg 1990: 84–5.

14 Jüngen 1982: 19.

15 RA: inventory nos. 640c–640g.

16 Faber 1978. Faber provided me with his research notes, which were helpful in determining the total number of cases in advance, as well as in coding variables as far as infanticide cases were concerned.

17 They alternately styled themselves "de gezworen chirurgijns van den gerechte" (the sworn surgeons of the court) or "de gequalificeerden tot het schouwen der lijken der nedergeslagenen" (the committee authorized to inspect the bodies of the slain), which clearly indicates that their task was to look for signs of a violent death.

18 There were 146 cases of strangulation altogether. In 1 case, however, a killer was mentioned. The body of the victim in question had been found in the water. Consequently, all cases with the combination "strangulation / found in the water" were listed as possible homicides. One more indication that strangulation was normally associated with suicide comes from Zierikzee. The committee performing the autopsies in that town was said to be dealing with three types of bodies: those drowned; those who had hanged themselves; (the wounds of) those slain – Slenders 1989: 30.

19 Based on Nusteling 1997: 75–9.

20 Ordinance inserted in RA: no. 640g.

21 Personal information from Jean Jüngen, who made no mention of this observation in his article.

22 In this case, the bodies of children who had never breathed were included in the figure. When they are left out, the percentages are 51.6 and 48.4, respectively.

23 Hoffer and Hull 1981: 183.

24 Franke 1991: 23.

25 Nieuwbeerta and Leistra 2007: 35.

26 Centraal Bureau voor de Statistiek at Voorburg: Library, no. 4 F 52, series B3. The series begins in the 1960s, but the system of classification used up to 1978 does not have a separate category of homicide.

27 Nieuwbeerta and Leistra 2007: 36.

28 Franke 1991: 28.

29 Leistra and Nieuwbeerta 2003: 25.

30 Gijswijt-Hofstra 1984: 139–49. For an analysis of contextual factors in nineteenth-century Northern France, see Parrella 1992.

31 RA: nos. 308–515 (interrogation protocols), 581–598 (justice books),

605–614 (sentence books). Additional data were extracted from nos. 639 (list of those executed), 640a (register 1795–1807), 640i-O (various dossiers of criminal cases), 1867–1927 (role of cases handled without jailing the victim), and Library of the archive: diary of Jacob Bicker Raye.

32 In the 1710s there were also several trials of members of the Jaco band and some of them had murdered their victims. These trials were left out of consideration, because it was unclear who exactly was charged with murder. In any case, the operations of the Jaco band all took place outside Amsterdam.

33 RA: no. 611, sentence 41.

34 RA: no. 389, fos. 200v, 206, 210, 227.

35 van Ruller 1987: 126–9. Since petitioning for pardon was a routine matter in this period and the records include rejected pardons, the representativeness of van Ruller's sample is much greater than that of Gijswijt-Hofstra's sample.

2 Homicide and the Law in the Dutch Republic: A Peaceful Country?

Originally published as "L'Homicide et la loi en République des Pays-Bas du Nord: un pays pacifique?" in: Laurent Mucchielli and Pieter Spierenburg (eds.), Histoire de l'homicide en Europe: de la fin du Moyen Âge à nos jours. Paris (La Découverte) 2009: 53–82. Copyright: © La Découverte, Paris, 2009. Reprinted with permission. Paragraphs overlapping with my History of Murder and some examples have been suppressed.

1 See esp. Dekker 1982 and 2008.

2 All non-Dutch rates are from Spierenburg 2008.

3 Franke 1991: 28; Leistra and Nieuwbeerta 2003: 21–6.

4 RA 327, fos. 21v, 22, 25, 25v, 54.

5 GA Amsterdam, Keurboek S, fo. 86v; Handvesten 1748: 1049.

6 RA 376, fos. 111, 116v.

7 RA 387, fos. 254v, 259v.

8 RA 640f, Dec. 15, 1720, and May 29, 1724; Keurboek S, fo. 131v.

9 Spierenburg 1984: 172.

10 RA 477 pp. 462, 482, 512; RA 478 pp. 9, 19, 37, 55, 89, 107, 124, 150, 153.

11 RA 502, pp. 261ff.; RA 503, pp. 34ff.; RA 504, pp. 212–13.

12 Egmond 1993: 129–51.

13 For a more detailed analysis of the popular duel in Amsterdam including several examples, see Spierenburg 2008: 82–93.

14 van den Brink 1995: 306–8.

15 Castan 1980a: 57–8; Hanlon 1985: 258; Beattie 1986: 92–3; Brennan 1988: 45–8, 61–3, 74–5; Farr 1988: 180; Kiernan 1988: 72; Dinges 1994: 213–15, 341–2; Greenshields 1994: 72, 83–5; Boschi in Spierenburg 1998a; Jansson 1998: 114–20; Ylikangas 1998; Foyster 1999: 177–9; Shoemaker 2001: 195–6, 198; Tlusty 2001: 127–33; McMahon 2004: 167; Mantecón 2007.

16 Hollands Placcaet-boeck 1645, vol. I: 365–6. A few military ordinances preceded this law.

17 Dewald 1993: 88–91.

18 Schmidt 1986: 50–1.
19 Counted from van den Berg 1985. See also Ridderikhoff 1985.
20 RA 327, fos. 6, 10, 20, 22v, 28v, 43v, 51, 54v. Other Amsterdam duels are recorded in 1672, 1712 and 1795.
21 GA Amsterdam, Keurboek O, fo. 168; P, fos. 112, 163.
22 RA 367, fos. 182, 229v.
23 van Weel 1977; Spierenburg 2006b: 10–13, 24–5.
24 RA 344, fos. 255v, 265; RA 345, fos. 7v, 12v, 14, 17 (year: 1697).
25 RA 321, fos. 188, 189v–190v, 202–203v; RA 322, fos. 4vs-5v, 11v; RA 588, fo. 231v.
26 RA 374, fos. 219, 252v, 253; RA 375, fo. 14; RA 640i-2: year (1717).
27 RA 388, fo. 160v; RA 640K, year 1730.
28 RA 398, fos. 102v, 110v, 157v, 160v, 190v; RA 613, no. 61.
29 RA 415, fos. 97, 110, 126v; RA 1896: Nov. 5, 1756; RA 640g: Sept. 4, 1756; University Library Amsterdam, Handschriften, no. IV A 18–II (collection Petrus Camper).
30 RA 398, fos 161v, 168v, 172, 173, 176.
31 RA 378, fos. 39v, 43v, 50.
32 RA 501, pp. 98, 271, 276, 280, 286, 365.
33 Spierenburg 2006b: 12–15.
34 Spierenburg 1999: 123–4.
35 RA 352, fos. 192, 194, 200, 201, 202, 204, 206, 212v, 214, 217, 220v.
36 RA 339, fos. 81, 83v, 84, 87v, 90v, 108vs (year: 1693).
37 RA 368, fos. 61v, 69, 218v, 220v.
38 RA 368, fos. 241vff.; RA 369, fos. 54v, 75v, 77, 107, 107v.
39 van den Brink 1995: 309.
40 RA 321, fos. 209v, 211v; RA 322, fos. 5v, 11v.
41 RA 336, fos. 129v, 132v, 138, 140v.
42 RA 363, fos. 53, 57v, 136, 164v, 180, 182v, 199v.
43 RA 349, fos. 241, 244v, 247, 249v, 250, 278.
44 Spierenburg 1984: 11.
45 RA 371, fos. 113, 128, 142, 15.
46 RA 429, pp. 79, 111, 156, 233.
47 RA 450, pp. 438, 481; RA 451, pp. 315, 319, 328, 329, 340, 348.
48 RA 477, pp. 189, 211, 317, 398, 492.

3 Violence and Culture: Bloodshed in Two or Three Worlds

Originally delivered as the New History Lecture at the Academia Sinica, Taipei, in April 2005 and published, in Chinese translation, in the Taiwanese journal *New History* (September 2006: vol.17,3, pp. 145–82). Reproduced with permission. The section on Europe has been considerably shortened to minimize overlap with my *History of murder*. The section on America has been updated, taking account of various publications not cited in the original version. A few studies of American violence, however, were unavailable in Dutch libraries.

1 The outline here is based on Spierenburg 2008. See also chapters 1–2 of this volume.
2 See Eisner 2003 and Spierenburg 2008.
3 Turner 1953 (first edn. 1920, consisting mostly of essays written and published separately in the 1890s).
4 Roth 2009: 38–9 (graphs 1.2 and 1.3).
5 See the debate between Roth and myself in the Forum section of *Crime, Histoire & Sociétés / Crime, History & Societies* 15,2 (2011): 123–50.
6 Lane 1997: 310. For the West, he adds Chinese and Mexicans.
7 Monkkonen 2001: 16 (my own rough conclusion from his graph), 178–9.
8 Lane 1999: 60.
9 Butterfield 1995: 8.
10 Vandal 2000: 13.
11 For information on intimate violence, see Daniels and Kennedy 1999 and Roth 2009: chs. 3 and 6.
12 Claimed, based on homicide rates from prosecuted cases, in, among others, Lane 1997: 344.
13 McKanna 1997: 6–10, 162. Michael Bellesiles, for example, makes unfounded statements about the level of violence in American and European history. See his introduction to Bellesiles 1999.
14 McKanna 1997: 163. California rates are in the appendix to that work and in McKanna 2002. On homicide in the West, see also Peterson del Mar 2002 and Roth 2009: 355.
15 McKanna 1997: 17 (my emphasis).
16 McKanna 1997: 22.
17 McKanna 1997: 76.
18 See Adler 2006. He further demonstrates that, by the early twentieth century, Chicago was by far the most violent city in the USA. In many American cities the YMCA was the principal organization attempting to counter the rowdy culture of working-class men. See Winter 2002.
19 Hamm 2003: 8.
20 The democracy-came-too-early thesis is presented also in Spierenburg 2006a.
21 Cornell 2008: 4, 21–3, 138–44. See also Bellesiles 2000: 215 and *passim*. The scandal about this author's gun count should not make us discard his entire research effort. See, further, Robert E. Shalhope, review of H. Richard Uviller and William G. Merkel, *The Militia and the Right to Arms, or, How the Second Amendment Fell Silent* (Constitutional Conflicts). Durham, NC: Duke University Press, 2002, in *American Historical Review* 5 (2003): 1442–3. The book itself is unavailable in Dutch libraries.
22 Bellesiles 2000: 224.
23 Only occasionally did state courts deal with African Americans. See Waldrep and Nieman 2001.
24 Reproduced as an illustration to Rodriguez' contribution to Bellesiles 1999: 138.
25 Ayers 1984: 18. See also Wyatt-Brown 1982: ch. 14. The jury system

need not automatically lead to easy acquittals, but it tends to do so where violence is viewed with leniency, as in Ireland in the second half of the nineteenth century: "The jury system meant that crimes could only be punished severely if the community saw them as truly criminal" (Conley 1999: 40).

26 Ingalls 1988: xvi.

27 Culberson 1990: 3–4.

28 Ingalls 1988; Lane 1997: 69, 131–5.

29 James H. Madison, review of Christopher Waldrep, *The Many Faces of Judge Lynch: Extralegal Violence and Punishment in America.* New York: Palgrave Macmillan, 2002, in *American Historical Review* 1 (2004): 194–5. See also the subsequent review on lynching in Colorado. Neither book is available in Dutch libraries. See, further, Tolnay and Beck 1995 and Waldrep 2006. For Central Texas, William D. Carrigan (2004: 132–3) speaks of a "racialization of lynching" between 1870 and 1900. The term "strange fruit" derives from a well-known Billie Holiday song.

30 Pfeifer 2004. He argues that the death penalty, technocratically administered, functioned as a substitute for the rough justice of lynching. That argument is reminiscent of Zimring's views (see chapter 6).

31 Lane 1997: 164–5.

32 McKanna 1997: 30–2. Yet McKanna explains Western violence primarily in terms of "the rapid convergence of diverse cultures, industrialization and differing social systems" (155).

33 Employers sometimes relied on private agencies, such as the Worsted Committee in Northern England, to detect workplace embezzlement. See Godfrey 1999 a and b.

34 Anderson 1994 (quote) and 1999.

35 Clarke 1998 argues, in a narrative fashion, that violence was central to race relations throughout American history.

36 Schulte Nordholt 2002. See also Ricklefs 2002.

37 Mennell in Goudsblom et al. 1996: 117–34.

38 On violence and state formation in the warring states period, see also Lewis 1990 and Hui 2005.

39 Rowe 2007. On homicide related to conflicts over land in South-East China in the eighteenth century: Buoye 2000.

40 Brook et al. 2008.

41 Krug et al. 2002: pp. 308ff. (table A.8). Note that considering one year only results in a limited validity. For Japan, Leistra and Nieuwbeerta (2003: 25) also list a figure of 0.6 based on mortality statistics, but in their column for police data, the Japanese homicide rate is 1.0.

42 Chuang Ying-chang et al. 2006 results from a project in which the Netherlands and Taiwan were compared with respect to demographic and family history.

43 Leistra and Nieuwbeerta 2003: 21.

44 Berghuis and Jonge 1993; Leistra and Nieuwbeerta 2003: 23.

45 See Maguire 1997.

4   Punishment, Power and History: Foucault and Elias

Published originally under the same title in *Social Science History* 28,4 (2004): 607–36. Copyright, 2004, the Social Science History Association. All rights reserved. Reprinted by permission of the publisher, Duke University Press.

1 All quotes are my own translations from this original French edition.
2 Camus and Koestler 1957: 130, 222. See also Affaire Weidmann 1939 (a dossier containing the pleas of the attorneys of Weidmann and his principal accomplice, whose death sentence was commuted).
3 Cited in Spierenburg 1991: 49–50.
4 The king suffered only a light wound, but he feared that the knife had been poisoned. Damiens probably had no intention of killing him, but influential circles at court believed in a conspiracy. Cf. Lavisse 1909: 244–5.
5 In Spierenburg 1984, in particular, as well as in several other publications and numerous conference contributions.
6 See Garland 1990: 135, who remarks that it is not a "difficult" text. Garland (1990: 155) also stresses that Foucault never claimed that *Surveiller et punir* comprised a general theory of punishment.
7 "L'éclat des supplices" – Foucault 1975: 36–72.
8 Gatrell 1994: 14–16.
9 Behrens 1999: 46–8.
10 Dinges 1994: 30–5.
11 Dinges 1996: 159, 161–2, 170–1.
12 Gellately 1990: 12.
13 Gellately 1996: 203. Surprisingly, Gellately 2001 has no references to Foucault.
14 The first publication, resulting from a conference in 1977, is Perrot 1980. See also Petit 1984 and Petit et al. 2002, a practically unchanged reprint of a collection first published in 1981.
15 Farge and Foucault 1982. For a few critical notes on this collection's introduction, see Spierenburg 1991: 242, 247–8.
16 Robert in Mucchielli 1995: 435.
17 Notably in his contribution to the conference "Crime and Criminal Justice in Preindustrial and Industrial Societies" held at the University of Maryland in September 1980.
18 See Spierenburg 1991. In fairness it should be added that Rothman later recognized this, since he included a chapter on these early modern institutions in a book he co-edited. Recently, Guy Geltner 2008 showed that, even in late-medieval Italy, penal imprisonment was more common than previously thought.
19 Foucault 1961. I have no argument with this book except about the term "great confinement" itself (see Spierenburg 1991: 10).
20 Scull 1979 and 1993: esp. 1–10, with reference to Foucault 1961.
21 Roding 1986: 7; Frey 1997: 17–18.
22 Brieler 1998: 277–8.

23 Foucault 1975: 78.
24 Hufton 1974: 266–83; Castan 1980b: 223–8.
25 Hufton 1974: 277.
26 Cobb 1970; see also Brown 1997.
27 See Spierenburg 2001 and the literature referred to there.
28 For a similar critique on Foucault, see Garland 1990: 161.
29 Nye 1984 and 1993: 72–97; Wiener 1990; Wetzell 2000; Becker 2002; Kaluszynski 2002.
30 See various contributions to Mucchielli 1995.
31 Garland 1990: 3–10.
32 "Allgegenwärtigkeit der Machtfenomene" – Kim 1995: 88.
33 Even a mild critic such as Garland (1990: 138) does so.
34 Foucault 1976a: 114–23. This cheap German edition identifies the essay as a lecture at the Collège de France in 1973. I was unable to trace the French original.
35 Elias 1971 [1970]: 101.
36 Elias 1984: 251.
37 Szakolczai 1998: 78.
38 "[C'est] le pouvoir-savoir, les processus et les luttes qui le traversent et dont il est constitué, qui déterminent les formes et les domaines possibles de la connaissance" – Foucault 1975: 32.
39 Cf. Szakolczai 1998: 77–82, 238–9.
40 "L'effet le plus important peut-être du système carcéral et de son extension bien au-delà de l'emprisonnement légal, c'est qu'il parvient à rendre naturel et légitime le pouvoir de punir, à abaisser du moins le seuil de tolérance à la pénalité" – Foucault 1975: 308.
41 Compare Kim (1995) who criticizes Foucault's concept of power and opposes it to that of Elias.
42 "Il [le pouvoir] prend à bras-le-corps le corps sexuel. . . . sans doute . . . aussi sensualisation du pouvoir. . . . Le plaisir découvert reflue vers le pouvoir qui le cerne. . . . Il [le pouvoir] attire, il extrait ces étrangetés sur lesquelles il veille. Le plaisir diffuse sur le pouvoir qui le traque" – Foucault 1976b: 61.
43 Franke 1995: 294 (quote), 763.
44 Evans 1996: 880–99. Neither does Gatrell (1994) have a theory of his own.

5   Monkey Butt's Mate: On Informal Social Control, Standards of Violence and Notions of Privacy

Based on my inaugural lecture as Professor of Historical Criminology at Erasmus University, Sept. 7, 2007. This lecture was published in expanded form as "Apegatjes Achtervolgers: Sociale Controle Tussen Verschuivende Geweldsdrempels en Veranderende Noties van Privacy" in: Henk van de Bunt, Pieter Spierenburg, René van Swaaningen, *Drie perspectieven op sociale controle*. Den Haag (Boom Juridische Uitgevers) 2007: 67–112.

Reproduced with permission of Boom publishers. An earlier version of the English text was presented as a plenary lecture at the Second British Crime Historians Symposium, Sheffield, Sept. 3, 2010.

1 www.volkskrant.nl/binnenland/article158486.ece/Inhakken_op_een_al_dan_niet_gevaarlijke_kassadief; www.parool.nl/artikelen/NIE/1055568329865.html; www.parool.nl/nieuws/2007/MRT/27/ams3.html; www.zibb.nl/retail/food/artikel_start/asp/artnr/689035/index.html (all sites accessed March 30, 2007).

2 RA 377, fos. 157v, 162v, 184vs (trial of Hendrik Hendriks de Ridder = Monkey Butt); fos. 160, 162v, 170v, 174, 184 (trial of Willem Coerten = Big Mouth); RA 640f: 5–7–1719 (body inspection report).

3 Spierenburg 1984: 11.

4 www.hetccv.nl/nieuws/2011/04/aanmelden-voor-de-hein-roethofprijs-2011.html (accessed May 12, 2011).

5 Fijnaut and Spierenburg 1990 resulted from a conference at the occasion of the end of the report's first five-year period of action.

6 *Eindrapport*: 63–6.

7 *Interimrappport*: 28–31. Cited, with new examples added, in *Eindrapport*: 13–14.

8 The collective volumes: Roodenburg and Spierenburg 2004 and Emsley et al. 2004.

9 In Roodenburg and Spierenburg 2004. See also van der Heijden 1998 and, for Amsterdam, Roodenburg 1990.

10 See, among others, Schilling's contribution to Roodenburg and Spierenburg 2004.

11 In his contribution to Roodenburg and Spierenburg 2004.

12 In his contribution to Roodenburg and Spierenburg 2004.

13 Sleebe 1994. See also his contribution to Emsley et al. 2004.

14 See, among others, Lis and Soly 1992. For a critical reviw of English studies: Colls 2004.

15 Gould 1995: 153–94.

16 See also his contribution to Emsley et al. 2004.

17 "Elle apparaît, au contraire, comme un espace où les relations de parenté et de voisinage sont, dans la période étudiée, un aspect essentiel de la vie quotidienne" – Burdy 1989: 107.

18 Published posthumously as Dijkhuis 1940 – not to be confused with the master's thesis which he did finish and which was also published.

19 Roché 1998. See also his contribution to Emsley et al. 2004.

6 **"The Green, Green Grass of Home": Reflections on Capital Punishment and the Penal System in Europe and America from a Long-term Perspective**

Originally published as "The Green, Green Grass of Home: Capital Punishment and the Penal System from a Long-Term Perspective" in: Austin Sarat and Jürgen Martschukat (eds), *Is the death penalty dying?* (2011), copyright by Cambridge University Press, reproduced with permission. The earlier version has been shortened by about one-fifth.

1 See www.youtube.com/watch?v=vgd426QrtJQ (accessed Dec. 24, 2009; attempt at access on June 8, 2010 led to the notification that the video had been removed).

2 See, among others, Zimring 2003 and Whitman 2003 and the debate raised by these works in *Punishment and Society* (Garland 2005; Whitman 2005; Zimring 2005). Garland presents his own conclusions in Garland 2010.

3 Spierenburg 1984: 87–9; Evans 1996: 86–98.

4 Royer 2004: 70.

5 Merback 1999: 150–7.

6 Spierenburg 1984: 59.

7 Banner 2002: 36–9. In China, executions always remained profane. See Brook et al. 2008.

8 Rappaz 2009: 8.

9 Bastien 2006: 114–42.

10 Spierenburg 2004: 107.

11 As I have noted in my review (*American Historical Review*, Feb. 2009: 198), nor does he refer to the sacralization of executions in Whitman 2008, where religious concern in relation to criminal trials is the central issue.

12 Whitman 2003: 243 (note 28).

13 Arasse 1989: 136–42.

14 Arasse 1989: 28–32.

15 Bosch 2008: 32–3. The rope meant hanging for men and garroting for women.

16 Evans 1996: 215–25; Martschukat 2000: 140–234.

17 Arasse 1989: 158.

18 I will refer here to Franke 1995, which is an abbreviated version of his Dutch dissertation of 1990.

19 Franke 1995: 203–7.

20 Franke 1995: 246–74.

21 Rotman 1995: 192.

22 Chesnais 1976: graph 9. Chesnais' graph is per 100,000 which I converted to per million for convenience's sake.

23 Banner 2002: 208. The most detailed and recent quantitative analysis is in Allen and Clubb 2008.

24 Evans 1996: 914–16 (table 1). The table goes back to 1860 but it presents no per capita figures and has gaps.

25 Portugal abolished the death penalty in 1867, having executed its last death sentence either in 1843 (Hood 1999: 10) or 1849 (Hood 2002: 23).

26 See van Ruller 1987: 94–6 (count of death sentences based on number of pardon dossiers; since 1814, all death sentences were apparently followed by a pardon procedure) and 200 (tables 9b and 9c, indicating the increase in the percentage of pardons).

27 Bot 2005: 8–12, 20.

28 On Chris Meijer: www.dodenakkers.nl/oorlog/grafmonumenten/20–vuur-peloton.html (accessed May 26, 2010).
29 Belinfante 1978: 17–50; Bot 2005: 15–19, 22.
30 Most recent figures in Bosch 2008: 83–4.
31 For the most recent analyses of these episodes, see Hammel 2011 (Europe) and Gottschalk 2011 (United States).
32 Noted earlier in Banner 2002: 301.
33 See also my review, *Journal of Social History* 44,1 (2010): 290–2, where I argue that the situation before the sacralization of executions provides counter-evidence to her thesis about the religious nature of punishment.
34 As pointed out in Downes and van Swaaningen 2007: 33.
35 Salle 2009: 135.
36 Downes and van Swaaningen 2007: 36–9.
37 Spierenburg 2008: 218–22.
38 See esp. Gottschalk 2006: chs. 5 and 6. She argues that in the US the anti-rape and battered women's movements became much more aligned with law-and-order politics than in Europe. Simon (2007: 108) also briefly comments on the link between feminism and the victims' movement in the US, but he identifies the 1968 Safe Streets Act as the real root of the trend toward compassion with victims.
39 Mennell 2007: 151.

7 Elites and Etiquette: Changing Standards of Personal Conduct in the Netherlands until 1800

The research into Dutch books of etiquette was performed in the early 1970s, leading to an unofficial publication in Dutch in 1973. The original version of this article also was published unofficially, as a paper in the series Centrum voor Maatschappijgeschiedenis in 1981 under the title of *Elites and etiquette. Mentality and social structure in the early modern Northern Netherlands*. In the present version some quotations from manner books have been suppressed; it takes account of the most relevant studies of elites and the state in the Dutch Republic published since then. I am grateful to Manon van der Heijden for reading this chapter and making suggestions for improvement.

1 This specification of the selection of sources should have been provided also in my original article. Its absence there caused Herman Roodenburg (1991: 179, note 6) to call the original article an incomplete overview, because it lacked a reference to C. van Laar, *Het groot ceremonieboek der beschaafde zeden* (1735). Van Laar's work was one of those listed in the card-box that lacked concrete rules.
2 te Brake (1989) is one of the few authors who correctly writes "Estates." He does, however, write "regents."
3 Bouc van Seden 1844: 581, 582–3, 586. Originally in verse.
4 Dit is Hovesheit 1846: 118–24. Similar rules in Goetman 1860 [1488]: 16–17.
5 Goede manierlijcke Zeden 1864 [1546]: 352, 353, 354.

6 Valcoogh 1875 [1591]: 47–9. Originally in verse.
7 Cierlycke Voorsnydinge 1664: 14–15.
8 Nieuwe Verhandeling 1677: 109–10, 120. Rules mostly copied in Blankaart 1683: 139–40.
9 Chalmot 1786–93, vol. IX: entry "viesheid."
10 van Oostrom 1987: 27–8.
11 van Lennep and Hofdijk 1854–60: third series, second part, 94–6.
12 Aitzema 1664: 859–60.
13 Chalmot 1786–93, vol. IX: entry "viesheid."
14 This is a passage from Erasmus' *De civilitate morum puerilium* (see *Opera omnia*, vol. I: 1045) not included in Elias' book. The last quotation under the heading of bodily functions deals with the same subject. The quotations from 1546 and 1626 should be compared with that about farting provided by Elias (1969, vol. I: 175–6).
15 From Charles V's decree against begging. Quoted in Kemper 1851: 322.
16 Goede manierlijcke Zeden 1864 [1546]: 343–4.
17 From the Dutch school-edition of Erasmus' *De civilitate morum puerilium*. Quoted in Kuiper 1958: 115–18.
18 Chomel and Chalmot 1778, vol. V: entry "pis."
19 For a more detailed analysis of the role of hygiene in civilizing processes, see Goudsblom 1977.
20 Original text quoted in Elias 1969, vol. I: 176–7. Bowlerized Dutch translation: Casa 1715: 6.
21 Goede manierlijcke Zeden 1864 [1546]: 339.
22 Valcoogh 1875 [1591]: 25. Originally in verse.
23 Nieuwe Verhandeling 1677: 26.
24 Betz 1900: 83–4.
25 Goede manierlijcke Zeden 1864 [1546]: 341.
26 Valcoogh 1875 [1591]: 25. Originally in verse.
27 Nieuwe Verhandeling 1677: 27, 37.
28 Bouc van Seden 1844: 585. Originally in verse.
29 Goede manierlijcke Zeden 1864 [1546]: 361.
30 Nieuwe Verhandeling 1677: ch. XIII.
31 van der Heijden 1998: 108–9.
32 In the sixteenth century, Dutch was a conglomerate of regional languages, from which modern Dutch and Flemish developed. The difference between modern Dutch and Flemish is as small as that between British and American English.
33 Information on editions of *De civilitate* are from Haeghen and Arnold 1893, and from www.erasmus.org (accessed Nov. 23, 2011).
34 Information from Hans Trapman. A Leiden bookseller sold books printed by Plantin in Antwerp, but the Leiden list dates only from the end of the sixteenth century – Coppens 2001: 32–3, 41. Den Bosch booksellers regularly ordered loads of books from Plantin just after mid-century: van den Oord 1989.
35 See ten Brink (Jan) 1887.

36 Kuiper 1958: 152.
37 Komans 1693: 11, 25–8.
38 Rabus 1702.
39 See Frank-van Westrienen 1983.
40 Hoofsche welleventheid 1733, 1737, 1742, 1768. Because of the "letter by Erasmus" various bibliographies ascribe the whole book to him.
41 See Egmond 1989.
42 Porta 1975: 254; de Jongste 1993: 11–12.
43 This argument was not present in the original version of this article. I first put it forward in my dissertation (Spierenburg 1978: 49). Without referring to my dissertation, Prak (1989: 43) notes the original absence of a dual monopoly in one hand but not its appearance in the mid eighteenth century.
44 Compare Tilly 1990: 30 (to which van Zanden and Prak also refer) who ranks the Dutch Republic with the "capital-intensive" modes of government. On Dutch taxation also: 't Hart and van der Heijden 2006 and van der Heijden 2010. On the civil militia: Knevel 1994.
45 Reinders (2008: 97–9) flatly denies the existence of a process of aristocratization, but with unconvincing arguments.
46 Eysten 1916: 39.
47 Price 1974: 34–5, 124–5.
48 Dijkshoorn 1925: 16.
49 Elias (Johan Engelbert) 1923: 100–1.
50 Robert Fruin's epilogue to Droste 1879 [1720]: 267–74.
51 Heringa 1961: 77–9.
52 Betz 1900: 77; Japikse 1915: 20–2, 102–3, 204; Dijkshoorn 1925: 219–25. For the most recent biography of Johan de Witt and his brother, see Panhuysen 2005.
53 Valkenier 1675: 249–66. My emphasis.
54 Nieuwe Verhandeling 1677: ch. 17.
55 Heringa 1961: 168–9.
56 Mountague 1696: 164–5.
57 Feith 1906: 20.
58 Quoted in Dijkshoorn 1925: 41–2.
59 [Swildens] 1789: LXXXIX–XCI.
60 Several elite studies published in the 1980s focus especially on family life: de Jong 1985, Kooijmans 1985 and Prak 1985 (on three smaller cities). See also de Jong 1987.
61 Most references to the Great World are in Hartog 1890. Sturkenboom 1998 analyzes the observing magazines with a view on emotional standards. See also Spierenburg 2004: 5–9.
62 Hubner 1732: Voorrede.
63 P. van der Schelling's preface to the third volume of Alkemade and van der Schelling 1732–5.
64 Elias 1939, vol. I: 47–50.
65 [Swildens] 1789: V–VI.

8   Civilizing Celebrations: An Exploration of the Festive Universe

Originally published as "Hebben historici iets te vieren? Een verkenning van het festieve universum" in: *Leidschrift* 16,2 (2001): 7–23. Reproduced with permission of the *Stichting Leidschrift*.

1   The published text has "*postiliminaires*," but he had wanted to replace this with "*postliminaires*." See addendum to van Gennep 1969 [1909].
2   Turner 1969. See also Babcock 1978 (a collection inspired by Turner, applying his ideas to, among other things, festivals).
3   De Waardt 1995: 308–10.
4   The theme of the world upside-down is discussed in greater detail in Spierenburg 1998b: 109–15.
5   Burke 1978: 201.
6   Muir 1993: prologue and chs. 4–6; Ladurie 1980.
7   Bakhtin 1968. On Bakhtin's work see Gardiner 1993. See also Noëlle Gérôme in Corbin et al. 1994: 15.
8   Klaniczay 1990: 22.
9   Durkheim 1995 [1912]: 386–7. This work primarily deals with Australia, but Durkheim accorded a wider theoretical significance to his observations.
10   Mitchell 1991: 44.
11   McNeill 1995: 13.
12   Compare McNeill 1995: 74–81.
13   Heers 1983.
14   Shoshan 1993: 40–51.
15   Corbin in Corbin et al. 1994: 30.
16   Anna Esposito in Matheus 1999: 11–30.
17   Ozouf 1976: 324.
18   Jacqeline Lalouette in Corbin et al. 1994: 223–35.
19   Rosemonde Sanson in Corbin et al. 1994: 117–19.
20   See various contributions to Corbin et al. 1994. Compare Mezger (in Matheus 1999: 143–50) about the use of carnival by the Nazis.
21   Brophy 1997; Fransen and Schwedt in Matheus 1999.
22   Wijers 1995.
23   Compare André Simon (in Corbin et al. 1994: 391–7) on multi-cultural festivals in Avignon.

9   The Body's End: Death and Paradise in Human History

Written on the occasion of Joop Goudsblom's retirement and published in abbreviated form as "Het Paradijs en de dood: een kanttekening bij Goudsbloms mensheidshistorische perspectief" in: Nico Wilterdink et al. (eds.), *Alles Verandert: Opstellen voor en over J. Goudsblom*. Amsterdam (Meulenhoff) 1997: 268–78. Reprinted with permission.

1   See the analysis in Pagels 1988: xi–xiv. The second tale of creation begins in chapter 2, verses 4–7, where the "editor" of Genesis makes a hardly successful attempt to connect the two stories.

2 In addition, Adam and Eve became ashamed of their nudity, which is merely a sideline in the story. According to Pagels 1988, the story's sexual connotation was not emphasized until about AD 200, culminating in the work of St. Augustine. From then onwards, the dominant interpretation involved an absence of sexual intercourse in Paradise, the forbidden knowledge of good and evil being primarily carnal knowledge. According to this interpretation, Adam's sin, which became original sin, consisted of sexual lust rather than disobedience.

3 Goudsblom 1992 (references to *Fire and Civilization* are to the original Dutch edition); Goudsblom et al. 1996.

4 Eric Jones (in Goudsblom et al.1996) calls this extensive growth.

5 Goudsblom 1992: 128–9. Compare Barber (1988: in particular 125–35). In a similar vein to Goudsblom, Barber explains many rituals and magical beliefs concerning death from a realistic perspective. Medieval people believed that wolves loved to eat soldiers slain on the battlefield – Salisbury 1994: 69.

6 On Hesiod, see also Goudsblom et al. 1996: 18–19, 51.

7 Graf 1982 [1892]; Delumeau 1992–2000, vol. I (1992: *Le jardin des délices*): 13–15.

8 Boserup, quoted in Goudsblom 1992: 74. For the relationship with the transition from gathering/hunting to agriculture, see Goudsblom et al. 1996: 38.

9 I developed this idea independently in the 1980s when reading Goudsblom's preliminary studies on fire in prehistory published in *De Gids*. Later, I also encountered it in Spier 1990 (115–16, note 10).

10 Delumeau 1992–2000, vol. I: 146, 150.

11 Pangritz 1963: 53–90; Thomas 1983: 17–25, 150–65.

12 Sälzle 1965: 66–7.

13 Serpell 1986: 57–8.

14 Noske 1989: 41–2.

15 McNeill 1963: 10.

16 Elias 1982: 13ff.

17 Ariès (1977) indeed maintains that people accepted their own death until some five to six centuries ago, but this argument has been criticized by Chaunu as well as Elias. Summary of their arguments in Spierenburg 1998b: 167–8 (based mainly on Ariès 1977; Chaunu 1978; Elias 1982).

18 Goudsblom et al. 1996: 45–6.

19 Goudsblom et al. 1996: 54.

20 Delumeau 1992–2000, vol. I: 13–15.

21 Graf 1982 [1892]: 72.

22 Spier (1990: 93–4) identifies death as one of the problems of orientation – next to the phases of life, disease and the task of hunting and gathering itself – with which religious specialists in gathering and hunting societies occupied themselves. However, he does not pose the question of the rise of, or changes in the awareness of, death. He takes the concept of religious specialist from Bax 1988.

23 For a brief but clear summary, see Carroll 1992: 9–11; see also Thomas 1973

[971]: 27–89. According to Kieckhefer (1989: 37), the analytical distinction between religion and magic originated in early Christianity.

24 Weber 1922; Winckelmann 1980. Compare Spierenburg 1998b: 21–4, 80–7.
25 Ginzburg 1980 (original Italian edn. 1966).
26 Compare Martin 1992.
27 McNeill 1995: 43–4. He associates this with the emergence of an animistic view of the world and believes that this emergence began before *Homo sapiens* had spread over the entire globe.
28 Goudsblom et al. 1996: 24.
29 Goudsblom 1992: 40.
30 Elias 1991: 117–18.
31 This implies that a principle from the blind process of biological evolution reappeared in cultural form – of course without the people involved knowing this. In the evolutionary process of selection the (relative) immortality of the species is based on the mortality of its individual members.
32 Goudsblom et al. 1996: 34–8 (rejection of theological reasoning), 61 (world religions "attuned to the ideal of individual salvation"). The English word "salvation," moreover, appears to combine the German notions of *Erlösung* and *Heil*. Weber (1976: 245–381) speaks mostly of *Erlösung*, of which the "Heilsmethodik" (324–48) forms part.
33 The long struggle of competition and the mutual interpenetration of official religion on the one hand and magic and local religion on the other constitute a prominent theme in socio-cultural history. Excellent studies are Christian 1981 and Schmitt 1994.
34 Because of this division of tasks, priests tended to belittle the importance of the community's collective survival. This may be a partial explanation for the sexual taboos that characterize various religious faiths.
35 Janssen 1993: 95.
36 According to Bernstein (1993: 3), the idea that the dead are judged by a standard of known criteria and then rewarded or punished was expressed first in Egypt in the middle of the second millennium BC.
37 Vergil's cyclical view of history, in which the Golden Age was to return somewhere in the future (see Delumeau 1992–2000, vol. I), implies a secular version of this belief. Christians often viewed the heavenly Paradise, like Eden, as a garden. From the twelfth century on, with the rise of towns, the notion of heaven as the new Jerusalem became more important: McDannel and Lang 1988: 70–80.
38 Spier (1990: 92) points at Protestantism as the great exception, officially denying the mediating role of priests. It cannot be a coincidence that several Protestant doctrines also deny that the faithful can reach heaven by living a good life. Unofficially, however, this idea lived on.
39 According to Barber (1988: 25) the battle of the Orthodox Church against popular magical beliefs, concerning death and other subjects, was much less intense than that of the Catholic and Protestant Churches. Consequently, such beliefs were more tenacious in Eastern compared to Western and Central Europe.

40 Papenheim (1992) coined the concept of *innerweltliche Unsterblichkeit*. See also McManners 1981: 167–72 and Helsdingen n.d.

Epilogue: A Personal Recollection of Norbert Elias and How I Became a Crime Historian

In the mid-1990s a group of Amsterdam sociologists edited a collection with recollections of Norbert Elias. When I expressed to an English scholar my disappointment at not having been asked to contribute, he told me that he wished to edit an English counterpart. I wrote this piece in early 1997 for his collection, which never materialized. In this version, I have introduced some corrections and one new paragraph.

1 My recollection was that the posters were hanging there in connection with John Lennon and Yoko Ono's "bed-in" for peace, but according to Wikipedia (http://en.wikipedia.org/wiki/Bed-In, accessed Dec. 15, 2011) this was in March 1969, hence before Norbert came to Amsterdam.

2 A pdf of my letter is available on request. The letter published in the *New York Review of Books* was from J. Goudsblom.

Archival Sources

All archival references are to the Stadsarchief (City Archive) Amsterdam. They include archive no. 5020 (keurboeken – in notes, "Keurboek" plus identifying letter) and archive no. 5061 (oud-rechterlijk archief – abbreviated in the notes as RA, followed by inventory number).

Bibliography

Adler (Jeffrey S.), First in violence, deepest in dirt. Homicide in Chicago, 1875–1920. Cambridge MA (Harvard University Press) 2006.

Affaire Weidmann (l'), in: Revue des grands procès contemporains 45 (October–December 1939): 417–85.

Aitzema (Lieuwe van), Historie of verhaal van saken van staet en oorlogh. Vol. IX. Den Haag (Jan Veely, Johannes Tongerloo, Jasper Doll) 1664.

Alkemade (Kornelis van) + P. van der Schelling, Nederlands displegtigheden, vertoonende de plegtige gebruiken aan den dis . . . 3 vols. Rotterdam (Philippus Losel) 1732–5.

Allen (Howard W.) + Clubb (Jerome M.), Race, class, and the death penalty. Capital punishment in American history. With assistance from Vincent A. Lacey. Albany (State University of New York Press) 2008.

Anderson (Elijah), The code of the streets, in: Atlantic Monthly (May 1994): 81–94.

Anderson (Elijah), Code of the street. Decency, violence and the moral life of the inner city. New York, London (Norton) 1999.

Arasse (Daniel), De machine van de Revolutie. Een geschiedenis van de guillotine. Nijmegen (SUN) 1989.

Ariès (Philippe), L'homme devant la mort. Paris (Editions du Seuil) 1977.

Ayers (Edward L.), Vengeance and justice. Crime and punishment in the 19th-century American South. New York (Oxford University Press) 1984.

Babcock (Barbara A.) (ed.), The reversible world. Symbolic inversion in art and society. Ithaca, London (Cornell University Press) 1978.

Bairoch (Paul) et al., La population des villes Européennes. Banque de données et analyse sommaire des résultats, 800–1850. Geneva (Droz) 1988.

Bakhtin (Mikhail), Rabelais and his world. Cambridge MA, London (Harvard University Press) 1968.

Banner (Stuart), The death penalty. An American history. Cambridge (Harvard University Press) 2002.

Barber (Paul), Vampires, burial and death. Folklore and reality. New Haven, London (Yale University Press) 1988.

Baroja (Julio Caro), Le carnaval. Paris (Gallimard) 1979.

Barton (Carlin A.), Roman honor. The fire in the bones. Berkeley (University of California Press) 2001.

Bastien (Pascal), L'exécution publique à Paris au 18e siècle. Une histoire des rituels judiciaires. Seyssel (Champ Vallon) 2006.

Bax (Mart), Religieuze regimes in ontwikkeling. Verhulde vormen van macht en afhankelijkheid. Hilversum (Gooi & Sticht) 1988.

Beattie (J[ohn] M.), Crime and the courts in England, 1660–1800. Oxford (Oxford University Press) 1986.

Becker (Peter), Verderbnis und Entartung. Eine Geschichte der Kriminologie des 19. Jahrhunderts als Diskurs und Praxis. Göttingen (Vandenhoeck & Ruprecht) 2002.

Behrens (Ulrich), Sozialdisziplinierung als konzeption der frühneuzeitforschung, in: Historische Mitteilungen 12 (1999): 35–68.

Belinfante (A[ugust] D[avid]), In plaats van bijltjesdag. De geschiedenis van de Bijzondere Rechtspleging na de Tweede Wereldoorlog. Assen (Van Gorcum) 1978.

Bellesiles (Michael A.) (ed.), Lethal imagination. Violence and brutality in American history. New York, London (New York University Press) 1999.

Bellesiles (Michael A.), Arming America. The origins of a national gun culture. New York (Knopf) 2000.

Bennassar (Bartolomé), L'homme espagnol. Attitudes et mentalités du 16e au 19e siècle. Paris (Hachette) 1975.

Bercé (Yves-Marie), Fête et révolte. Des mentalités populaires du XVIe au XVIIIe siècle. Essai. Paris (Hachette) 1976.

Berents (Dirk Arend), Misdaad in de middeleeuwen. Een onderzoek naar de criminaliteit in het laat-middeleeuwse. Utrecht (Diss. University of Utrecht) 1976.

Berents (D[irk] A[rend]), Het werk van de vos. Samenleving en criminaliteit in de late middeleeuwen. Zutphen (Walberg Pers)1985.

Berg (P. A. J. van den), Lijsten van dossiers inzake criminele en civiele processen, in: Nienes (A. P. van), De archieven van de universiteit te Franeker, 1585–1812. Leeuwarden (Rijksarchief in Friesland) 1985: 227–81.

Berghuis (A.C.) + Jonge (L. K. de), Moord en doodslag in 1989 en 1992. Een secundaire analyse, in: Tijdschrift voor Criminologie 35,1 (1993): 55–62.

Bernstein (Alan E.), The formation of hell. Death and retribution in the Ancient and early Christian worlds. London (University College London Press) 1993.

Betz (G. H.), Het Haagsche leven in de tweede helft der 17e eeuw. Den Haag (Hols) 1900.

Blankaart (Steven), De borgerlyke tafel. Amsterdam (J. ten Hoorn) 1683.

Blok (Anton), The mafia of a Sicilian village, 1860–1960. A study of violent peasant entrepreneurs. New York (Harper & Row) 1974.

Blok (Anton), Zinloos en zinvol geweld, in: Amsterdams Sociologisch Tijdschrift 18,3 (1991): 189–207.

Blok (Anton), Honour and violence. Cambridge (Polity) 2001.

Body-Gendrot (Sophie) + Spierenburg (Pieter) (eds.), Violence in Europe: historical and contemporary perspectives. New York (Springer) 2008.

Boomgaard (Jan), Het Amsterdamse criminaliteitspatroon in de late mid-deleeuwen, in: Diederiks (H. A.) + Roodenburg (H. W.) (eds.), Misdaad, zoen en straf. Aspekten van de middeleeuwse strafrechtsgeschiedenis in de Nederlanden. Hilversum (Verloren) 1991: 102–19.

Boomgaard (Jan), Misdaad en straf in Amsterdam. Een onderzoek naar de strafrechtspleging van de Amsterdamse schepenbank, 1490–1552. Zwolle, Amsterdam (Waanders) 1992.

Bosch (A.G.), De ontwikkeling van het strafrecht in Nederland van 1795 tot heden. 5th edn. Nijmegen (Ars Aequi Libri) 2008.

Bot (Erwin), De doodstraf onder de Bijzondere Rechtspleging. Master's thesis Erasmus University Rotterdam 2005.

Bouc van Seden, in: Kausler (Eduard) (ed.), Denkmäler altniederländischer Sprache und Literatur, Vol. II. Tübingen (Fues) 1844 : 561–86.

Bourdieu (Pierre), Esquisse d'une théorie de la pratique, précédé de trois études d'ethnologie Kabyle. Geneva (Droz) 1972.

Bourdieu (Pierre), Le sens pratique. Paris (Editions de Minuit) 1980.

Brake (Wayne Ph. te), Regents and rebels. The revolutionary world of an eight-eenth-century Dutch city. Cambridge (Basil Blackwell) 1989.

Brennan (Thomas), Public drinking and popular culture in 18th-century Paris. Princeton (Princeton University Press) 1988.

Brieler (Ulrich), Foucault's Geschichte, in: Geschichte und Gesellschaft 24 (1998): 248–82.

Brink (Gabriël van den), De grote overgang. Een lokaal onderzoek naar de modernisering van het bestaan: Woensel, 1670–1920. Amsterdam (Diss. Universiteit van Amsterdam) 1995.

Brink (Jan ten), Gerbrand Adriaensz. Bredero. Derde boek. De kluchten en de blijspelen. Leiden 1887.

Brook (Timothy), Bourgon (Jérôme) + Blue (Gregory), Death by a thousand cuts. Cambridge MA (Harvard University Press) 2008.

Brophy (James M.), Carnival and citizenship. The politics of carnival culture in the Prussian Rhineland, 1823–48, in: Journal of Social History 30,4 (1997): 873–904.

Brown (Howard G.), From organic society to security state. The war on brig-andage in France, 1797–1802, in: Journal of Modern History 69 (1997): 661–95.

Buoye (Thomas M.), Manslaughter, markets, and moral economy. Violent dis-putes over property rights in eighteenth-century China. Cambridge (Cambridge University Press) 2000.

Burdy (Jean-Paul), Le soleil noir. Un quartier de Saint-Etienne, 1840–1940. Lyon (Presses Universitaires de Lyon) 1989.

Burke (Peter), Popular culture in early modern Europe. New York (Harper & Row) 1978.

Burke (Peter), The translation of culture. Carnival in two or three worlds, in: Burke, Varieties of cultural history. Cambridge (Polity) 1997: 148–61.

Butterfield (Fox), All God's children. The Bosket family and the American tradition of violence. New York (Alfred A. Knopf) 1995.

Bynum (Caroline Walker), Holy feast and holy fast. The religious significance of food to medieval women. Berkeley (University of California Press) 1987.

Bynum (Caroline Walker), Fragmentation and redemption. Essays on gender and the human body in medieval religion. New York (Zone Books) 1991.

Bynum (Caroline Walker), The resurrection of the body in Western Christianity, 200–1336. New York (Columbia University Press) 1995.

Cadden (Joan), Meanings of sex difference in the Middle Ages. Medicine, science and culture. Cambridge (Cambridge University Press) 1993.

Cameron (Iain A.), Crime and repression in the Auvergne and the Guyenne, 1720–1790. Cambridge (Cambridge University Press) 1981.

Camporesi (Piero), The incorruptible flesh. Bodily mutation and mortification in religion and folklore. Cambridge (Cambridge University Press) 1988.

Camus (Albert) + Koestler (Arthur), Réflexions sur la peine capitale. Introduction et étude de Jean Bloch-Michel. Paris (Calmann-Lévy) 1957.

Carrigan (William D.), The making of a lynching culture. Violence and vigilantism in Central Texas, 1836–1916. Urbana (University of Illinois Press) 2004.

Carroll (Michael P.), Madonnas that maim. Popular Catholicism in Italy since the 15th century. Baltimore, London (Johns Hopkins University Press) 1992.

Casa (Giovanni della), Galateus, of welgemanierdheid. Amsterdam (Johannes Oosterwyk en Hendrik van de Gaete) 1715.

Castan (Nicole), Justice et répression en Languedoc à l'époque des Lumières. Paris (Flammarion) 1980a.

Castan (Nicole), Les criminels de Languedoc. Les exigences d'ordre et les voies du ressentiment dans une société pré-révolutionnaire, 1750–1790. Toulouse (Université de Toulouse-le-Mirail) 1980b.

Chalmot (J. A.), Algemeen huishoudelijk-, natuur-, zedekundig- en konst-woordenboek. 9 vols. Kampen, Amsterdam (J. Yntema) 1786–93.

Chaunu (Pierre), La mort à Paris. XVIe, XVIIe et XVIII siècles. Paris 1978.

Chesnais (Jean-Claude), Les morts violentes en France depuis 1826. Comparaisons internationales. Paris (Presses Universitaires de France) 1976.

Chomel (Noël) + Chalmot (J. A.), Algemeen huishoudelijk-, natuur-, zedekundig- en konst-woordenboek. 7 vols. Leiden, Leeuwarden 1778.

Christian (William A., Jr.), Local religion in 16th-century Spain. Princeton (Princeton University Press) 1981.

Chuang Ying-chang et al. (eds.), Positive or preventive? Reproduction in Taiwan and the Netherlands, 1850–1940. Amsterdam (Aksant) 2006.

Cierlycke Voorsnydinge aller tafelgerechten. Amsterdam (Hiëronymus Sweerts) 1664.

Clarke (James W.), The lineaments of wrath. Race, violent crime and American culture. New Brunswick (Transaction Publishers) 1998.

Cobb (Richard), The police and the people. French popular protest, 1789–1820. Oxford (Clarendon) 1970.

Cockburn (J. S.), Patterns of violence in English society. Homicide in Kent, 1560–1985, in: Past and Present 130 (1991): 70–106.

Cohen (Esther), The crossroads of justice. Law and culture in late medieval France. Leiden (Brill) 1993.

Cohen (Thomas V.) + Cohen (Elizabeth S.), Words and deeds in Renaissance Rome. Trials before the Papal Magistrates. Toronto (University of Toronto Press) 1993.

Colls (Robert), When we lived in communities. Working-class culture and its critics, in: Colls (Robert) + Rodger (Richard) (eds.), Cities of ideas. Civil society and urban governance in Britain, 1800–2000. Aldershot (Ashgate) 2004: 283–307.

Conley (Carolyn A.), Melancholy accidents. The meaning of violence in post-famine Ireland. Lanham MD (Lexington Books) 1999.

Coppens (Chris), Fondscatalogi als marketingstrategie. Een onderzoek naar lijsten van drukkers en boekhandelaren tot 1600, in: Jaarboek voor Nederlandse Boekgeschiedenis 8 (2001): 27–41.

Corbin (Alain) et al. (eds.), Les usages politiques des fêtes au 19e–20e siècles. Paris (Publications de la Sorbonne) 1994.

Cornell (Saul), A well-regulated militia. The Founding Fathers and the origins of gun control in America. Oxford (Oxford University Press) 2008.

Crawford (Katherine), European sexualities, 1400–1800. Cambridge (Cambridge University Press) 2007.

Culberson (William C.), Vigilantism. Political history of private power in America. New York (Praeger) 1990.

Culianu (Ioan P.), A corpus for the body. Review article, in: Journal of Modern History 63,1 (1991): 61–80.

Cusac (Anne-Marie), Cruel and unusual. The culture of punishment in America. New Haven, London (Yale University Press) 2009.

Daniels (Christine) + Kennedy (Michael V.) (eds.), Over the threshold. Intimate violence in early America. New York (Routledge) 1999.

Dekker (Rudolf), Holland in beroering. Oproeren in de 17e en 18e eeuw. Baarn (Ambo) 1982.

Dekker (Rudolf), Meer verleden dan toekomst. Geschiedenis van verdwijnend Nederland. Amsterdam (Bert Bakker) 2008.

Delumeau (Jean), Une histoire du paradis. 3 vols. Paris (Fayard) 1992–2000.

Deursen (A.Th. van), Bavianen en slijkgeuzen. Kerk en kerkvolk ten tijde van Maurits en Oldenbarnevelt. Assen (Van Gorcum) 1974.

Dewald (Jonathan), Aristocratic experience and the origins of modern culture. France, 1570–1715. Berkeley (University of California Press) 1993.

Dinges (Martin), Der Maurermeister und der Finanzrichter. Ehre, Geld und soziale Kontrolle im Paris des 18. Jahrhunderts. Göttingen (Vandenhoeck & Ruprecht) 1994.

Dinges (Martin), Michel Foucault's impact on the German historiography of criminal justice, social discipline, and medicalization, in: Finzsch (Norbert) + Jütte (Robert) (eds.), Institutions of confinement. Hospitals, asylums, and prisons in Western Europe and North America, 1500–1950. Cambridge (Cambridge University Press) 1996: 155–74.

Dit is Hovesheit. Uit een handschrift van het klooster Bursveld in Westfalen, in: Geldersche Volks-almanak 12 (1846): 118–24.

Downes (David) + Swaaningen (René van), The road to dystopia? Changes in the penal climate of the Netherlands, in: Tonry (Michael) + Bijleveld (Catrien) (eds.), Crime and justice in the Netherlands. Chicago (University of Chicago Press) 2007: 31–72.

Droste (Coenraad), Overblyfsels van geheugchenis der bisonderste voorvallen. Edited by Robert Fruin. Leiden (Brill) 1879 [1720].

Durkheim (Emile), The elementary forms of religious life. Translated and with an introduction by Karen E. Fields. New York (The Free Press) 1995 [1912].

Dijkhuis, (H. Tj.), De Jordaan. De ontwikkeling van een volkswijk in een grote stad, in: Economisch-Historisch Jaarboek 21 (1940): 1–90.

Dijkshoorn (Johannes Arend), L'influence française dans les moeurs et les salons des Provinces-Unies. Paris (Louis Arnette) 1925.

Egmond (Florike), Fragmentatie, rechtsverscheidenheid en rechtsongelijkheid in de Noordelijke Nederlanden tijdens de 17e en 18e eeuw, in: Faber (Sjoerd) (ed.), Nieuw licht op oude justitie. Misdaad en straf ten tijde van de Republiek. Muiderberg (Coutinho) 1989: 9–23.

Egmond (Florike), Underworlds. Organized crime in the Netherlands, 1650–1800. Cambridge (Polity) 1993.

Eindrapport van de Commissie kleine criminaliteit. Den Haag (Staatsuitgeverij) 1986.

Eisner (Manuel), Modernization, self-control and lethal violence. The long-term dynamics of European homicide rates in theoretical perspective, in: British Journal of Criminology 41 (2001): 618–38.

Eisner (Manuel), Long-term historical trends in violent crime, in: Crime and Justice. A Review of Research 30 (2003): 83–142.

Elias (Johan Engelbert), Geschiedenis van het Amsterdamsche regentenpatriciaat. Den Haag (Nijhoff) 1923.

Elias (Norbert), Über den Prozess der Zivilisation. Soziogenetische und psycho-genetische Untersuchungen. 2 vols. Bern (Haus zum Falcken) 1939.

Elias (Norbert), Die höfische Gesellschaft. Untersuchungen zur Soziologie des Königtums und der höfischen Aristokratie. Berlin (Luchterhand) 1969.

Elias (Norbert), Wat is sociologie? Utrecht (Spectrum) 1971 [1970].

Elias (Norbert), Über die Einsamkeit der Sterbenden in unseren Tagen. Frankfurt am Main (Suhrkamp) 1982.

Elias (Norbert), Knowledge and power. An interview by Peter Ludes, in Stehr (Nico) + Meja (Volker) (eds.), Society and knowledge. Contemporary perspectives in the sociology of knowledge. New Brunswick, NJ (Transaction Publishers) 1984: 251–91.

Elias (Norbert), On human beings and their emotions. A process-sociological essay, in: Mike Featherstone et al. (eds.), The body. Social process and cultural theory. London (Sage) 1991: 103–25.

Emsley (Clive) et al. (eds.), Social control in Europe, Vol. II: 1800–2000. Columbus (Ohio State University Press) 2004.

Evans (Richard J.), Rituals of retribution. Capital punishment in Germany, 1600–1987. Oxford (Oxford University Press) 1996.

Eysten (J.), Het leven van prins Willem II, 1626–1650. Amsterdam (n.p.) 1916.

Faber (S[joerd]), Kindermoord, in het bijzonder in de 18e eeuw te Amsterdam, in: Bijdraagen en Mededelingen betreffende de Gischiedenis der Nederlanden 93 (1978): 224–40.

Faber (Sjoerd), Strafrechtspleging en criminaliteit te Amsterdam, 1680–1811. De nieuwe menslievendheid. Arnhem (Gouda Quint) 1983.

Farge (Arlette) + Foucault (Michel), Le Désordre des familles. Lettres de cachet des Archives de la Bastille au XVIIIe siècle. Paris (Gallimard) 1982.

Farr (James R.), Hands of honor. Artisans and their world in Dijon, 1550–1650. Ithaca (Cornell University Press) 1988.

Feher (Michel), Naddaff (Ramona) + Tazi (Nadia) (eds.), Fragments for a history of the human body. 3 vols. New York (Urzone) 1989.

Feith (J. A.), De Ommelander borgen en hare bewoners in de 17e en 18e eeuw. Groningen (Wolters) 1906.

Foucault (Michel), Folie et déraison. Histoire de la folie à l'age classique. Paris (Gallimard) 1961.

Foucault (Michel), Surveiller et punir. Naissance de la prison. Paris (Gallimard) 1975.

Foucault (Michel), Mikrophysik der Macht. Michel Foucault über Strafjustiz, Psychiatrie und Medizin. Berlin (Merve Verlag) 1976a.

Foucault (Michel), Histoire de la sexualité, Vol. 1: La volonté de savoir. Paris (Gallimard) 1976b.

Foyster (Elizabeth A.), Manhood in early modern England. Honour, sex and marriage. London, New York (Longman) 1999.

Frank-van Westrienen (Anna), De Groote Tour. Tekening van de educatiereis der Nederlanders in de 17e eeuw. Leiden (Diss. University of Leiden) 1983.

Franke (Herman), Geweldscriminaliteit in Nederland. Een historisch-sociologische analyse, in: Amsterdams Sociologisch Tijdschrift 18,3 (1991): 13–45.

Franke (Herman), The emancipation of prisoners. A socio-historical analysis of the Dutch prison experience. Edinburgh (Edinburgh University Press) 1995.

Frevert (Ute), Ehrenmänner. Das Duell in der bürgerlichen Gesellschaft. Munich 1991.

Frey (Manuel), Der reinliche Bürger. Entstehung und Verbreitung bürgerlicher Tugenden in Deutschland, 1760–1860. Göttingen (Vandenhoeck & Ruprecht) 1997.

Gallagher (Catherine) + Laqueur (Thomas) (eds.), The making of the modern body. Sexuality and society in the 19th century. Berkeley (University of California Press) 1987.

Gardiner (Michael), Ecology and carnival. Traces of a "green" social theory in the writings of M. M. Bakhtin, in: Theory and Society 22 (1993): 765–812.

Garland (David), Punishment and welfare. A history of penal strategies. Aldershot (Gower) 1985.

Garland (David), Punishment and modern society. A study in social theory. Chicago (University of Chicago Press) 1990.

Garland (David), The culture of control. Crime and social order in contemporary society. Chicago (University of Chicago Press) 2001.

Garland (David), Capital punishment and American culture, in: Punishment and Society 7,4 (2005): 347–76.

Garland (David), Peculiar institution. America's death penalty in an age of abolition. Cambridge MA (Belknap Press of Harvard University Press) 2010.

Gatrell (V. A. C.), The decline of theft and violence in Victorian and Edwardian
England, in: Gatrell (V. A. C.) et al. (eds.), Crime and the law. The social
history of crime in Western Europe since 1500. London (Europa Publishers)
1980: 238–370.

Gatrell (V. A. C.), The hanging tree. Execution and the English people, 1770–
1868. Oxford (Oxford University Press) 1994.

Gauvard (Claude), "De grace especial." Crime, état et société en France à la fin
du Moyen Age. 2 vols. Paris (Publications de la Sorbonne) 1991.

Gellately (Robert), The Gestapo and German Society. Enforcing Racial Policy,
1933–1945. Oxford (Clarendon) 1990.

Gellately (Robert), The prerogatives of confinement in Germany, 1933–1945.
"Protective custody" and other police strategies, in: Finzsch (Norbert) + Jütte
(Robert) (eds.), Institutions of confinement. Hospitals, asylums, and prisons
in Western Europe and North America, 1500–1950. Cambridge (Cambridge
University Press) 1996: 191–211.

Gellately (Robert), Backing Hitler. Consent and coercion in Nazi Germany.
Oxford (Oxford University Press) 2001.

Geltner (G[uy]), The medieval prison. A social history. Princeton (Princeton
University Press) 2008.

Gennep (Arnold van), Les rites de passage. Etude systématique des rites de la
porte et . . . Reprint. New York (Johnson Reprint Corp) 1969 [1909].

Ginzburg (Carlo), Les batailles nocturnes. Sorcellerie et rituels agraires en Frioul,
XVIe–XVIIe siècle. Lagrasse (Editions Verdier) 1980.

Ginzburg (Carlo), Ecstasies. Deciphering the witches' sabbath. London
(Hutchinson Radius) 1990.

Godfrey (Barry), Law, factory discipline and "theft." The impact of the factory
on workplace appropriation in mid to late nineteenth-century Yorkshire, in:
British Journal of Criminology 39,1 (1999): 56–71 (1999a).

Godfrey (Barry), Judicial impartiality and the use of criminal law against labour.
The sentencing of workplace appropriators in Northern England, 1840–1880,
in: Crime, Histoire & Sociétés / Crime, History & Societies 3,2 (1999): 57–72
(1999b).

Godfrey (Barry), Counting and accounting for the decline in non-lethal violence
in England, Australia and New Zealand, 1880–1920, in: British Journal of
Criminology 43 (2003): 340–53.

Godfrey (Emelyne), Masculinity, crime and self-defence in Victorian literature.
Houndmills (Palgrave Macmillan) 2011.

Goede manierlijcke Zeden [1546]. Edited by J. van Vloten, in: De Dietsche
Warande 6 (1864): 337–61.

Goetman (Lambertus), De spiegel der jongers. Gent (Annoot-Braeckman) 1860
[1488].

Gottschalk (Marie), The prison and the gallows. The politics of mass
incarceration in America. Cambridge (Cambridge University Press) 2006.

Gottschalk (Marie), The long shadow of the death penalty. Mass incarceration, capital punishment and penal policy in the United States, in: Sarat (Austin) + Martschukat (Jürgen) (eds.), Is the death penalty dying? European and American perspectives. Cambridge (Cambridge University Press) 2011: 292–321.

Goudsblom (Johan), Zivilisation, Ansteckungsangst und Hygiene. In Gleichmann (Peter) et al., Materialien zu Norbert Elias' Zivilisationstheorie. Frankfurt (Suhrkamp) 1977: 215–53.

Goudsblom (Johan), Vuur en beschaving. Amsterdam (Meulenhoff) 1992.

Goudsblom (Johan), De paradox van de pacificatie, in: Amsterdams Sociologisch Tijdschrift 25,3 (1998): 395–406.

Goudsblom (Johan), Jones (Eric) + Mennell (Stephen), The course of human history. Economic growth, social process and civilization. Armonk, NY (M. E. Sharpe) 1996.

Gould (Roger V.), Insurgent identities. Class, community and protest in Paris from 1848 to the Commune. Chicago (University of Chicago Press) 1995.

Graafhuis (A.) et al., Misdaad en straf in de stad Utrecht in de tweede helft van de 16e eeuw, in: Recht en Slecht. Een registratie van misdaad en straf in de stad Utrecht, 1550–1575. Gemeentelijke Archiefdienst Utrecht 1976: 17–89.

Graf (Arturo), Il mito del paradiso terrestre. Con un saggio introduttivo di Gianfranco de Turris. Rome (Edizioni del Graal: Manilo Basaia 1982 [1892].

Greenberg (Kenneth S.), Honor and slavery. Princeton (Princeton University Press) 1996.

Greenshields (Malcolm), An economy of violence in early modern France. Crime and justice in the Haute Auvergne, 1587–1664. University Park, PA (Pennsylvania State University Press) 1994.

Gijswijt-Hofstra (Marijke), Wijkplaatsen voor vervolgden. Asielverlening in Culemborg, Vianen, Buren, Leerdam en IJsselstein van de 16e tot eind 18e eeuw. Dieren (Bataafsche Leeuw) 1984.

Haar (Barend J. ter), Rethinking "violence" in Chinese culture, in: Aijmer (Göran) + Abbink (Jon) (eds.), Meanings of violence. A cross-cultural perspective. Oxford, New York (Berg) 2000: 122–39.

Haeghen (Ferd. vander) + Arnold (Th. J. J.), Bibliotheca Erasmiana: répertoire des oeuvres d'Erasme. 2 vols. Gand 1893.

Halttunen (Karen), Humanitarianism and the pornography of pain in Anglo-American culture, in: American Historical Review 100 (1995): 303–34.

Hamm (Richard F.), Murder, honor and law. Four Virginia homicides from Reconstruction to the Great Depression. Charlottesville (University of Virginia Press) 2003.

Hammel (Andrew), Civilized rebels. Death-penalty abolition in Europe as cause, mark of distinction and political strategy, in: Sarat (Austin) + Martschukat (Jürgen) (eds.), Is the death penalty dying? European and American perspectives. Cambridge (Cambridge University Press) 2011: 173–203.

Handvesten ofte privilegien ende octroyen mitsgaders willekeuren, costumen, ordonnantien en handelingen der stad Amstelredam. 3 vols. Amsterdam 1748.

Hanlon (Gregory), Les rituels de l'agression en Aquitaine au 17e siècle, in: Annales: Economies, Sociétés, Civilisations 40,2 (1985): 244–68.

Hart (Marjolein 't) + Heijden (Manon van der), Het geld van de stad. Recente historiografische trends in het onderzoek naar stedelijke financiën in de Nederlanden, in: Tijdschrift voor Sociale en Economische Geschiedenis 3,3 (2006): 3–35.

Hartog (J.) De spectatoriale geschriften van 1741–1800: bijdrage tot de kennis van het huiselijk, maatschappelijk en kerkelijk leven onder ons volk, in de tweede helft der 18de eeuw. 2nd edn. Utrecht (Gebr. van der Post) 1890.

Hay (Douglas), Property, authority and the criminal law, in: Hay (Douglas) et al., Albion's fatal tree. Crime and society in 18th-century England. New York (Pantheon Books) 1975: 17–63.

Heers (Jacques), Fêtes des fous et carnavals. Paris (Fayard) 1983.

Helsdingen (Hans-W. van), Politiek van de dood. Begraven tijdens de Franse Revolutie, 1789–1800. Amsterdam (SUA).

Heringa (Jan), De eer en hoogheid van de staat. Groningen (Wolters) 1961.

Heijden (Manon van der), Huwelijk in Holland. Stedelijke rechtspraak en kerkelijke tucht, 1550–1700. Amsterdam (Bert Bakker) 1998.

Heijden (Manon van der), Introduction: new perspectives on public services in early modern Europe, in: Journal of Urban History 20,10 (2010): 1–14.

Hoeven (Anton van den), Ten exempel en afschrik. Strafrechtspleging en criminaliteit in Haarlem, 1740–1795 (unpublished thesis University of Amsterdam 1982).

Hoffer (Peter C.) + Hull (N. E. H.), Murdering mothers. Infanticide in England and New England, 1558–1803. New York, London (New York University Press) 1981.

Hollandts Placcaet-boeck . . . 1580 tot 1645. Amsterdam (Jan Janssen) 1645.

Hood (Roger), Introduction. The importance of abolishing the death penalty, in: The death penalty. Abolition in Europe. Strasbourg (Council of Europe Publishing) 1999: 9–16.

Hood (Roger), The death penalty. A worldwide perspective. 3rd edn. revised and updated. Oxford (Oxford University Press) 2002.

Hoofsche welleventheid en loffelijke welgemaniertheid, by alle voortreffelyke luiden in Nederland gebruykelyk. Amsterdam (Jacob Graal) 1733, 1737, 1742, 1768.

Hubner (Johan), De Staats- en Koeranten-tolk . . . door den heer Johan Hubner, Rector van St. Jan te Hamburg. En nu volgens de twaalfden druk vertaalt. Leiden 1732.

Hufton (Olwen H.), The poor of eighteenth-century France, 1750–1789. Oxford (Clarendon) 1974.

Hughes (Steven C.), Politics of the sword. Dueling, honor and masculinity in modern Italy. Columbus (Ohio State University Press) 2007.

Hui (Victoria Tin-bor), War and state formation in ancient China and early modern Europe. Cambridge (Cambridge University Press) 2005.

Ignatieff (Michael), A just measure of pain. The penitentiary in the iIndustrial revolution, 1750–1850. New York (Pantheon) 1978.

Ignatieff (Michael), State, civil society and total institution. A critique of recent social histories of punishment, in: Sugarman (David) (ed.), Legality, ideology and the state. London (Academic) 1983: 183–211.

Ikegami (Eiko), The taming of the samurai. Honorific individualism and the making of modern Japan. Cambridge MA (Harvard University Press) 1995.

Ingalls (Robert P.), Urban vigilantes in the New South. Tampa, 1882–1936. Knoxville (University of Tennessee Press) 1988.

Ingram (Martin), Church courts, sex and marriage in England, 1570–1640. Cambridge (Cambridge University Press) 1987.

Interimrapport van de Commissie kleine criminaliteit. Den Haag (Staatsuitgeverij) 1984.

Janssen (Louis), Nicolaas, de duivel en de doden. Opstellen over volkscultuur. Baarn (Ambo) 1993.

Jansson (Arne), From swords to sorrow. Homicide and suicide in early modern Stockholm. Stockholm (Almqvist & Wiksell International) 1998.

Japikse (Nicolaas), Johan de Witt. Amsterdam (Meulenhoff) 1915.

Jong (Jacob Johannes de), Met goed fatsoen. De elite in een Hollandse stad. Gouda, 1700–1780. Utrecht (Diss. University of Utrecht) 1985.

Jong (Joop de), Een deftig bestaan. Het dagelijks leven van regenten in de 17e en 18e eeuw. Utrecht (Kosmos) 1987.

Jongste (Jan A. F. de), De Republiek der verenigde Nederlanden, in: Leidschrift 9,3 (Staatsvorming in vroegmodern Europa) (1993): 101–15.

Jüngen (Jean A. G.), Een stad van justitie? Een verkenning van misdaad en maatschappij in Amsterdam in de 2e helft van de 16e eeuw (unpublished thesis Free University Amsterdam 1979).

Jüngen (Jean A. G.), God betert. De Amsterdamse lijkschouwingsrapporten in de jaren 1560, 1570, 1580 en 1590 (unpublished thesis Free University Amsterdam 1982).

Kalof (Linda) + Bynum (William) (eds.), A cultural history of the human body. 6 vols. Oxford (Berg) 2010.

Kaluszynski (Martine), La République à l'épreuve du crime. La construction du crime comme objet politique, 1880–1920. Paris (LGDJ) 2002.

Kemper (J. de Bosch), Geschiedkundig onderzoek naar de armoede in ons vaderland. Haarlem (Loosjes) 1851.

Kieckhefer (Richard), Magic in the middle ages. Cambridge (Cambridge University Press) 1989.

Kiernan (V. G.), The duel in European history. Honour and the reign of aristocracy. Oxford (Oxford University Press) 1988.

Kim (Eun-Young), Norbert Elias im Diskurs von Moderne und Postmoderne. Ein Rekonstruktionsversuch der Eliasschen Theorie im Licht der Diskussion von Foucault und Habermas. Marburg (Tectum) 1995.

Klaniczay (Gábor), The uses of supernatural power. The transformation of popular religion in medieval and early-modern Europe. Cambridge (Polity) 1990.

Knevel (Paul), Burgers in het geweer. De schutterijen in Holland, 1550–1700. Hilversum (Verloren) 1994.

Komans (Michiel), D. Erasmus van Rotterdam, van de borgerlyke wellevendheid der kinderlyke zeden. In vaersen gebracht door Michiel Komans. Amsterdam 1693.

Kooijmans (Luuc), Onder regenten. De elite in een Hollandse stad. Hoorn, 1700–1780. Utrecht (Diss. University of Utrecht) 1985.

Krug (Etienne G.) et al. (eds.), World report on violence and health. Geneva (World Health Organization) 2002.

Kuiper (Ernst Jan), De Hollandse "schoolordre" van 1625. Een studie over het onderwijs op de Latijnse scholen in Nederland in de 17e en 18e eeuw. Groningen (Wolters) 1958.

Ladurie (Emmanuel Le Roy), Carnival in Romans. A people's uprising at Romans, 1579–1580. Harmondsworth (Penguin), 1980.

Lane (Roger), Murder in America. A history. Columbus (Ohio State University Press) 1997.

Lane (Roger), Violent death in the city. Suicide, accident and murder in 19th-century Philadelphia. Second ed. Columbus (Ohio State University Press) 1999.

Laqueur (Thomas W.), Making sex. Body and gender from the Greeks to Freud. Cambridge MA (Harvard University Press) 1990.

Lavisse (Ernest), Histoire de France depuis les origines jusqu'à la Révolution. Vol. 8, pt. 2, Le regne de Louis XV, 1715–1774. Paris (Hachette) 1909.

Lees (Clare A.) (ed.), Medieval masculinities. Regarding men in the middle ages. Minneapolis (University of Minnesota Press) 1994.

Leistra (Gerlof) + Nieuwbeerta (Paul), Moord en doodslag in Nederland, 1992–2001. Amsterdam (Prometheus) 2003.

Lennep (Jacob van) + Hofdijk (Willem Jacob), Merkwaardige kasteelen in Nederland. 6 vols. Amsterdam 1854–60.

Lewis (Mark Edward), Sanctioned violence in early China. Albany (SUNY Press) 1990.

Lis (Catharina) + Soly (Hugo), "Beter een goede buur dan een verre vriend." Buurschap en buurtleven in Westeuropese steden aan het eind van het Ancien Régime, in: Vries (Boudien de) et al. (eds.), De kracht der zwakken. Studies over arbeid en arbeidersbeweging in het verleden. Opstellen aangeboden aan Theo van Tijn. Amsterdam (Stichting Beheer IISG) 1992: 81–107.

Maguire (Keith), Modernisation and clean government. Tackling crime, corruption and organised crime in modern Taiwan, in: Crime, Law and Social Change 28 (1997): 73–88.

Mantecón (Tomás), Long-term changes of ritualized interpersonal violence. The early modern Spanish desafíos. Paper presented at the conference "Crime, Violence and the Modern State," Rethymon, Greece, March 2007.

Martin (John), Journeys to the world of the dead. The work of Carlo Ginzburg, in: Journal of Social History 25,3 (1992): 613–26.

Martschukat (Jürgen), Inszeniertes Töten. Eine Geschichte der Todesstrafe vom 17. bis zum 19. Jahrhundert. Cologne (Böhlau) 2000.

Matheus (Michael) (ed.), Fastnacht/Karneval im europäischen Vergleich. Stuttgart (Franz Steiner) 1999.

McDannell (Colleen) + Lang (Bernhard), Heaven. A history. New Haven, London (Yale University Press) 1988.

McKanna (Clare V., Jr.), Homicide, race and justice in the American West, 1880–1920. Tucson (University of Arizona Press) 1997.

McKanna (Clare V., Jr.), Race and homicide in 19th-century California. Reno (University of Nevada Press) 2002.

McLennan (Rebecca M.), The crisis of imprisonment. Protest, politics and the making of the American penal state, 1776–1941. Cambridge (Cambridge University Press) 2008.

McMahon (Vanessa), Murder in Shakespeare's England. London (Hambledon and London) 2004.

McManners (John), Death and the Enlightenment. Changing attitudes to death among Christians and unbelievers in 18th-century France. Oxford (Oxford University Press) 1985.

McNeill (William H.), The rise of the West. A history of the human community. Chicago (University of Chicago Press) 1963.

McNeill (William H.), Plagues and peoples. Oxford (Basil Blackwell) 1977.

McNeill (William H.), Keeping together in time. Dance and drill in human history. Cambridge, MA (Harvard University Press) 1995.

Meeteren (Aries van), Op hoop van akkoord. Instrumenteel forumgebruik bij geschilbeslechting in Leiden in de 17e eeuw. Hilversum (Verloren) 2006.

Mennell (Stephen), The American civilizing process. Cambridge (Polity) 2007.

Merback (Mitchell B.), The thief, the cross and the wheel. Pain and the spectacle of punishment in medieval and Renaissance Europe. Chicago (University of Chicago Press) 1999.

Mitchell (Timothy), Blood sport. A social history of Spanish bullfighting. With an essay and bibliography by Rosario Cambria. Philadelphia (University of Pennsylvania Press)1991.

Mitterauer (Michael) + Sieder (Reinhard), Vom Patriarchat zur Partnerschaft. Zum Strukturwandel der Familie. Munich (Beck) 1977.

Monkkonen (Eric H.), Murder in New York City. Berkeley (University of California Press) 2001.

Monkkonen (Eric), Homicide. Explaining America's exceptionalism, in: American Historical Review 111,1 (2006): 76–94.

Mountague (William), The delights of Holland, or a three months travel about that and the other provinces. London 1696 (available through Early English Books Online)

Mucchielli (Laurent) (ed.), Histoire de la criminologie française. Paris (L'Harmattan) 1995.

Muchembled (Robert), La violence au village. Sociabilité et comportements populaires en Artois du 15e au 17e siècle. Turnhout (Brepols) 1989.

Muir (Edward), Mad blood stirring. Vendetta & factions in Friuli during the Renaissance. Baltimore (Johns Hopkins University Press) 1993.

Nieuwbeerta (Paul) + Leistra (Gerlof), Dodelijk geweld. Moord en doodslag in Nederland. Amsterdam (Balans) 2007.

Nieuwe Verhandeling van de hoofsche wellevendheit en loffelijke welgemanierdheit. Amsterdam (Jan Claessen te Hoorn) 1677.

Noske (Barbara), Humans and other animals. Beyond the boundaries of anthropology. London (Pluto Press) 1989.

Nusteling (Hubert), The population of Amsterdam in the golden age, in: Kessel (Peter van) + Schulte (Elisja), Amsterdam, Rome. Two growing cities in 17th-century Europe. Amsterdam (Amsterdam University Press) 1997: 71–84.

Nye (Robert A.), Crime, madness and politics in modern France. The medical concept of national decline. Princeton (Princeton University Press) 1984.

Nye (Robert A.), Masculinity and male codes of honor in modern France. New York, Oxford (Oxford University Press) 1993.

Oord (Kees van den), Nederlandse boekhandelaren in de grootboeken van de Officina Plantiniana, 1566–1589, in: De Gulden Passer 67 (1989): 391–7.

Oostrom (Frits P. van), Het woord van eer. Literatuur aan het Hollandse hof omstreeks 1400. Amsterdam (Meulenhoff) 1987.

Ozouf (Mona), La fête révolutionnaire, 1789–1799. Paris (Gallimard) 1976.

Pagels (Elaine), Adam, Eve and the serpent. New York (Random House) 1988.

Pangritz (Walter), Das Tier in der Bibel. Munich, Basel (Ernst Reinhardt) 1963.

Panhuysen (Luc), De ware vrijheid. De levens van Johan en Cornelis de Witt. Amsterdam (Atlas) 2005.

Papenheim (Martin), Erinnerung und Unsterblichkeit. Semantische Studien zum Totenkult in Frankreich, 1715–1794. Stuttgart (Klett-Cotta) 1992.

Parrella (Anne), Industrialization and murder. Northern France, 1815–1904. Journal of Interdisciplinary History 22, 4 (1992): 627–54.

Peristiany (J[ohn] G.) + Pitt-Rivers (Julian) (eds.), Honor and grace in anthropology. Cambridge (Cambridge University Press) 1992.

Perrot (Michelle) (ed.), L'impossible prison. Recherches sur le système pénitentiaire au 19e siècle. Débat avec Michel Foucault. Paris (Seuil) 1980.

Peterson del Mar (David), Beaten down. A history of interpersonal violence in the West. Seattle, London (University of Washington Press) 2002.

Petit (Jacques-Guy) (ed.) La Prison, le bagne et l'histoire. Geneva (Librairie des Méridiens) 1984.

Petit (Jacques-Guy), Ces peines obscures. La prison pénale en France, 1780–1875. Paris (Fayard) 1990.

Petit (Jacques-Guy) et al., Histoire des prisons en France, 1789–2000. Le système pénitentiaire et les bagnes d'outre-mer. Toulouse (Privat) 2002.

Pfeifer (Michael J.), Rough justice. Lynching and American society, 1874–1947. Urbana (University of Illinois Press) 2004.

Porta (Antonio), Joan en Gerrit Corver. De politieke macht van Amsterdam, 1702–1748. Assen (Van Gorcum) 1975.

Pouchelle (Marie-Christine), Corps et chirurgie à l'apogée du moyen age. Savoir et imaginaire du corps chez Henri de Mondeville, chirurgien de Philippe le Bel. Paris (Flammarion) 1983.

Prak (Maarten), Gezeten burgers. De elite in een Hollandse stad. Leiden, 1700–1780. Utrecht (Diss. University of Utrecht) 1985.

Prak (Maarten), Republiek en vorst. De stadhouders en het staatsvormingsproces in de Noordelijke Nederlanden, 16e–18e eeuw, in: Bruin (Kees) + Verrips (Kitty (eds.), Door het volk gedragen. Koningschap en samenleving. Groningen (Wolters-Noordhoff) 1989: 28–52.

Price (J. L.), Culture and society in the Dutch Republic during the 17th century. London (Batsford) 1974.

Rabus (Pieter), Boekzaal van Europe. Twee-maandelijkse uittreksels. Rotterdam 1702.

Rappaz (Sonia Vernhes), La noyade judiciaire dans la République de Genève, 1558–1619, in: Crime, Histoire & Sociétés / Crime, History & Societies 13,1 (2009): 5–24.

Reinders (Michel), Printed pandemonium. The power of the public and the market for popular political publications in the early modern Dutch Republic. Rotterdam (Diss. Erasmus University) 2008.

Ricklefs (Merle), De Verenigde Oost-Indische Compagnie en de gewelddadige wereld van het vroegmoderne Azië, in: Knaap (Gerrit) + Teitler (Ger) (eds.), De Verenigde Oost-Indische Compagnie tussen oorlog en diplomatie. Leiden (KITLV Press) 2002: 355–78.

Ridderikhoff (C. M.), De Franequer Los-Kop, in: Jensma (G.Th.) et al. (eds.), Universiteit te Franeker, 1585–1811. Bijdragen tot de geschiedenis van de Friese hogeschool. Leeuwarden (Fryske Akademy) 1985: 119–32.

Robinson (David), Bandits, eunuchs and the son of heaven. Rebellion and the economy of violence in mid-Ming China. Honolulu (University of Hawai'i Press) 2001.

Roché (Sebastian), Sociologie politique de l'insécurité. Violences urbaines, inégalités et globalisation. Paris (Presses Universitaires de France) 1998.

Roding (Juliette), Schoon en net. Hygiëne in woning en stad; de cultuurgeschiedenis van bad en toilet. The Hague (Staatsuitgeverij) 1986.

Roodenburg (Herman), Onder censuur. De kerkelijke tucht in de Gereformeerde gemeente van Amsterdam, 1578–1700. Hilversum (Verloren) 1990.

Roodenburg (Herman), The "hand of friendship." Shaking hands and other gestures in the Dutch Republic, in: Bremmer (Jan) + Roodenburg (Herman) (eds.), A cultural history of gesture from Antiquity to the present day. With an introduction by Keith Thomas. Cambridge (Polity) 1991: 152–89.

Roodenburg (Herman), Spierenburg (Pieter) (eds.), Social control in Europe, Vol. I: 1500–1800. Columbus (Ohio State University Press) 2004.

Roorda (Daniel Jeen), Partij en factie. Groningen (Wolters-Noordhoff) 1961.

Roorda (Daniel Jeen), The ruling classes in Holland in the seventeenth century, in: Britain and the Netherlands II. Groningen (Wolters-Noordhoff) 1964: 109–32.

Roth (Randolph), American homicide. Cambridge MA (Belknap Press of Harvard University Press) 2009.

Rothman (David J.), The discovery of the asylum. Social order and disorder in the New Republic. Boston (Little, Brown) 1971.

Rothman (David J.), Conscience and convenience. The asylum and its alternatives in Progressive America. Boston (Little, Brown) 1980.

Rotman (Edgardo), The failure of reform: United States, 1865–1965, in: Morris

(Norval) + Rothman (David J.) (eds.), The Oxford history of the prison. New York, Oxford (Oxford University Press) 1995: 169–97.

Rowe (William T.), Crimson rain. Seven centuries of violence in a Chinese county. Stanford (Stanford University Press) 2007.

Royer (Katherine), Dead men talking. Truth, texts and the scaffold in early modern England, in: Devereaux (Simon) + Griffiths (Paul) (eds.), Penal practice and culture, 1500–1900. Punishing the English. Basingstoke (Palgrave Macmillan) 2004: 63–84.

Ruller (Sibo van), Genade voor recht. Gratieverlening aan ter dood veroordeelden in Nederland, 1806–1870. Amsterdam (De Bataafsche Leeuw) 1987.

Sabean (David Warren), Power in the blood. Popular culture and village discourse in early modern Germany. Cambridge (Cambridge University Press) 1984.

Salisbury (Joyce E.), The beast within. Animals in the middle ages. New York, London (Routledge) 1994.

Salle (Grégory), La part d'ombre de l'état de droit. La question carcérale en France et en République fédérale d'Allemagne depuis 1968. Paris (Editions EHESS) 2009.

Sälzle (Karl), Tier und Mensch, Gottheit und Dämon. Das Tier in der Geistesgeschichte der Menschheit. Munich (Bayerischer Landswirtschaftsverlag) 1965.

Schick (Irvin Cemil), The erotic margin. Sexuality and spatiality in alteritist discourse. London, New York (Verso) 1999.

Schmidt (Cornelis), Om de eer van de familie. Het geslacht Teding van Berkhout, 1500–1950. Amsterdam (De Bataafsche Leeuw) 1986.

Schmitt (Jean-Claude), Les revenants. Les vivants et les morts dans la société médiévale. Paris (Gallimard)1994.

Schreiner (Klaus) + Schwerhoff (Gerd) (eds.), Verletzte Ehre. Ehrkonflikte in Gesellschaften des Mittelalters und der frühen Neuzeit. Cologne (Böhlau) 1995.

Schulte Nordholt (Henk), A genealogy of violence, in: Colombijn (Freek) + Lindblad (Thomas) (eds.), Roots of violence in Indonesia. Contemporary violence in historical perspective. Leiden (KITLV Press) 2002: 33–61.

Schuster (Peter), Eine Stadt vor Gericht. Recht und Alltag im spätmittelalterlichen Konstanz. Paderborn (Ferdinand Schöningh) 2000.

Schuster (Peter), Hinrichtungsritualen in der frühen Neuzeit. Anfragen aus dem Mittelalter, in: Rudolph (Harriet) + Schnabel-Schüle (Helga) (eds.), Justiz = Justice = Justicia. Rahmenbedingungen von Strafjustiz im frühneuzeitlichen Europa. Trierer Historische Forschungen, no. 48. Trier (Kliomedia) 2003: 213–33.

Scull (Andrew T.), Museums of madness. The social organization of insanity in nineteenth-century England. London (Allen Lane) 1979.

Scull (Andrew T.), The most solitary of afflictions. Madness and society in Britain, 1700–1900. New Haven, CT (Yale University Press) 1993.

Serpell (James), In the company of animals. A study of human–animal relationships. Oxford, New York (Oxford University Press) 1986.

Sharpe (J[ames] A.), Last dying speeches. Religion, ideology and public execution in 17th-century England, in: Past and Present 107 (1985a): 144–67.

Sharpe (J[ames] A.), The history of violence in England. Some observations, in: Past and Present 108 (1985b): 206–15.

Sharpe (James A.), Civility, civilizing processes, and the end of public punishment in England, in: Burke (Peter), Harrison (Brian) + Slack (Paul) (eds.), Civil histories. Essays presented to Sir Keith Thomas. Oxford (Oxford University Press) 2000: 215–30.

Shilling (Chris), The body and social theory. London (Sage) 1993.

Shoemaker (Robert B.), Male honour and the decline of public violence in 18th-century London, in: Social History 26,2 (2001): 190–208.

Shoshan (Boaz), Popular culture in medieval Cairo. Cambridge (Cambridge University Press) 1993.

Simon (Jonathan), Governing through crime. How the war on crime transformed American democracy and created a culture of fear. Oxford (Oxford University Press) 2007.

Sleebe (Vincent), In termen van fatsoen. Sociale controle in het Groningse kleigebied, 1770–1914. Assen (Van Gorcum) 1994.

Slenders (J. A. M.), Het Theatrum Anatomicum in de Noordelijke Nederlanden, 1555–1800 (Scripta Tironum no. 17/18, University of Nijmegen, Faculty of Medicine) 1989.

Spier (Fred), Religie in de mensheidsgeschiedenis. Naar een model van de ontwikkeling van religieuze regimes in een lange-termijnperspectief, in: Amsterdams Sociologisch Tijdschrift 16,4 (1990): 88–122.

Spierenburg (Pieter), Judicial violence in the Dutch Republic. Corporal punishment, executions and torture in Amsterdam, 1650-1750. Amsterdam (Diss. University of Amsterdam) 1978.

Spierenburg (Pieter), The spectacle of suffering. Executions and the evolution of repression: from a preindustrial metropolis to the European experience. Cambridge (Cambridge University Press) 1984.

Spierenburg (Pieter), The prison experience. Disciplinary institutions and their inmates in early modern Europe. New Brunswick, NJ (Rutgers University Press) 1991.

Spierenburg (Pieter), Four Centuries of Prison History: Punishment, Suffering, the Body and Power, in: Finzsch (Norbert) + Jütte (Robert) (eds.), Institutions of confinement. Hospitals, asylums and prisons in Western Europe and North America, 1500–1950. Cambridge (Cambridge University Press) 1996: 17–35.

Spierenburg (Pieter) (ed.), Men and violence. Gender, honor and rituals in modern Europe and America. Columbus OH (Ohio State University Press) 1998a.

Spierenburg (Pieter), De Verbroken Betovering. Mentaliteit en Cultuur in Preïndustrieel Europa. 3rd edn. Hilversum (Verloren) 1998b.

Spierenburg (Pieter), Sailors and violence in Amsterdam, 17th–18th centuries, in: Lappalainen (Mirkka) + Hirvonen (Pekka) (eds.), Crime and control in Europe from the past to the present. Helsinki (Publications of the History of Criminality Research Project) 1999: 112–43.

Spierenburg (Pieter), Crime, in: Stearns (Peter N.) (ed.), Encyclopedia of European social history from 1350 to 2000. Detroit (Charles Scribner's Sons) 2001. Vol. III: 335–50.

Spierenburg (Pieter), Written in blood. Fatal attraction in Enlightenment Amsterdam. Columbus OH (Ohio State University Press) 2004.

Spierenburg (Pieter), Democracy came too early: a tentative explanation for the problem of American homicide, in: American Historical Review 111,1 (2006a): 104–14.

Spierenburg (Pieter), Protestant attitudes to violence. The early Dutch Republic. in: Crime, Histoire & Sociétés / Crime, History & Societies 10,2 (2006b): 5–31.

Spierenburg (Pieter), A history of murder. Personal violence in Europe from the middle ages to the present. Cambridge (Polity) 2008.

Stewart (Frank Henderson), Honor. Chicago, London (University of Chicago Press) 1994.

Stone (Lawrence), Interpersonal violence in English society, 1300–1980, in: Past and Present 101 (1983): 22–33.

Stone (Lawrence), A rejoinder, in: Past and Present 108 (1985): 216–24.

Sturkenboom (Dorothée), Spectators van hartstocht. Sekse en emotionele cultuur in de 18e eeuw. Hilversum (Verloren) 1998.

[Swildens (Jan Hendrik)], Over den tegenwoordigen toestand der samenleving in onze republiek, in: Knigge (van), Over de verkeering met menschen. Amsterdam 1789: I–CVIII.

Szakolczai (Arpád), Weber (Max), Foucault (Michel), Parallel life-works. London (Routledge) 1998.

Thoden van Velzen (H. U. E.), De Aukaanse (Djoeka) beschaving, in: Sociologische Gids 29 (1982): 243–78.

Thomas (Keith), Religion and the decline of magic. Studies in popular beliefs in 16th- and 17th-century England. Harmondsworth (Penguin) 1973 [1971].

Thomas (Keith), Man and the natural world. A history of the modern sensibility. New York (Pantheon Books) 1983.

Tilly (Charles), Coercion, capital and European states, AD 990–1990. Oxford (Basil Blackwell) 1990.

Tlusty (B. Ann), Bacchus and civic order. The culture of drink in early modern Germany. Charlottesville, London (University Press of Virginia) 2001.

Tolnay (Stewart E.) + Beck (E. M.), A festival of violence. An analysis of Southern lynchings, 1882–1930. Urbana (University of Illinois Press) 1995.

Tsung-Hsueh Lu, Changes in injury mortality by intent and mechanism in Taiwan, 1975–98, in: Injury Prevention 8 (2002): 70–3.

Turner (Frederick Jackson), The frontier in American history. New York (Henry Holt) 1953 [1920].

Turner (Victor W.), The Ritual Process. Structure and Anti-Structure. New York (Aldine) 1969.

Valcoogh (Dirck Adriaensz), Regel der Duytsche schoolmeesters. Den Haag (Ykema) 1875 [1591].

Valkenier (Petrus), 't Verwerd Europa . . . Tweede druk. Amsterdam (Hendrik en Dirk Boom) 1675.

Vandal (Gilles), Rethinking Southern violence. Homicides in post-Civil War Louisiana, 1866–1884. Columbus (Ohio State University Press) 2000.

Vries (Jan de), European urbanization, 1500–1800. London (Methuen) 1984.

Waardt (Hans de), Ehrenhändel, Gewalt und Liminalität. Ein Konzeptualisierungsvorschlag, in: Schreiner (Klaus) + Schwerhoff (Gerd) (eds.), Verletzte Ehre. Ehrkonflikte in Gesellschaften des Mittelalters und der frühen Neuzeit. Cologne (Böhlau) 1995: 303–19.

Wacquant (Loïc J. D.), Decivilisering en diabolisering. De transformatie van het Amerikaanse zwarte getto, in: Amsterdams Sociologisch Tijdschrift 24 (1997): 320–39.

Wacquant (Loïc J. D.), Crafting the neoliberal state. Workfare, prisonfare and social insecurity, in: Sociological Forum 25,2 (2010): 197–221.

Waldrep (Christopher) (ed.), Lynching in America. A history in documents. New York (New York University Press) 2006.

Waldrep (Christopher) + Nieman (Donald G.) (eds.), Local matters. Race, crime and justice in the 19th-century South. Athens GA (University of Georgia Press) 2001.

Weber (Max), Gesammelte Aufsätze zur Religionssoziologie, Vol. I. Tübingen 1922.

Weber (Max), Wirtschaft und Gesellschaft. Grundriss der verstehenden Soziologie. Fünfte Auflage, Studienausgabe. Tübingen 1976.

Weel (A. J. van), De wetgeving tegen het duelleren in de Republiek der Verenigde Nederlanden, in: Nederlands Archievenblad 81 (1977): 282–96.

Wetzell (Richard F.), Inventing the criminal. A history of German criminology, 1880–1945. Chapel Hill, London (University of North Carolina Press) 2000.

Whitman (James Q.), Harsh justice. Criminal punishment and the widening divide between America and Europe. New York (Oxford University Press) 2003.

Whitman (James Q.), Response to Garland, in: Punishment and Society 7,4 (2005): 389–96.

Whitman (James Q.), The origins of reasonable doubt. Theological roots of the criminal trial. New Haven, London (Yale University Press) 2008.

Wiener (Martin J.), Men of blood. Violence, manliness and criminal justice in Victorian England. Cambridge (Cambridge University Press) 2004.

Wilterdink (Nico), Inleiding [introduction to special issue on violence in Dutch society], in: Amsterdams Sociologisch Tijdschrift 18,3 (1991): 7–12.

Winckelmann (Johannes), Die Herkunft von Max Webers "Entzauberungs" Konzeption, in: Kölner Zeitschrift für Soziologie und Sozialpsychologie 32 (1980): 12–53.

Winter (Thomas), Making men, making class. The YMCA and workingmen, 1877–1920. Chicago (University of Chicago Press) 2002.

Wouters (Cas), Informalization. Manners and emotions since 1890. London (Sage) 2007.

Wyatt-Brown (Bertram), Southern honor. Ethics and behavior in the Old South. Oxford (Oxford University Press) 1982.

Wijers (Clara Leonarda Johanna), Prinsen en clowns in het Limburgse narrenrijk.

Het carnaval in Simpelveld en Roermond, 1945–1992. Amsterdam (Meertens Instituut) 1995.

Ylikangas (Heikki), The knife fighters. Violent crime in Southern Ostrobothnia, 1790–1825. Helsinki (Academia Scientiarium Fennica) 1998.

Zanden (Jan Luiten van) + Prak (Maarten), Towards an economic interpretation of citizenship. The Dutch Republic between medieval communes and modern nation-states, in: European Review of Economic History 10 (2006): 111–45.

Zimring (Franklin E.), The contradictions of American capital punishment. New York (Oxford University Press) 2003.

Zimring (Franklin E.), Path dependence, culture and state-level execution policy. A reply to David Garland, in: Punishment and Society 7,4 (2005): 377–84.

Index